~THE~

UEST

CONTINUES

HERE IS WHAT KEY LEADERS HAVE SAID ABOUT DR. DAUGHERTY, VALLEY CHRISTIAN SCHOOLS, AND VCS STUDENTS OVER THE LAST 25 YEARS:

As a career research scientist, VCS alumni parent, and member of Valley Christian's AMSE (Applied Math, Science, and Engineering) Advisory Board, I have seen the remarkable impact of Dr. Clifford Daugherty's vision for American education. In *The Quest Continues,* he outlines the foundational principles and values that have driven educational excellence at Valley Christian Schools, and reveals how applying the "self-evident truths" of our Founding Fathers can restore excellence and transform K–12 education throughout America. It is a must-read for educators and parents.

—DR. BRUCE ROTH,
Ph.D. in Synthetic Chemistry
Inventor of Lipitor – 2008 American Chemical Society Hero of Chemistry;
2013 American Chemical Society Medicinal Chemistry Division Hall of
Fame; 2013 Perkin Medal from the Society of Chemical Industry; 2015
National Academy of Sciences Award for Chemistry in Service of Society

Dr. Daugherty, your literary achievement is wonderful and truly inspiring. I am excited and moved beyond words that you would include the precious journey surrounding Faith Christian High School that compelled and transported us all beyond the bounds of gravity!

—DR. YVONNE D. CAGLE,
NASA Astronaut

The principles of goodness, peace, and joy, as well as Light, Life, and Learning, are evident in *The Quest Continues.* Valley Christian Schools and Andrew Hill High School student mentors put Common Virtues into action for our elementary students through the Junior University and Lighthouse Initiative. Examples include funding from VCS students for the Holistic Playground, our Lighthouse after-school program of Christian values, music instruction by VCHS Conservatory students, reading partners, student tutors, "Splish! Splash! Learn to Swim" program, and Christmas gifts for our students.

—DR. RICARDO BALDERAS,
Principal, Los Arboles Literacy & Technology Academy
Franklin–McKinley School District, San Jose, California

Dr. Daugherty's book *The Quest Continues* describes the journey that opened the door for public schools and private Christian schools to collaborate and create a mentoring program to enrich the lives of all our students. Dr. Daugherty is a true creative spirit who found ways within the legal system to bring "goodness, peace, and joy" to our schools and enrich the lives of our students, no matter their background. Through the work of Dr. Daugherty and the Junior University program, elementary students are mentored by high school students from both Valley Christian Schools and Andrew Hill High School. The "Splish! Splash!" program provides swimming lessons, friendship, and guidance to our students. It is wonderful to observe our younger students learn to swim while being supported socially and mentally by the broader community. As principal of a 4–8th grade public school, I applaud the work of a great leader, Dr. Daugherty, who continues to amaze me with his dedication and perseverance as he leads us on the journey to spread "goodness, peace, and joy" as part of our teaching and learning. I feel honored to be part of this team of educators, who go above and beyond the classroom experience.

—**DR. MARIA DEHGHANFARD,**
Principal, Lairon College Preparatory Academy
Franklin–McKinley School District, San Jose, California

The Junior University and Lighthouse Initiative offers such a great opportunity for our students, and we see nothing but growth in the future. We are thankful for our successful partnership with Valley Christian and Andrew Hill High School. Their students serve as amazing mentors for our elementary students at Hellyer, Lairon, and Los Arboles elementary schools. I'm so proud of all the effort and the relationships we have built through this program. —**CARLA HAAKMA,**
Administrator
Former Principal, Los Arboles Elementary School
Franklin–McKinley School District, San Jose, California

The Junior University and Lighthouse Initiative has given our high school students exceptional opportunities to develop leadership and mentoring skills while giving back to their own community. They easily connect with and impact younger students in ways parents and teachers can only dream of. We're grateful to the Quest Institute for addressing the need and implementing these programs in our neighborhood public schools, allowing our most vulnerable and impressionable kids to feel loved and appreciated, and to become the next generation to find joy and meaning in giving back. It's a great joy to be included in this movement to reclaim our neighborhoods and schools and give our children the opportunities they deserve.

—JOSHUA GREENE,
E.L.D. Teacher, 504 Coordinator, CAS House Coordinator
Guidance Office, Junior University/Community Service Opportunities
Andrew P. Hill High School
East Side Union High School District, San Jose, California

The State of California wants all schools to reach API achievement scores of 800—and when I became principal at Hellyer Elementary, the school was below that benchmark. With the help of the Junior University and Lighthouse Initiative, our student achievement scores have catapulted above 800 and continue to grow each year. Outstanding high school mentors exhibiting "goodness, peace, and joy" really connect with our students and influence them to emulate those important character qualities we call Common Virtues. Amazing results are evident on a day-to-day basis. The Quest Institute and the Junior University and Lighthouse Initiative provide tremendous academic, artistic, and athletic opportunities for our students. Dr. Daugherty's book *The Quest Continues* describes the Light, Life, and Learning principles we discovered to guide our journey.

—JERRY MERZA,
Principal, Hellyer Elementary School
Franklin–McKinley School District, San Jose, California

Our partnership with the Quest Institute for Quality Education enriches our entire neighborhood community. Andrew Hill High School is honored to serve with Valley Christian Schools to provide mentors who tutor and enhance the lives of elementary school students through the Junior University and Lighthouse Initiative. Our partnership promotes joy and learning, and hundreds of students are inspired to higher achievement. We are dedicated to continue seeing our neighborhood community grow this passion.

— BETTINA LOPEZ,
Principal, Andrew P. Hill High School
East Side Union High School District, San Jose, California

I enjoyed reading this very thoughtfully written book. The high school students of Valley Christian deserve a personal thanks from the Board of Trustees and myself for being the wonderful role models you are for our students, and for your devotion and dedication to the work you do with us. I've never seen a partnership like this between a parochial school and an elementary school district. This has been a unique opportunity for us, and we are all grateful.

— DR. JOHN PORTER,
Superintendent
Franklin–McKinley School District, San Jose, California

Dear Students, I hope you take pride in all your hard work and accomplishments. America needs students like you who are working hard in school, dreaming big dreams, and improving our communities. Our country faces great challenges, but we will overcome them if we join together in common purpose. I encourage you to continue to put your best effort into everything you do, and please know I expect great things from you. Young people like you—the future leaders of our Nation—inspire me and give me great hope for the future. Michelle and I wish you all the best.

— BARACK OBAMA,
President of the United States

I am pleased to send greetings to all those gathered to celebrate the 25th anniversary of the founding of Valley Christian Schools. For a quarter of a century your institution has provided its students with the best—not only the best academic content but the best values as well. By recognizing the importance of the Judeo-Christian values in education, you offer your students a treasure that both trains the mind and fills the heart with hope. Nancy and I congratulate you and wish you every success in your efforts. God bless you.

—RONALD REAGAN,
President of the United States

To the ISS Team—Aim high in all you do!   —TOM JONES,
NASA Astronaut
(completed four space shuttle flights)

To the ISS and Satellite Development Teams—of Valley Christian High School—with congratulations.   —JOHN GLENN,
NASA Astronaut, U.S. Senator

To Valley Christian, Great work on your ISS experiments!

—BUZZ ALDRIN,
Apollo XI Astronaut
(2nd man to walk on the moon)

To the ISS Team of Valley Christian High School: Your pursuit of knowledge in the confines of your experiment that will soon fly into the glorious free fall of space is a sign of hope for us all. You are not merely asking questions of nature, you are seeking answers—of the two, the much more difficult and provocative activity. Anyone can ask a question, but it takes something much more to seek the answers. Ignore the poor typing of this letter, for my old typewriter lacks spellcheck in lieu of permanence—as will your experiment. Your result will be proof of a great truth. Bravo and God speed. You are gifted, each of you, and I exhort you.   —TOM HANKS,
Actor

Dear Students, I understand that you and your fellow students from Valley Christian High School recently became the first high school students in the nation to have an experiment aboard the International Space Station. I applaud your hard work. I know you and your teams have earned this honor through much dedication and perseverance. I am pleased to have this opportunity to join your family and friends in offering my congratulations. By sending the first student-designed experiment into space, you will be sure to inspire future generations to come. Again, congratulations and my very best wishes to you. Keep up the outstanding work and I wish you the best of luck in school.　—BARBARA BOXER,
U.S. Senator

I am pleased to offer warm greetings and congratulations as you receive the *2004 No Child Left Behind—Blue Ribbon Schools Program Award.* The education and creative development of our youth is a vital responsibility, one which can only be fulfilled through the exemplary efforts of schools like yours. I commend your work to foster academic achievement among your students. I am proud to join the U.S. Department of Education in honoring you as the first private high school in California to receive the prestigious *Blue Ribbon Award*—a designation reflecting the achievement of your students in the top 10 percent of all high school students in the nation. This national recognition is a worthy tribute to your dedicated pursuit of excellence. I also commend each Valley Christian student for your commitment to working hard and realizing your goals. The strength of this state is found in the accomplishments of Californians such as yourself, and I am confident your future will hold even greater achievement and fulfillment. Please accept my best wishes for a memorable event and every future success.
—ARNOLD SCHWARZENEGGER,
Governor of California

To the Valley Christian High ISS Team, with best wishes.
—GEORGE W. BUSH,
President of the United States

Dear Students, Congratulations! I recently learned that you designed, built, tested, and are now flying an experiment on the International Space Station, and I wanted to send a note to let you know that I am incredibly proud of your achievements. I am encouraged by your interest in math and science—excelling in these areas will be critical to our Nation's success in the 21st century. I am confident your experience will motivate other students to take part in similar hands-on projects and become America's next great inventors and innovators. You have already discovered that you have the power to change our Nation and our world, and it is my greatest wish that you continue to exercise that power throughout your life. Your generation is our future—and when I hear about students like you, I know that future will be bright. I look forward to hearing the outcome of your experiment, and I wish you much success and happiness in the years ahead. Keep up the great work.

—JOSEPH R. BIDEN, JR.,
Vice President of the United States

Valley Christian High School is one of the finest schools in America. The Quest for Excellence™ should be lived out in every Christian school throughout the world. The Excellence Brings Influence™ strategy and the Quest for Excellence journey of Valley Christian Schools is a model for every committed Christian. If we are going to reclaim our culture for the cause of Christ, we must pursue a Quest for Excellence.

—JOSH D. McDOWELL,
Author/Communicator

The NFL family life can be emotionally challenging. When we answered God's call to coach, we put our seven children in His hands and He has delivered. Valley Christian Schools' Quest for Excellence offers academic quality and an amazing athletic program that is so important to our children. They are flourishing! The book *Quest for Excellence* is for all who passionately seek to achieve what God intends!

—MIKE SINGLETARY,
NFL Hall of Fame and San Francisco 49ers Assistant Defensive Head Coach

DR. CLIFFORD E. DAUGHERTY

FOREWORD BY ED SILVOSO

~THE~ QUEST

CONTINUES

LIGHT, LIFE, *and* LEARNING

QUEST *for* EXCELLENCE | MEDIA

Published by Quest for Excellence Media
100 Skyway Drive
San Jose CA 95111

The phrases "Quest for Excellence," "Excellence Brings Influence," and "Quest Institute" throughout this book are trademarked by Valley Christian Schools.

Unless otherwise noted, all scripture quotations are taken from the New King James Version®, (NKJV). Copyright © 1982 by Thomas Nelson. Used by permission. All rights reserved.

Scripture quotations marked "HCSB" are taken from the Holman Christian Standard Bible®, Copyright © 1999, 2000, 2002, 2003, 2009 by Holman Bible Publishers. Used by permission. Holman Christian Standard Bible®, Holman CSB®, and HCSB® are federally registered trademarks of Holman Bible Publishers.

Scripture quotations marked "KJV" are taken from the King James Version of the Bible. Public domain.

Scripture quotations marked "NASB" are taken from the New American Standard Bible®, Copyright © 1960, 1962, 1963, 1968, 1971, 1972, 1973, 1975, 1977, 1995 by The Lockman Foundation. Used by permission. www.Lockman.org

Scripture quotations marked "NIV" are taken from the Holy Bible, New International Version®, NIV®. Copyright © 1973, 1978, 1984, 2011 by Biblica, Inc.™ Used by permission of Zondervan. All rights reserved worldwide. www.zondervan.com The "NIV" and "New International Version" are trademarks registered in the United States Patent and Trademark Office by Biblica, Inc.™

Scripture quotations marked "NLT" are taken from the Holy Bible, New Living Translation, copyright © 1996, 2004, 2007, 2013 by Tyndale House Foundation. Used by permission of Tyndale House Publishers, Inc., Carol Stream, Illinois 60188. All rights reserved.

Note from the author: When quoting Old Testament scripture, I follow the convention of these Bible versions in using small capitals (e.g. "Lord") to signify a translation from the Hebrew of the divine name YHWH. In my personal writing, I use the usual form of initial capital followed by lower case (e.g. "Lord"), as is found in the New Testament.

Library of Congress Cataloging-in-Publication Data

Daugherty, Clifford E.
    The quest continues: light, life, and learning / Clifford E. Daugherty, Ed. D.
p. cm.

ISBN: 978-0-9964207-2-3
        978-0-9964207-3-0 (eBook)

Printed in the United States of America
21 20 19 18 17 16 15 (DP) 10 9 8 7 6 5 4 3 2 1

Design by Peter Gloege | LOOK Design Studio

T H A N K   Y O U !

Without the support and participation of many contributors to the success of Valley Christian Schools and the Junior University and Lighthouse Initiative, our Quest for Excellence journey would not be possible. Please see the Acknowledgments at the back of this book.

To Loved Ones Who Have Preceded Us

My mother and father
Cletus O'Henry (1923–2004) and Geneva May (1929–2003) Daugherty
who prayed for all their children and grandchildren

My grandparents
Abner Nathan (1882–1955) and Melvina (1887–1961) Daugherty
Audie Earl (1903–1956) and Ruth Elizabeth (1908–2009) Sutherland

To My Loving Wife, Kris

To Our Growing Family

Our daughter, Kristin, and her husband, Mike Annab
Their children and our grandchildren, Emily, Kaitlyn, and Jacob

Our son, Zane, and his wife, Rebecca
Their children and our grandchildren, Josiah and Hannah
and future grandchildren and great-grandchildren
whom God may graciously add to our family

"AND THIS IS MY COVENANT WITH THEM,"
SAYS THE LORD. "MY SPIRIT WILL NOT
LEAVE THEM, AND NEITHER WILL THESE WORDS
I HAVE GIVEN YOU. THEY WILL BE ON YOUR LIPS
AND ON THE LIPS OF YOUR CHILDREN AND YOUR
CHILDREN'S CHILDREN FOREVER.
I, THE LORD, HAVE SPOKEN!"
—ISAIAH 59:21, NLT

TABLE OF CONTENTS

FOREWORD

NEXT TO PARENTING, teaching is the noblest of professions on earth. Indeed, schools around the world were conceived to be extensions of the home—a place to impart life-giving knowledge in a warm and wholesome learning environment.

We all fondly remember indelible moments when our parents taught us values that shaped our character and, later, teachers who led us on a learning journey to provide the skills needed to pursue our destiny.

The first day of school is often on par with pivotal occasions such as weddings and births in the family, with vivid recollections of the excitement and the anxiety triggered by meeting new friends and, above all, the teacher under whose care we were entrusted. To many of us, teachers became surrogate parents.

Teaching is a calling and a career chosen less for the monetary rewards than for the desire to guide students through the labyrinth of life to face the challenges of adulthood. Teachers are noble, selfless people who sacrifice towards that end.

However, many teachers and schools today are under crushing pressure. More often than we dare admit, our once-honored learning centers have become failure zones for too many students. Brave teachers who longingly work to lead their pupils to victory find themselves reduced to "holding the fort." The invigorating idealism that led them to become educators is being tarnished by the brutal reality of disempowerment. It's as if the hands of outstanding educators are tied behind their backs by the removal of character-building values, to placate misguided political correctness or from a fear of violating the establishment clause of the First Amendment. They are expected to achieve higher academic performance with fewer resources. Teachers in many schools can rarely count on parent or community support due to the drain of energy and time so prevalent in homes where, on one extreme, both parents must work to make ends meet or, on the other, neither parent has a job.

Parents who can afford it frequently flee with their children to private and most often religious schools, further widening the public–private school gap by siphoning talent and resources from our public schools.

In *The Quest Continues,* Dr. Clifford Daugherty provides inspiring hope to the challenge at hand. He narrates the tale of a Christian school rated among the very top in the nation that partners with public schools to make every student a winner. Valley Christian Schools has fully embraced the idea expressed by Rick Warren's opening line in his book *The Purpose-Driven Life:* "It's not about you." Life is about others.

This book documents how public schools established a partnership with a thriving faith-based school to significantly improve student achievement and enrich the lives of all students, including both mentors and mentees. I will never forget Dr. Daugherty's words as he watched Valley Christian High School student mentors boarding the bus after pouring their talent into the students at Hellyer Elementary School: "More rides back on the bus than comes over on the bus."

This book will inspire you. More importantly, it will show you how to join hands, hearts, and faith with your neighborhood schools to

make the world a better place by bringing transformation to education.
Read, rejoice, and get envisioned!

Dr. Ed Silvoso
Founder, International Transformation Network
Author, *TRANSFORMATION: Change the Marketplace and You Change the World*

PREFACE

AS I BEGAN MY WORK DAY on July 21, 2006, I printed and reread an email I had received the day before. In it Dave Dolphin, director of production at Tate Publishing, reported the news that my first book, *Quest for Excellence,* was off to the printer.

Wow! I thought. *What an anniversary gift! It was exactly twenty years ago today when I starting working at Valley Christian Schools.* The date was Monday, July 21, 1986, and the *San Jose Mercury News* called for an interview. The reporter asked me, "What is your vision for Valley Christian Schools?"

"Valley Christian Schools needs permanent facilities," I responded. Before long an article appeared with my photo announcing me as the new VCS superintendent. Our goal of acquiring permanent facilities seemed so remote. The facts were ugly: We faced more than a million dollars of debt, imminent loss of campus leases, and several hundred thousands of deficit spending on a less than $3 million budget. The prospects of raising funds to buy fifty acres at $1 million per acre to build a $60 million campus seemed as likely to succeed as a local campaign to eliminate the national debt.

As I looked back, in 2006, at over twenty years of God's provision of fifty-three acres, a balanced budget of multiple tens of millions, and 2,106 students attending school in more than 200,000 square feet of permanent facilities valued at more than $100 million, it all seemed so incredible. Hey, let's take on the national debt too! (Since 2006, VCS has built another 66,000 square feet with another 450 students and $21 million added to the annual budget.)

But there it was: an email arriving on the last day of a twenty-year period since my first day at VCS, with news that *Quest for Excellence,* a book describing VCS's miraculous journey, had gone to print.

When I proposed the Quest for Excellence theme for Valley Christian Schools in 1991, I thought it was a catchy, inspirational phrase. My hope was it would send a message that Valley Christian Schools would always strive for quality. I wondered if the theme would even resonate well with our constituents.

In truth, the power of the Quest for Excellence caught me off guard. Its potency not only inspired people; it seemed to have a life of its own. It spoke to us at a much deeper and more profound level than I had imagined. Almost everyone associated with Valley Christian Schools, it seemed, was captured by the power of the Quest for Excellence. The courage to dream unimaginable dreams, to discover the unknown, and to predict seemingly impossible success as though it could not fail (and with repeated accuracy) is either something akin to illegal insider trading, or nothing less than a divine infusion of God's creative works!

In the years since my first book was published, the most amazing and unexpected part of our Quest for Excellence journey has unfolded. Through a remarkable sequence of events, I have come to see how the power of the Quest reaches beyond our faith-based communities to touch and transform our wider communities, even our public schools.

The Quest Continues falls roughly into two sections. The first part, reflecting our school setting, explores the *principles* of character-based education and its underlying values. We at Valley Christian Schools continue to believe, along with those who laid the foundations of our nation, "that all men are created equal, that they are endowed by their Creator with certain unalienable Rights, that among these are Life, Liberty, and the pursuit of Happiness." These "self-evident" truths serve as the bedrock of true wisdom, knowledge, and success among all people everywhere, including our neighborhood public schools. They also serve as a singular, unifying set of principles for all students in the quest for academic excellence—regardless of race, religion, creed, nationality, ethnicity, or socioeconomic circumstances. Part I culminates with an examination of the true nature of excellence and our guide for the pursuit of excellence in any arena.

In the second part of *The Quest Continues,* I share stories about the *practice* of what we have learned, with concrete examples of the Quest for Excellence concepts in action—both in the United States and abroad.

Throughout both sections—the *vision* described in Part I and the *action* in Part II—my goal is to reaffirm the insight that the universal, self-evident truths of the Declaration of Independence, which gave birth to our nation, can—and will—provide the foundation for a rebirth of America's public schools and transformation of K–12 education. The United States can once again rank among the world's leading education systems.

This book recounts my journey of discovery about the transforming power of the Quest for Excellence. Let's take the journey together. Here we go!

Clifford E. Daugherty, Ed. D.
March 2015

Note: All faith-based activities described in this book in conjunction with public schools have taken place in compliance with First Amendment court rulings, including after-school scheduling and positive written parent permission for student participation.

PART ONE

THE QUEST
FOR EXCELLENCE
VISION

CHAPTER 1

Sink the *Bismarck!*

THE CREW OF THE GERMAN battleship
Bismarck was proud, confident, and convinced their ship was unsinkable.
Many of the sailors would have scoffed at any prediction of doom. Yet
within a forty-eight-hour sequence of events in 1941, most would be
dead—entombed within the broken steel of the sunken vessel, 16,000
feet below the surface of the North Atlantic Ocean.

As the pride of Hitler's naval forces, the heavily armed and armored
Bismarck was a beast on the seas—an 823-foot tiger displacing 50,300
tons, ready to pounce on her prey as she prowled the northern sea
lanes. She saw action for only eight months, but struck fear into the
hearts of Allied nations as a killer of their supply ships.

It was with some excitement, then, when on the morning of May
24, 1941, the British naval vessels *HMS Hood* and *HMS Dorsetshire*
intercepted the *Bismarck* in the narrow strait between Iceland and
Greenland. On a cold spring day, the three warships went head-to-head
at the Battle of the Denmark Strait.

The *HMS Hood*, though the flagship of the Royal Fleet, was wholly
inferior to the battleship built by Nazi Germany. The vast superiority of
the *Bismarck* proved the *Hood's* doom: Ten minutes into the battle, the

Hood exploded into flames, and within three minutes sunk below the icy waters. Of the 1,400 British sailors on board, only three survived.

The main deck of the *Bismarck* erupted in cheers as the *Hood* slipped beneath the frigid waves. The *Dorsetshire* hastily retreated with minimal damage. In response, British Prime Minister Winston Churchill issued an order to the entire British fleet: "Sink the *Bismarck!*"

"I don't care how you do it," he said. "You must sink the *Bismarck*."[1]

Sixteen British warships scrambled into action, descending upon the *Bismarck's* last known position south of Greenland. The British command ordered them to hunt the *Bismarck* down, even if they risked running out of fuel. Finally, three royal vessels cornered their enemy 300 miles off the Irish coast.[2]

Her position compromised, German Admiral Lütjens ordered the *Bismarck* to make a sweeping circular maneuver behind her pursuers—a brilliant tactic allowing her to slip away undetected from her Majesty's Royal Navy. The *Bismarck* made a run for occupied France, and it looked as if she would indeed reach French shores and the protection of the German *Luftwaffe*.

On the morning of May 26, however, a British reconnaissance aircraft spotted the *Bismarck*. Though the bulk of Britain's naval vessels still lagged far behind the German battleship, the aircraft carrier *Ark Royal* was in the vicinity. Her flying arsenal included Swordfish biplanes, an aircraft resembling those of World War 1 vintage, with a top speed of a mere 125 miles per hour and a payload consisting of a single torpedo.

Late in the day, fifteen Swordfish launched from the *Ark Royal* during a heavy storm. The biplanes descended upon the *Bismarck* like a buzzing cloud of tiny mosquitoes attempting to penetrate an elephant's thick hide. One of the German officers commented, "It was incredible to see such obsolete-looking planes having the nerve to attack a fire-spitting mountain like the *Bismarck*."[3]

The Fairey Swordfish biplane

Though most of the fifteen Swordfish torpedoes missed the *Bismarck,* two hit their mark. One exploded harmlessly against the ship's thick hull, while a second struck portside near the port rudder shaft.[4] It was an unlikely shot, hitting the seemingly invulnerable *Bismarck* at her Achilles heel—the rudders of her steering mechanism. The torpedo blast jammed the port rudder into a locked twelve-degree turn to port. Unbelievably, the tiny mosquito, incapable of piercing the armor of the great beast, forced the *Bismarck* to steam in out-of-control circles—helplessly awaiting the attack of the Royal Navy.[5]

A day later, on May 27, 1941, with the *Bismarck* dangerously exposed and unable to maneuver, the British naval forces finally caught up with her. Four British warships pummeled the *Bismarck* with more than 2,800 shells, scoring 400 hits. After the withering ninety-minute assault, the German ship lay devastated, with fires breaking out, water penetrating the decks, and many lives lost.[6]

The battleship's upper works were almost completely destroyed, but her engines still functioned. Survivor Johannes "Hans" Zimmermann, a boiler-room stoker, confirms salt water had entered the boiler feed lines. Fearing an explosion, the engineers reduced speed to seven knots, placing the ship in even greater danger. Despite the deadly British barrage, surviving crew members of the *Bismarck* said the hull appeared to be relatively sound. Rather than risk the ship's capture, however, its First Officer gave the order to scuttle and then abandon ship.[7]

Thus German-rigged scuttling explosives did what more than 400 shells could not achieve: At 10:40 a.m. the *Bismarck* disappeared below the ocean's surface.[8] Of the 2,200-member crew, only 115 survived.[9]

Decades later, Germany insisted the crew had scuttled the *Bismarck* to avoid capture, while the British claim the ship was already sinking from British fire. Underwater video footage from the expeditions of Robert Baillard, the explorer who discovered the wreck of the *Bismarck* in 1991, and later James Cameron, of *Titanic* fame, revealed very little damage to *Bismarck's* hull below the waterline. The consensus? Eventually, the *Bismarck* would have sunk—minutes or hours later. But rather than give the British the satisfaction of sinking her, the Germans scuttled their own ship.

What a David and Goliath story! The fate of Europe's fiercest warship was sealed by a tiny, archaic-style biplane carrying a single torpedo.

A CALL TO ACTION

Educators, parents, and students living in 21st-century America can take the following important insights from the story of the *Bismarck:*

1. Europe's greatest naval warship was built to empower Nazi Germany as Hitler threatened freedom worldwide. Then, as today, America's freedoms are endangered as school children often pass from grade to grade while failing to learn the values of our Founding Fathers—the values giving birth to the liberties and freedoms of our republic.

2. When the *Bismarck* sank the *HMS Hood*—the most advanced warship in the Royal Navy—in just thirteen minutes, Churchill could have succumbed

to discouragement and despair. Today, too many Americans have a sense of hopelessness toward our struggling public schools. Millions of parents believe the only good option is to send their children to expensive private schools, but most face the sad reality they cannot afford private school tuition.

3. In the face of seeming despair, Churchill's famous response was a commitment to find and "sink the *Bismarck*." Truth is on the side of freedom, and those who place their faith in the truth will ultimately prevail. The seemingly infinite problems of our public schools are not insurmountable. The same power of truth that gave birth to the freedoms and liberty of our nation can bring a rebirth of quality in our schools.

4. The crew who believed the *Bismarck* unsinkable, who just hours before her sinking had mocked the Swordfish biplanes, stopped scoffing when a single torpedo knocked out the ship's rudder and crippled the entire formidable warship. The lesson we can learn from Winston Churchill and the Royal Navy is to never give up on the defense of truth and the fight for freedom—even in the face of apparently impossible odds.

Despite the daunting challenge of winning liberty from what was then the greatest military force in the world, our Founding Fathers prevailed, establishing the United States of America on shining principles. Imagine the power of those "self-evident" truths our Founders so boldly affirmed in the Declaration of Independence: "We hold these truths to be self-evident, that all men are created equal, that they are endowed by their Creator with certain unalienable Rights, that among these are Life, Liberty, and the pursuit of Happiness." How quickly and dramatically the circumstances of our public schools could improve if American educators and parents once again called upon the power and legacy of our Founding Fathers to achieve this transformation. The dismal problems plaguing our schools—poor academic performance, delinquency, lack of funding, violence, and more—would give way to a bright shining light within a relatively short time. We need to keep a determined and positive view of the same self-evident truths. And today we understand how "the pursuit of Happiness" is an empty promise and a shallow dream without the opportunity for a quality education.

The demise of the *Bismarck* illustrates how an apparently unstoppable force can be defeated by the daring and determined efforts of a few brave men and women.[10] This reality restores hope for every child in American schools. To succeed, however, we must courageously pilot our seemingly insignificant biplanes toward the formidable armor of a "behemoth beast" of problems beleaguering our poor-performing schools. The power of our Founding Fathers' values, strategically aimed like the Swordfish torpedo, can foster a rebirth of excellence in American schools.

The *Bismarck* story is rich with analogies and metaphors. From another perspective, America's educational system is like the crippled battleship itself. Once the finest in the world, with noble intent to offer educational opportunity for all, public education in America is now in jeopardy of catastrophic failure: Having lost our rudder, we are turning in circles. The children aboard the foundering ship of public education need our rescue. Unlike the crew of the *Bismarck,* determined Americans can and must repair our educational rudder and restore the same moral compass that guided our nation's Founding Fathers.

THE GREAT ADVANTAGE

Can we really expect the restoration of a moral compass and rudder to transform our nation's schools and provide all students with the opportunity for quality education? My own story sheds some light on this question. During the amazing development of Valley Christian Schools, I often wondered what made the Quest for Excellence so powerful. Superb programs embracing Academic Achievement, Artistic Beauty, and Athletic Distinction—what we call "A to the third power," or A^3—made the school's beautiful facilities on a fifty-three-acre hill overlooking Silicon Valley even more appealing. The big question became *why?* Why Valley Christian Schools? It seemed as though VCS had some sort of great advantage. One well-respected leader of Christian schools told me during an administrative conference, "You just happened to be in the right place at the right time."

I reflected on his analysis. Does being "in the right place at the right time" adequately explain Valley Christian Schools' great advantage? The reasoning goes something like this: "The rain falls and the sun shines on the just and the unjust." We simply happened to build VCS in Silicon Valley while the sun shined and when generous "dot-com" philanthropists gave large capital gifts to develop our school. Other schools with less favorable, "rainy" economic circumstances could expect to struggle with less-than-excellent program offerings.

Somehow my heart hurt with those thoughts. Such an explanation led to a logical conclusion that "time and place"—not divine Providence—accounted for VCS's great advantage. Deep in my heart I wanted to shout, "No! It's not just being in the right place at the right time." One fact is certain, the Quest for Excellence and the Excellence Brings Influence strategy continued to bring amazing results for Valley Christian Schools.

But questions remained: Is the Quest for Excellence a model all schools—individuals, businesses, or professions—can emulate? Is such success repeatable anywhere, in any arena? Obviously, if being in the right place at the right time is VCS's great advantage, the answer is no. If VCS, however, was built and sustained by divine principles involving the Quest for Excellence, the VCS model for development may be repeatable in any community. As I pondered, I passionately wanted to tell everyone VCS has no advantage greater than any other school in the world. It's not just about being "in the right place at the right time," because the principles of the Quest for Excellence *will* work "any place, all the time"!

Any place at any time is the right place at the right time because, as our Founding Fathers described in the Declaration of Independence, we too can rely on "divine Providence" to bring "Life, Liberty, and the pursuit of Happiness"—or what I and our team of neighborhood educators describe as goodness, peace, and joy[11]—anywhere.[12]

Everyone who has read my first book, *Quest for Excellence,* knows I deeply believe God built and sustains Valley Christian Schools. I long to tell all school administrators and other marketplace professionals that God can be counted on to do the same great works in their community, their businesses, and their personal lives. When guests visit and tell me what a great job I have done building VCS, I am quick to say how thankful I am to serve at VCS while *God* does His great work.

It is true. A good look at the accomplishments of Valley Christian students elicits in me the same reaction others experience when they visit Valley Christian Schools. It's a sense of *awe!* When Josh McDowell, who will no doubt be remembered as one of the most scholarly and articulate Christian apologists of the 20th and 21st centuries, spoke to our VCS parents and students, he affirmed that "Valley Christian High School is one of the finest schools in America. The Quest for Excellence should be lived out in every Christian school throughout the world."

While speaking to more than 5,000 Valley Christian Schools graduates and guests, Dr. Paul Kienel, founder of the Association of

Christian Schools International (ACSI), said, "Over my long career I have visited hundreds of Christian schools around the world, and this campus is indeed the most beautiful I have seen."

Yes, VCS is an amazing place. Examples of national, state, and regional awards and recognition abound in almost every part of our schools. With such powerful results from the Quest for Excellence, I asked God to help me understand the reasons for this success. What really was catapulting our more than 2,800 students and staff to such heights? And can the godly principles of the Quest for Excellence do the same for anyone, for any school—or for any business or profession?

MY JOURNEY OF DISCOVERY

Three critical insights lie at the core of Valley Christian Schools' success, and serve as the fuel for the Quest for Excellence. The first two insights were described in my first book, and the third insight is the topic of this book. They are:

- ❖ *Excellence is the nature, character, and works of God.* — This definition and absolute standard of excellence challenges every student, teacher, parent, and person in the VCS community to achieve the highest standards. In the school arena, this measure of excellence answers the question, "*What* is the essence of a most excellent education?"

- ❖ *Excellence Brings Influence!* — VCS's Excellence Brings Influence strategy answers the question, "How can Christians positively influence their world?" Likewise, our theme verse, "Whatsoever ye do, do it heartily, as to the Lord,"[13] answers the question, "Why should Christians passionately pursue excellence?"

❖ *Access to the Omnis* — God is omnipotent, omnipresent, and omniscient. His very nature qualifies Him as
the only ultimate, all-powerful, everywhere-present,
and all-knowing God of the universe. "Access to the
Omnis" describes how God makes His inexhaustible
resources available to achieve His will through those
who "ask anything in My name. . . ."[14]

Hundreds of heads of schools, principals, and board members
come to visit Valley Christian Schools with questions and hopes
about building excellent Christian schools in their communities. I
often wondered if I could confidently say God is willing and able to
do the same miraculous works to build schools like Valley Christian
in other communities. Or is God's development of our school a unique
phenomenon in the sovereign plans of God?

Of course, I never doubted God is able to build a great school
anywhere He pleases, but I wondered if I might be presumptuous to
say God is willing to build a great school system in any community. As
I reflected on the approximately $150 million it would take to rebuild
Valley Christian Schools in today's economy, I wondered whether there
could possibly be enough money to build such great schools everywhere.
Not knowing the answer, I took the Apostle James' advice: "If any of
you lacks wisdom, let him ask of God, who gives to all liberally. . . ."[15]

I asked, and God, faithful to His Word, gave me insights. My
journey of discovery began with three big, central questions:

1. Can I confidently say God is willing and able to do the
    same miraculous works to build schools like VCS in
    any community where people are praying and working
    to bring His goodness, peace, and joy to the children
    in their schools?

2. Are there really enough resources to build great schools in every community, even during difficult economic times?

3. If the answers to the first two questions are yes, what can I say to help people find enough resources to build great schools like VCS? In other words, how can ordinary people with ordinary means get "Access to the Omnis" to accomplish the Quest for Excellence in their schools, their businesses, or their professional lives?

As the Quest for Excellence transformed education for students at Valley Christian Schools, I found myself longing for the same opportunity for all children everywhere. But it seemed like an impossible challenge. Given my default perspective at the time that only Christian schools could foster godly character in light of United States Supreme Court rulings, building quality K–12 Christian schools in every community seemed like our only option. Was I in for a big surprise! The huge paradigm shift for me involved a realization of how calling on the legacy of America's Founding Fathers can restore goodness, peace, and joy to all children in all our schools, including public schools—regardless of religious or socioeconomic circumstances.

This book describes my discovery of answers to the three central questions introduced above. As I began, I wanted to believe the Quest for Excellence journey is assuredly within reach of every school and student in America—and that it can be pursued by anyone, anywhere, any time.

Ready to restore the moral compass and take a deep dive to repair the rudder on our nation's ship of education? Let's launch!

CHAPTER 2

LIGHT, LIFE, AND LEARNING
IN A PUBLIC SCHOOL

MY THIRD-GRADE TEACHER introduced me to Jesus Christ—at a public school. Here is how it happened.

When I was eight years old, my father, a master sergeant in the Air Force, was transferred to Harmon Air Force Base in Newfoundland, Canada, where our family lived for three years. On the first day of third grade, during the 1957–58 school year, a beautiful blond teacher opened her Bible and read: "In the beginning God created the heavens and the earth. . . ." And then she prayed a simple prayer asking God to help every student have a great year and to learn how much God loves them.

I wanted to impress Mrs. Oehm. She was nice, and I wanted her to like me as much as I admired her. One day she mentioned the word "saint" and I did not know the meaning of the word. She asked, "Do you want to be a saint, Cliff?"

Not wanting to reveal my ignorance, I answered her question with a question: "Do you?"

"Yes," she answered.

"Then I want to be a saint too!" But as much as I tried, I certainly was no saint.

Mrs. Oehm's class during my third-grade year,
with the school in the background

In the winter, Newfoundland felt like a freezer with lots of snow and wind. My mother ordered special winter clothing from the Montgomery Ward catalog to keep us warm. During our first winter, I wore heavy socks, waterproof snow boots, snow pants, gloves, a brown hat with a strap and furry ear covers, and a blue parka. My brother, sister, and I walked to our nearby school. Before we left the classroom for recess, we put on our warm outer clothing, then hung it on the coat hooks when we returned.

We played hard outside, and as our bodies warmed we sometimes pulled off outer clothing like hats, scarves, and gloves. If we left them outside and it began to snow, we might lose them until after the spring snowmelt.

One day I pulled off my cap and used only my parka hood to protect my head. At the end of the school day, I couldn't find my brown cap. I told Mrs. Oehm someone took it. After we looked around, I think Mrs. Oehm realized I probably left my cap in the snow on the play yard at recess.

She then made a wise comment. "I'm going to pray for the person who is responsible for your missing cap. Sometimes God speaks through a person's conscience to make things right."

My conscience was already speaking loudly and I didn't like what I was hearing. I wished I could be good from the inside like Mrs. Oehm, but it seemed impossible no matter how much I tried. I couldn't admit I lost my hat.

On another day when Mrs. Oehm was directing a reading group, I impetuously raised my hand. We were not to interrupt her reading groups. After watching me wave my arm awhile, she relented and stopped the group to ask what I wanted.

"I need to go to the bathroom," I said.

"It's almost recess. Wait until then."

"I can't," I pleaded.

Mrs. Oehm relented. "All right, you may go, but hurry back."

I went into the bathroom with only one thing in mind: combing my hair. I wet my hair and combed it back on both sides with a big wave in front. After all, Debbie Faulkner and Nancy Nelson would be at recess and I wanted to look my best. When I returned to class, I walked right by the reading group toward my desk. Mrs. Oehm took one look at my hair and called me to stand in front of her while she remained seated in her reading-group chair. I noticed her blue eyes. They seemed to pierce right into my heart.

"Did you go into the bathroom just to comb your hair?"

"Oh, no!" I answered. "You see, I went to the bathroom and when I was passing the sink I saw my hair in the mirror so I combed it."

She looked at me with knowing blue eyes, which turned sad as she whispered, "You may sit down now."

Similar incidents followed, and sometimes I even thought I fooled Mrs. Oehm. Though I really tried, I just couldn't be like Mrs. Oehm on the inside.

I noticed the Bible on her desk. She really liked the Bible. One day I asked her if we could read the Bible together after school. I thought my request would impress her, and the privilege of spending time with Mrs. Oehm would be a bonus.

She said she would pray about it.

The next day I asked her, "What did God say about reading the Bible after school?"

"Well," she replied, "I sense we should read only a verse or two because it is more important to understand what we read than to read a lot."

So we read the Bible after school every day. Sometimes almost half the class came and took turns reading.

When third grade ended, I still had an empty place in my heart. I certainly was not a saint, like Mrs. Oehm, on the inside.

The summer passed. After a school baseball game just before fourth grade began, I walked to the school door and pulled the handle. To my surprise, it opened. Down an empty hallway I walked, looking through the glass windows on classroom doors, wondering if Mrs. Oehm might be there. Suddenly, she appeared in another room—unloading boxes. I put on my best behavior as I entered the room.

"Hello, Mrs. Oehm!"

She stopped unloading and returned my greeting. "Hi, Cliff! It's so good to see you!" Then, after a thoughtful pause, she asked, "Did you ever ask Jesus to forgive you of your sins?"

Her question stunned me. I didn't know what to say. *If I say yes, that means I've sinned. If I say no, I don't think that's a good answer either.*

I bowed my head without a reply. Mrs. Oehm answered my thoughts. "If you want, I can pray with you right now so you can ask Jesus to forgive you of your sins, and He will come into your heart."

She did, and I did! And for the first time, I didn't need to fake it anymore. Jesus forgave my sins, and Jesus lived in my heart!

Even now, decades later, I can still remember walking home with the joy of the Lord in my heart—a feeling like I was walking on clouds. My sins were gone! And I believed I might actually be a real saint on the inside—like Mrs. Oehm!

I never had a better teacher than Mrs. Oehm, even though I attended Bethany University, San Jose State University, Santa Clara University, the University of California Santa Cruz, Penn State University (where I began my doctoral degree), and the University of San Francisco (where I completed my doctoral degree). Mrs. Oehm led me to the Lord, and for that I am eternally grateful. She is the single most important teacher in my life.

She later taught at a Christian school in Walnut Creek, California, where her husband, Dr. Rudy Oehm, headed the cardiology department at the Diablo Kaiser Permanente Medical Group. After the 1962–63 U.S. Supreme Court rulings against prayer and Bible reading in public schools, she chose to teach in a Christian school so she could continue to pray with her students.

Ancient bronze oil "lamp of learning" with the "Chi Rho"
Christian symbol of the Messiah (replica)
Photograph by Rama; licensed by the Wikimedia Commons

LIGHT, LIFE, AND LEARNING

Mrs. Oehm made sure her students had a great moral compass and a strong rudder to help form a positive school culture of Light, Life, and Learning. Throughout this book I will refer to Light, Life, and Learning. This phrase uncovers the "magic" of our Founding Fathers' insights that gave birth to our nation. These truths are also profoundly critical for restoring academic excellence in American schools.

The Light, Life, and Learning paradigm is informed by and directly tied to the Declaration of Independence as follows:

> *Light* comes from the "self-evident" truth that all "are created equal." Not one person, not one student, is on this earth by happenstance. Our Founding Fathers declared that everyone is created by our Creator! This principle, when understood, illuminates a sense of absolute worth for every individual. Every student deserves to know they are "created equal" with innate and incredible value in the eyes of their Creator.

> *Life* proceeds from Light and involves the realization that every person, every student, has a purpose and a destiny for their lives to bring goodness, peace, and joy to their families, their communities, and their world.

> *Learning* naturally follows Life. Students passionately pursuing their life's purpose and destiny discover they are "endowed by their Creator with certain unalienable Rights" including "Life, Liberty, and the pursuit of Happiness," as described by our Founding Fathers in the Declaration of Independence.

The sequence of Light, Life, and Learning is critical because Light precedes Life, and Life precedes Learning. The sequence parallels growing plants: First, sunlight warms the soil to sprout a seed and give it life, then the plant can grow and thrive until it produces good fruit. In the same way, Light emanating from the self-evident truths of our Founding Fathers must inform the minds and warm the hearts of students so they will appreciate the value, purpose, and sense of destiny of their lives. Such an identity of value, destiny, and purpose, when matured, can produce the fruit of inspired academic learning.

The principles of our Founding Fathers can again enrich the sense of self-worth and purpose needed for learning, creating an emotional readiness in students to learn. Learning is exponentially accelerated when the Light, Life, and Learning sequence takes root in the minds and hearts of students in any school, whether private, public, charter, or home school.

The question is this: Given the fifty-year-old U.S. Supreme Court rulings restricting school prayer, what can be done to repair the Light, Life, and Learning rudder in public schools? If liberty, morality, and faith are critical ingredients for accelerated learning and academic excellence, then this question is crucial for American public schools and deserves an answer.

HISTORICAL ORIGINS

French writer and historian Alexis de Tocqueville wisely wrote after an in-depth study of American democracy during the 1830s, "Liberty cannot be established without morality, nor morality without faith."[16]

When asked if government schools should be relied upon to teach their children religion, even the most fundamental Christians would agree with the high court's rulings suggesting parents, not the government, are responsible for the religious training of their children. In fact, in *Abington Township School District v. Schempp* (1963), Supreme Court Justice Tom C. Clark, writing for the court majority, concluded, "The place of religion in our society is an exalted one, achieved through a long tradition of reliance on the home, the church, and the inviolable citadel of the individual heart and mind. We have come to recognize through bitter experience that it is not within the power of government to invade that citadel, whether its purpose or effect be to aid or oppose, to advance or retard. In the relationship between man and religion, the State is firmly committed to a position of neutrality."[17]

As president of Valley Christian Schools, I am fully aware of the powerful influence of Christian faith for creating a culture of Light, Life, and Learning. The Christian influence enjoyed a continuous presence in America's schools for 343 years—since the founding of Plymouth, Massachusetts, in 1620. But since 1963, after prayer and Bible reading were severely restricted in schools, our nation has experienced its most precipitous rise in teen pregnancy, drug use, murder, and teen suicide.[18] I am not suggesting that denying government schools from leading students in prayer or teaching religion is to blame for the moral decline of our children. I do believe, however, that our struggles to maintain a strong rudder and moral compass for our schools have dramatically contributed to the moral and academic decline among our youth.

As was the case with the *Bismarck,* the loss of a ship's rudder turns into a nightmare for her captain. The American public school system originated in one-room church schoolhouses where, with rare exception, Christian faith was inextricably integrated through the entire curriculum. Our moral rudder, at the time, was intact.

Regarding American schooling in the first half of the 19th century, Tocqueville concluded, "Almost all education is entrusted to the clergy."[19] He further acknowledged, "Christianity, which has declared that all men are equal in the sight of God, will not refuse to acknowledge that all citizens are equal in the eye of the law."[20]

As well, Christianity unquestionably shaped the formation of the Declaration of Independence, as reflected in statements such as "All men are created equal." Indeed, the influence of Christian faith on Thomas Jefferson, the principal author of the Declaration, through his formal education cannot be denied. He wrote that his father,

Peter Jefferson, ". . . placed me at the English school at 5 years of age and at the Latin school at 9, where I continued until his death." Notably, the Reverend William Douglas conducted the Latin school. Early in 1758 Jefferson began attending the school of Reverend James Maury, whom Jefferson credited as "a correct classical scholar." He continued studies with Reverend Maury for two years until entering the College of William and Mary in Williamsburg during the spring of 1760 at the age of seventeen.[21]

Jefferson's formal education included influences from the Reverend William Douglas, Reverend James Maury, and the faculty of the College of William and Mary (1760–62). At the time, William and Mary's faculty was composed entirely of clergymen except for one professor of natural philosophy and mathematics.[22] Given the influence of Christian educators in Jefferson's formal education, it is no wonder Jefferson was so eloquently able to include the profound Christian virtues written into the Declaration of Independence.

Today historians and theologians debate whether Jefferson was a traditional Christian or a Deist and Unitarian who respected the Bible and its tenets. Whatever Jefferson's personal faith, one thing is clear: The Bible and its principles were deeply inculcated into Jefferson, profoundly affecting the creation and content of the Declaration of Independence.

"APPEALING TO THE SUPREME JUDGE OF THE WORLD . . ."

One Saturday, I read the Declaration of Independence without interruption. The soaring prose of this document, signed July 4, 1776, inspired me. Somehow I had subconsciously overlooked the power of Thomas Jefferson's words, forever enshrined in the final paragraph of the Declaration:

We, therefore, the Representatives of the United States of America, in General Congress, Assembled, appealing to the Supreme Judge of the world for the rectitude of our intentions, do, in the Name, and by Authority of the good People of these Colonies, solemnly publish and declare, That these United Colonies are, and of Right ought to be Free and Independent States; that they are Absolved from all Allegiance to the British Crown, and that all political connection between them and the State of Great Britain, is and ought to be totally dissolved; and that as Free and Independent States, they have full Power to levy War, conclude Peace, contract Alliances, establish Commerce, and to do all other Acts and Things which Independent States may of right do. And for the support of this Declaration, with a firm reliance on the protection of divine Providence, we mutually pledge to each other our Lives, our Fortunes and our sacred Honor.

Clearly, I concluded, if those who had the courage and wisdom to found our great United States of America considered it necessary and appropriate to appeal "to the Supreme Judge of the world for the rectitude of [their] intentions . . . with a firm reliance on the protection of divine Providence," we should do no less for all the children of America.

Good intentions are important, but moral behavior is another. The Declaration of Independence uses the word "rectitude" in reference to the intentions of the Founders. The Free Dictionary (www. TheFreeDictionary.com) defines rectitude as:

1. Moral uprightness; righteousness.
2. The quality or condition of being correct in judgment.
3. The quality of being straight.

The moral authority for restoring the rudder and moral compass of "self-evident" truths in our nation's public schools is a treasure all Americans inherit from our Founding Fathers. This precious hidden treasure of moral authority, enabling students to better discern right from wrong, can be rediscovered and reinstated in all of our American schools by teaching and honoring our Declaration of Independence.

All American school children deserve to learn how our Founding Fathers supported the Declaration of Independence's acknowledgement of our Creator's existence. As well, they must be exposed to the goodness, peace, and joy message, expressed by Thomas Jefferson as "Life, Liberty, and the pursuit of Happiness." While public schools are not to teach religion, all schools should teach students about the Declaration of Independence and that our Founding Fathers believed "these truths to be self-evident, that all men are created equal, that they are endowed by their Creator with certain unalienable Rights, that among these are Life, Liberty, and the pursuit of Happiness." After all, our nation's foundational document makes it clear how our Founding Fathers appealed "to the Supreme Judge of the world for the rectitude" of their intentions. Without such a firm reliance on the protection of divine Providence to found an independent nation, the United States of America would not exist.

The children of America have a right to learn about the faith of our Founding Fathers. The authority of the legacy they have left all Americans in the Declaration of Independence and other documents provides a sound basis and strong foundation for working to restore the moral compass of our public schools.

CAN THE RUDDER BE REPAIRED?

Americans have seldom faced a more debated topic than whether or not government schools should include Bible reading and prayer during school hours. In 1962, the Supreme Court ruled in *Engel v. Vitale* that the New York schools did not have the right to require students to recite a prayer composed by the education board. A year later, the high court ruled in *Abington Township School District v. Schempp* that school-sponsored Bible reading and recitation of the Lord's Prayer is unconstitutional.

So starting in the early 1960s, official Bible reading and prayer in public schools were forbidden by Supreme Court rulings based on the First Amendment to the U.S. Constitution and its prohibition of state establishment of religion. This ban left many Christian parents with a sense of complete incompatibility between their values and the public schools. Over the next several decades, a wide range of Christians—both parents and educators—saw a link between the removal of prayer from schools and a rise in teen pregnancy, STDs, gang violence, and substance abuse (as mentioned earlier). For a number of reasons, the secularization of the schools has led to an increasingly radical shift wherein our society has become less family- and faith-centered in its values.

For many Christians, then, our schools and most of our nation have become like the crippled *Bismarck*—a ship without a rudder. But our American public school system has lost not only its rudder; it has also lost its moral compass. Many parents without the resources to pay for private schools have elected to homeschool their children. Since the 1960s, countless disillusioned families have abandoned economically challenged public schools with concerns or questions about marginal school safety and low academic achievement. Besides questionable moral standards and the absence of even student-led prayer, other parents cite severe program reductions in the arts, athletics, sciences, technology, and math as further reasons why they have opted for private schools or homeschooling alternatives.

The U.S Department of Education reported 1,770,000 students were homeschooled during the 2011–12 school year, up from 1,508,000 since the fall of 2007. Ninety-one percent of homeschooling parents reported concern about the environment of other schools as a reason for their decision to homeschool, and 77 percent indicated a desire to provide moral instruction at home. Moreover, 74 percent expressed dissatisfaction with academic instruction at other schools, and 64 percent indicated a desire to provide religious instruction at home.[23]

Other parents sacrifice to pay tuition in private religious or non-sectarian schools to provide formal education consistent with their family's faith and academic standards. Public school compliance with court mandates banning Bible reading and prayer, combined with the exodus of families concerned about low academic achievement or poor school environments, has had a darkening effect on a good number of public schools. Many public schools float aimlessly without a rudder or moral compass—suffering without curricula or programs to teach good character virtues.

Like numerous other Americans, I had concluded public schools were doomed to poor quality because the Light and Life, which prepare students for Learning, were stripped from our schools in the early 1960s by the Supreme Court rulings.

For years I grappled with these questions:

❖ Can the severely damaged rudder of America's schools be repaired, even though the Supreme Court has forbidden government-led prayer, Bible reading, and posting the Ten Commandments in our public schools? In effect, is there another way to reintroduce the continuum of Light, Life, and Learning into the curriculum of our public schools?

❖ Can schools tap into the legacy and values of our Founding Fathers in order to provide a strong underpinning for restoring the educational rudder of Light, Life, and Learning?

✧ Having laid the foundation of our Founding Fathers' legacy, might a partnership with parents, churches, and other community organizations complete the Light, Life, and Learning mosaic for all students— with parent permission, regardless of their religious or non-religious affiliations—in public, private, or charter schools?

In the next chapter, I will share my own personal quest as a Christian school educator in answer to these questions. What I discovered was eye-opening.

CHAPTER 3

THE HIGHEST COURT
IN THE LAND

GIVEN VALLEY CHRISTIAN Schools' firm commitment to prayer and Christian values, as found in the Bible and reflected in the life and teachings of Jesus, there was never a doubt in my mind about the strong rudder undergirding quality education for our students. But like many—if not most—Christians in America, I had written off the public schools as unreachable and without hope. Was my perspective an accurate assessment, or by some miracle might Life, Light, and Learning be within reach for all American school children? The crew of the crippled *Bismarck* tried to repair the ship's rudder but failed. Is the same true of American public schools? Has its rudder been irreparably damaged?

Massive amounts of resources have poured into the public schools in pursuit of quality education. For example, in the 2009–10 school year alone, $638 billion was spent on public education in the United States.[24] According to a study conducted by the Organisation for Economic Co-operation and Development (OECD), the United States in 2010 spent more money per student on education than any of the other thirty-four nations covered in the report. In spite of this, U.S.

student achievement lagged: "The United States ranked 31st in math and 23rd in science among 15-year-old students on the Program for International Student Assessment (PISA). This supports the argument that higher spending does not equal higher test scores."[25]

The Light and Life of the Light, Life, and Learning paradigm was tragically—and unnecessarily—lost in American schools when the Supreme Court ruled against government-led school prayer, Bible reading, and the posting of the Ten Commandments, rulings based on the establishment clause of the First Amendment to the U.S. Constitution. The establishment clause reads, "Congress shall make no law respecting an establishment of religion. . . ." But the free exercise clause of the First Amendment completes the sentence: ". . . or prohibiting the free exercise thereof." Only *government-led* school prayer and Bible reading were banned, and subsequent court rulings further define and uphold the free exercise clause for students attending public schools.

More about these issues later, but suffice it to say for now, Americans have misunderstood and overreacted to the Supreme Court rulings. With all of the confusion, we have stood by feeling helpless as the quality of Light, Life, and Learning has diminished in our schools.

Did American Christians become so reliant on government educators to teach our children how to pray and read the Bible that we lost our way? Have Christians failed to teach our children at home, at church, and through Bible clubs and many other opportunities to serve every student in our public schools? Certainly most Christians do not want their children taught a politically correct religion or generic prayers appropriate for all religions. Parents with or without religious beliefs should never support any form of coerced religious instruction by public educators.

No doubt a culture of Light, Life, and Learning is critical for quality education. So with the Supreme Court having enforced the establishment clause of the First Amendment, the question becomes:

Will Christians and other people of good will take advantage of the free exercise clause of the same First Amendment to help restore a culture of Light, Life, and Learning in all our schools—whether public, private, or charter schools? The Supreme Court did its duty to ensure the government does not establish religion in American schools. Now, more than five decades later, it's past time to do our duty to restore the Light, Life, and Learning rudder to American school children by calling on the legacy of our Founding Fathers. The First Amendment not only forbids the government from establishing religion; it also ensures "the free exercise thereof." Thankfully, the Supreme Court has ruled that students do not "shed their constitutional rights . . . at the schoolhouse gate."[26]

While giving my 2013 keynote address at Valley Christian Schools, I discovered that, with few exceptions, most of our more than 300 VCS faculty and staff were uninformed about the court and legislative rulings related to the free exercise clause. They were surprised to learn there are more than twice as many major court and legislative rulings protecting the religious rights of school students, as well as adults, to read the Bible, pray, and distribute information than the two Supreme Court rulings forbidding government-led Bible reading and prayer in public schools. I showed the following table during my keynote to prove the point.

If Christian faith has gone missing from our public schools, the fault lies at the doorstep of misguided Christians who believe the Supreme Court forbids all religious meetings, prayer, Bible reading, and other religious rights in our public schools. It's simply not true! In fact, the courts have consistently protected the free exercise of religion by students, including Christian faith in our public schools. I too had a blind spot and blamed the Supreme Court for America's "godless" public schools. I needed a change of attitude and a change of heart, with clear vision as to the facts.

COURT CASE OR LEGISLATION	ISSUE	FIRST AMENDMENT CLAUSE
Engel v. Vitale, **Supreme Court, 1962**	Government-directed prayer in public schools violates the establishment clause of the First Amendment	**Establishment Clause** *Congress shall make no law respecting an establishment of religion,*
Abington Township School District v. Schempp, **Supreme Court, 1963**	Sanctioned and organized Bible reading in public schools in the United States is unconstitutional	**Establishment Clause** *Congress shall make no law respecting an establishment of religion,*
Tinker v. Des Moines Independent Community School District, **Supreme Court, 1969**	Students have First Amendment rights that cannot be denied at the "schoolhouse gate"	**Free Exercise Clause** *or prohibiting the free exercise thereof*
Congress – Equal Access Act, 1984	Schools may not discriminate against any students who wish to conduct meetings ... for religious, political ... or other ... speech	**Free Exercise Clause** *or prohibiting the free exercise thereof*
Westside School District v. Mergens, **Supreme Court, 1990**	School districts may not prohibit Bible study groups from meeting on school premises if other groups meet on school premises	**Free Exercise Clause** *or prohibiting the free exercise thereof*
Good News Club v. Milford Central School District, **Supreme Court, 2001**	A district may not exclude an adult-initiated club on the basis of religious content. The First Amendment requires neutrality toward, not hostility against, a religious perspective	**Free Exercise Clause** *or prohibiting the free exercise thereof*
Hills v. Scottsdale Unified School District, **9th Circuit Court of Appeals,** **329 F.3d. 1044, 2003**	If a district allows other organizations to distribute similar information, then it cannot refuse distribution of literature advertising an off-campus summer program because it is taught from a Christian perspective	**Free Exercise Clause** *or prohibiting the free exercise thereof*

COMMON VIRTUES

So how do we move forward, since the First Amendment not only forbids the government from establishing religion but also protects "the free exercise thereof"? Remember, the Supreme Court has ruled students do not "shed their constitutional rights . . . at the schoolhouse gate."[27]

During my career as an educator, all kinds of initiatives to restore quality to our public schools have come and gone. There was the "New Math" of the '70s, individualized instruction and measurable objectives of the '80s, then project-based and outcome-based education and the school-wide learning results of the '90s. And today we have Common Core Standards and benchmark assessments. While having varied success, all of these programs focus only on the Learning piece of the Light, Life, and Learning paradigm. The result? American public education has lost its rudder and moral compass.

If you are an educator or parent who keeps current with educational trends, then you are familiar with the educational phrase "Common Core State Standards." The Common Core State Standards Initiative is a set of college- and career-ready standards for kindergarten through twelfth grade in English language arts and mathematics. Almost all states have adopted the Common Core Standards. The goal is to produce high school graduates proficient in English and math skills. I posit, however, our nation desperately needs a "Common Virtues Initiative" offering all children a moral foundation of good character.

Outstanding teachers care enough about their students to work tirelessly toward rigorous standards for math, English, and other curricula. Should not we also support a Common Virtues Initiative to affirm the conscience of every student as a moral compass to discern right from wrong? Based on the values of our Founding Fathers, Common Virtues could easily be understood as the virtues proceeding from the insights of America's Founders as affirmed and recorded in the Declaration of Independence, now a shared legacy of all Americans.

"All . . . are created equal," the Founders wrote. By this they meant all humans, as created beings, have inherent worth, and each person's inherent created worth is equivalent to every other person's. Out of this belief flow virtues such as mutual respect, the dignity of every person, the value of kindness, honesty, integrity, treating others the way you would want them to treat you (the "Golden Rule"), and much more. These Common Virtues form the building blocks of good schools, good communities, and good relationships of all kinds.

Isn't a Common Virtues Initiative an educational movement most Americans would support and all children deserve, regardless of race, religion, creed, nationality, or ethnicity? While I am a lover of the Bible and read it daily, a Common Virtues Initiative would not require official Bible reading and prayer in our public schools. Teachers in public schools may not teach students to *believe* "self-evident" truths "that all men are created equal [and] endowed by their Creator with certain unalienable Rights." However, all children should learn that Thomas Jefferson, the foremost author of the Declaration of Independence, and our Founding Fathers who adopted that historic document did in fact believe those truths. Given this historical fact, students should learn what our Founding Fathers considered "self-evident" truths on which our nation was successfully founded. Students should also have the opportunity to personally choose to accept or reject what our Founders believed, because our nation's founding firmly rests on those truths.

Common Virtues are a key ingredient to the continuum of Light, Life, and Learning. Our Founding Fathers left a legacy of self-evident truths in the Declaration of Independence—a legacy we can call on to help restore Common Virtues as the moral compass and a rudder to help guide American public schools. The Founders believed our Creator instilled unchanging self-evident truths as a clear, internal compass to direct our national conscience and help us teach students to discern between right and wrong. In a time when teachers are lacking a school-wide compass for standards of right and wrong (in the absence of any religious moral authority), the self-evident truths and moral legacy of our Founding Fathers can repair the rudder and realign the moral compass in our schools to point toward true north.

The Common Virtues of our Founding Fathers, contained in the Declaration of Independence, offer unchanging truths—a bright Light to warm the fertile soil of every student's soul, affirm the personal value of every student, cultivate emotional strength, and ready eager minds for Life and Learning. These "self-evident" truths not only illuminate the mind, nurture the soul, and affirm the equality and value of every person; they also have the power to transform the culture of every American public school into a citadel of goodness, peace, joy, and—yes—accelerated learning. The Common Virtues emphasis turns on the light of self-discovery for all students, allowing them to see and embrace their own incredible value and dignity. This wonderful Light inspires a love of Life and Learning with a sense of individual destiny enabling students to serve their families, their communities, and the world.

These ideas of nurturing the soul are not new. Nearly 2,500 years ago Socrates declared, "All men's souls are immortal, but the souls of the righteous are immortal and divine."[28] Wise men have always insisted the foundation of personal success and the well-being of society rely not only on acquiring knowledge but also on the acquisition and application of virtue and good moral character.

Plato said, "Education is teaching our children to desire the right things."[29] America's own George Washington declared, "Human happiness and moral duty are inseparably connected."[30]

Regarding the birth of our nation, Washington penned these words in a letter: "I receive with the greater satisfaction your congratulations on the establishment of the new constitution of government . . . because I believe its mild yet efficient operations . . . promise the restoration of order and our ancient virtues, the extension of genuine religion, and the consequent advancement of our respectability abroad, and of our substantial happiness at home."[31] Washington's hopes for what the new constitution's operations promised could not be more eloquently stated as a summary of what our public schools need now, in modern-day America.

How might a practical application of a Common Virtues Initiative work in public schools? Again, VCS does not claim to own a corner on such insights. However, we are having great success partnering with local public schools through what we call the Junior University and Lighthouse Initiative. This two-pillared endeavor is a mentoring and enrichment program whereby VCS students are transported by bus, during the school day and multiple times a week, to mentor and coach hundreds of nearby elementary school children.

Read on for the story of how VCS was led to launch this effort to bring Light, Life, and Learning to a nearby public elementary school. In the process of its development, I learned an invaluable lesson that corrected my own misguided thoughts about our public schools.

THE BIRTH OF JUNIOR UNIVERSITY

VCS students enjoy a beautiful campus on Skyway Drive atop a hill in South San Jose, California, with Silicon Valley as the skyline. Just below, near the bottom of our long, winding entrance and not far from the backside of the Skyway campus, lies G. W. Hellyer Elementary School. The story of Junior University began with a longing in the heart of Liz Nandakumar, a VCS parent and resource specialist at Hellyer. While working at Hellyer, Liz had often looked up the hill at Valley Christian and wondered if VCS might join in a partnership to help improve student learning at Hellyer.

During 2006, Liz shared her thoughts with Claude Fletcher, VCS chancellor. Their discussion led to a meeting in my office. In addition to

Liz and myself, the meeting included Sheilah Lane, Hellyer's principal at the time; Cindy Nardi, the Valley Christian Outreach Coordinator; and Dr. Joel Torode, Valley Christian High School principal.

As I listened to Principal Lane describe her school's situation, the plight of Hellyer Elementary public school students saddened my heart. A high percentage of the children at Hellyer were struggling academically. Many were English language learners whose parents spoke only Spanish, Vietnamese, or another native language at home. Teaching children to read a language they could not speak seemed an almost insurmountable challenge. In addition, 72 percent of the 460 students' families faced socioeconomic disadvantages.

Moreover, the state had put Hellyer on academic probation. The Academic Performance Index (API) was a metric public schools used to measure school-wide performance, and anything under 800 was considered unacceptable. Hellyer's average API score in 2006 was only 756, and falling.

Principal Lane made a plea for volunteer Valley Christian High School (VCHS) students to go down the hill to tutor, mentor, and inspire the elementary students at Hellyer. While I was sympathetic and convinced of the need to help Hellyer, releasing VCHS students during the school day from their own academic studies, along with arranging transportation, seemed to present major hurdles. Principal Lane remained unwavering, and we agreed to try to help.

Valley Christian student class schedules prohibited effective time on task with Hellyer students during the 2006–07 school year, and Hellyer's average API score for 2007 continued declining to 736. Principal Lane convinced VCHS administrators to persist in finding a way to coordinate the high school schedule to accommodate more volunteer students and more hours.

During the 2007–08 school year, thirty VCHS students made excursions to Hellyer Elementary for about three hours per week, giving one-on-one academic, artistic, and athletic mentoring opportunities to the younger children. Having secured 3,060 hours of student volunteer time, Mrs. Lane named the program Junior University, with hopes VCHS college-bound juniors and seniors would help improve student learning and inspire Hellyer students to set goals to attend college.

When the 2008 API scores were reported, the results stunned everyone. The school's average API score for 2008 advanced fifty-seven points from the 2007 base of 736 to a new API high of 793. The home page of the Franklin–McKinley School District (K–8th grade) website reported the results with much deserved pride, along with considerable recognition and appreciation to VCHS students.

After settling back a few points in 2009, in 2010 Hellyer achieved an API score of 808 while meeting growth targets in all subgroups, including Asian, Hispanic or Latino, Socioeconomically Disadvantaged, and English Learners. District Superintendent Dr. John Porter invited Cindy Nardi, VCHS's Junior University director, and me to a Franklin–McKinley School District board meeting where members expressed appreciation for our students' good work.

By the fall of 2011, VCHS was entering its fifth full year offering the Junior University program in partnership with Hellyer Elementary School. We developed a great relationship with Jerry Merza, who in 2009 had followed Sheilah Lane as the school's principal after her retirement.

By 2013, Hellyer Elementary became one of the highest academic performing elementary schools in Santa Clara County among those with a student population at or above the region's average of 23 percent "Spanish-speaking English Language Learners." In fact, among elementary schools in Santa Clara County with at least the regional average percentage of "Spanish-speaking English Language Learners," Hellyer Elementary ranked first of all non-charter schools in 2013, with an API score of 828. Even including charter schools, Hellyer ranked fifth in all of Santa Clara and San Mateo Counties.[32]

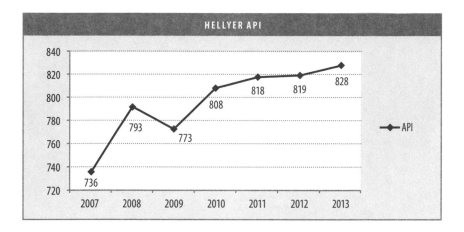

EMPIRICAL EVIDENCE

Dr. Stephen McMinn, Chief Operating Officer of VCS, did his doctoral dissertation study to examine academic achievement differences between mentored Junior University students at Hellyer Elementary School and students who were not mentored. Both groups were randomly selected. The results of the study—statistically significant at the .0001 level of confidence—are astounding, as demonstrated by the two scatterplots shown on the following pages.

The Figure 1 scatterplot of mentored Junior University students clearly tells the story, showing the change in the students' scores for English/language arts and math on tests given before and after their Junior University mentoring. The graph is divided into four quadrants. The upper left quadrant represents students in the mentored group who showed improvement in math but a decline in language. The lower left quadrant illustrates students with declines in both English/language arts and math year-to-year. The upper right quadrant is comprised of students who improved their test scores in both English/language arts and math. Finally, the lower right quadrant shows students who declined in math but improved in English/language arts skills.

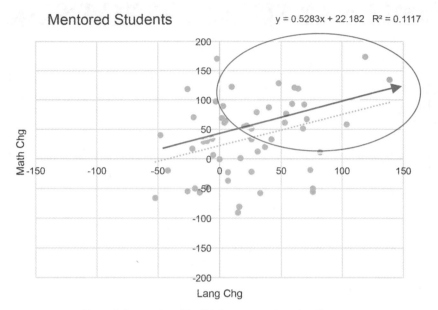

Figure 1. Scatterplot of English/language arts and math score changes for Junior University mentored students

The data clearly show a discernable increase in test scores for the mentored group of students as measured on a year-to-year basis. Only six of the fifty-four students showed declines in both English/language arts and math during their before and after testing in the mentoring group, whereas twenty-six showed improvement in both English/language arts and math. Twenty showed improvement in one of the two disciplines (ten in each), and two showed marginal or no improvement in either discipline.

Turning to the control group, we see quite a contrast. The following Figure 2 scatterplot for students in the control group tells a considerably different story.

As displayed, the control group data show little or no pattern consistency. As contrasted with the mentored group, eighteen of the fifty-three students had a decline in scores for both English/language arts and math, compared to only six of the mentored Junior University students. Moreover, the data are widely scattered to indicate no discernable trend.

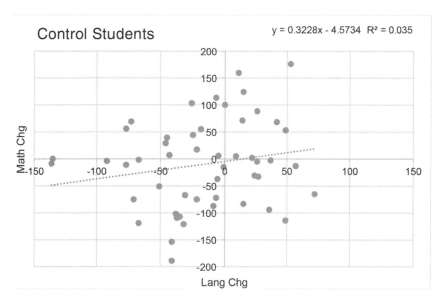

Figure 2. Scatterplot of English/language arts and math
score changes for control group students

Convincingly, the probability calculation is less than .0001—meaning the likelihood that increased Junior University student achievement occurred by random chance or sampling error is less than one in 10,000 such random samples.

The evidence is unambiguous. Junior University students who were mentored by Valley Christian High School students gained statistically significant higher achievement than students who did not participate in the Junior University mentoring program.

A CONVERSATION WITH GOD

The rise in Hellyer's API scores delighted everyone, but the school was still seriously hampered by state budget restraints and other hurdles. One cold morning in January 2012, the ongoing plight of Hellyer

Elementary School distressed my heart as I drove to work. Compared to VCS students, Hellyer public school students still faced a huge gap in the educational opportunities available to them. VCS students enjoyed a multitude of amazing programs—what we call "A to the third power," or A³, including Academic Achievement, Artistic Beauty, and Athletic Distinction—while Hellyer students did not have even one music, fine art, instrumental, dance, or physical education teacher.

"It's not fair!" I grieved at the injustice.

Though I didn't realize my blindness until later, like many Christians I had partly written off the public schools of America as hopeless, with nothing I could do to help. Disheartened and frustrated, I believed the lost rudder of the public schools could not be repaired because of the 1962–63 Supreme Court rulings.

To state it mildly, my commute prayer time was not pleasant as I drove north on Highway 101 from Morgan Hill to my South San Jose office that morning.

My deep burden and sadness continued. "It's not fair!" I complained to God. "The Hellyer students deserve the same opportunities as Valley Christian students." I recognized the huge advantages our students had as they experienced the benefits of daily prayer and Bible study to help frame their view of reality.

Certainly Junior University and its hundreds of our high school mentors had truly helped public school students on an academic level for the past four years. But I found myself longing for a new reality in our public schools—one incorporating respect for the U.S. Supreme Court rulings but also embracing the same knowledge of and regard for our Creator that America's Founding Fathers had when they established our nation. I was troubled as I thought about the seeming finality of the rulings forbidding prayer and Bible reading in public schools.

I reasoned with God. "The Court's rulings appear as insurmountable barriers to restoring Christian values into public schools. It seems our judicial system has walled off important character development values from public school students. Lord," I prayed, "is there nothing we can do to open the doors of public schools to Your goodness, peace, and joy? It's wonderful for Christian schools to have amazing opportunities to teach children, but the children at Hellyer Elementary School are just as precious to You as the children at VCS. The schoolhouse doors of our public schools seem shut and padlocked to Christian values."

Having lodged my complaint, I sensed an immediate reply from the Lord.

"So you think the highest law in the land is the United States Supreme Court?"

His response stunned me. I backpedaled as fast as I could. "Oh, no! I'm so sorry, Lord. Please forgive my faithlessness. I know You are the Supreme Judge of the Supreme Court of the Heavens and the Earth."

A verse raced through my mind: "The king's heart is in the hand of the LORD. . . ."[33]

The Lord spoke again: "If you believe the Supreme Court of the Heavens and the Earth is the highest court in the land, then why don't you put the rulings of the 1962 and 1963 United States Supreme Court on appeal to the Supreme Court Judge of the Heavens and the Earth? I'll take the case."

TIMELESS TRUTHS

At our next weekly prayer meeting later in January, I fully disclosed the whole matter to the VCS prayer intercessors. We made an earnest appeal to the Supreme Court Judge of the Heavens and the Earth to "judge righteously, and defend the rights of the afflicted and needy"[34] by overturning the effects resulting from these rulings of the Supreme Court of the United States.

A huge metamorphosis began taking place in my understanding. As it turned out, God overturned many of my misconceptions that rulings by the U.S. Supreme Court had in any way stopped God's ability to do His good work for students at Hellyer Elementary or any other public school.

As our understanding grew, our prayers matured. We prayed that all children, whether or not their parents could afford private Christian school tuition, would have opportunity to learn the same timeless "self-evident" truths our Founding Fathers declared. We prayed God would restore the legal possibility for public school children to learn from the Bible and to pray, so they could thrive with Light, Life, and Learning in a school culture of goodness, peace, and joy. As we lifted our petitions before God, our hearts filled with faith. We grew confident God was opening doors to transform and dramatically improve the opportunities for students in our public schools.

We wondered how the Supreme Court Judge of the Heavens and the Earth would do it, but new ideas came to life in my heart through prayer. What if the children across the land could *really* learn about the Declaration of Independence? Then American children in all schools could hear the truths spoken from our Founding Fathers themselves: "... all men are *created* equal ..." and our Creator is the ultimate source of all rights, including "Life, Liberty, and the pursuit of Happiness."

We were inspired to believe that the legacy of our Founding Fathers, proclaimed in the Declaration of Independence, could birth the "Common Virtues Initiative" as an added emphasis in our Junior University program. We imagined how this initiative could restore the rudder and moral compass of our public schools, so students could discover their equal and infinite value, and learn that our Creator "endowed" every person with great worth and a purposeful destiny. We wondered how God would do such marvelous things, but we became faith filled that He would.

With this new insight, God demolished a huge stronghold in my understanding. But the story had just begun, and we had more lessons to learn.

CHAPTER 4

PRAYERS FOR HEALING—
AT THE PUBLIC SCHOOL

AFTER MY CONVERSATION with the Lord in January 2012, when He corrected my thinking about the highest court in the land, the Valley Christian Schools intercessors and I prayed about how God might use VCS as a model and facilitator to help students everywhere embrace a Common Virtues Initiative. Ed Silvoso, founder of Harvest Evangelism and the International Transformation Network who also serves as VCS board chaplain, approached me about giving the educational keynote address at the Global Transform Our World conference in Hawaii the next October, and I began ruminating about how to share what we had learned.

Even after hearing from God, I found it hard to imagine how public educators could view themselves as "neutral" to Christian teachings and the tenets of other major faiths such as Buddhism, Hinduism, and Islam, then at the same time embrace the values of America's Founding Fathers powerfully shaped by Christian faith.

But the Supreme Court Judge of the Heavens and the Earth had indeed made a high court ruling to open the doors of Hellyer Elementary School to the Common Virtues of our Founding Fathers. To remove my doubt and to help me believe public school educators can teach, and students can learn, about the virtues of the Founders who birthed our nation, God orchestrated three significant events on Monday, January 23, 2012:

1. Jerry Merza (Principal at Hellyer Elementary), Shirley Hitchcock (Director of Curriculum at VCS), and I met that Monday to further develop the curricular features of the Hellyer School outreach during the coming 2012–13 school year. I had recently met Miguel and Lisa Sanchez, developers of a values-based curriculum program called Light Up Your World (LUYW), at the Annual Leadership Summit of Harvest Evangelism and the International Transformation Network, so we invited them to come the following fall to train the 180 VCHS students taking part in Junior University that year.[35] We will talk more about LUYW in Chapter 6.

2. Ed Silvoso had arranged for a visit to VCS—beginning January 23—from Caroline Oda, an outstanding educator, a key transformation leader in Honolulu, and wife of International Transformation Network chairman Francis Oda. That visit led to an introduction to Gail Hanneman, then CEO of the Girl Scouts of Hawaii. Gail visited for a full day the next week. Her visit resulted in a remarkable series of events linking Valley Christian Schools, the Quest Institute for Quality Education,[36] and the Hawaiian Girl Scouts.

3. Ed Silvoso contracted a video crew to create a documentary about Valley Christian Schools during the week starting January 23. During the second day of

Caroline Oda's visit, an excellent impromptu idea presented itself. The idea was to squeeze in a short video about the VCHS–Hellyer Elementary School Junior University outreach program. (The video is now featured online.[37])

During the video shoot at Hellyer Elementary, I learned grim news: Principal Jerry Merza's wife, Lyn, had contracted ovarian cancer. The malignancy had advanced to Stage IIIC. Survival rate of five years or longer for Stage IIIC ovarian cancer is frighteningly low, a reported 35 percent. My heart went out to Jerry, Lyn, and their children: three-year-old Brayden and his fourth-grade sister, Cameron. The thought of them losing their mother devastated me.

As our VCS intercessors and I prayed for Lyn, I had a strong sense of God's leading to invite Jerry to lunch and offer for our students to pray for Lyn. I honestly felt awkward about it since I didn't know Jerry well and wondered how he might respond.

By the last week of March, Jerry and I scheduled a lunch meeting at Applebee's restaurant in The Plant shopping center in San Jose. I chose Applebee's since its warm lobby greets guests with scores of Valley Christian High School photos.

We had a pleasant lunch as I waited for the right time to ask Jerry if he thought his wife would like Valley Christian students to pray for her. It was difficult and uncomfortable for me to pose the question, but Jerry's immediate and wise response put me at ease.

"I really appreciate your offer, Cliff. Let me ask Lyn if she would like to gather with your students for prayer."

April Fools' Day came and went without an answer from Jerry as to whether Lyn wanted to have Valley Christian students pray for her. I began to wonder whether it would happen. *It's in God's hands,* I concluded.

THE LIGHTHOUSE INITIATIVE

This offer of prayer set in motion a wonderful sequence of events. Along with Cindy Nardi, director of Junior University, our intercessors and I had long prayed for opportunity to offer a weekly after-school Bible program based on parental consent, where public school children could learn Bible stories, Christian songs, and how to pray to Jesus. When the Junior University program began during the 2006–07 school year, Hellyer Elementary School did not allow an after-school Bible club, perhaps out of concerns rooted in the establishment clause of the First Amendment and mandates about separation of church and state.

A ship is useless without its rudder; it is also useless without fuel. Our desire was not only to bring the Junior University program to Hellyer School, but also for our high school students to launch, with parental permission, an after-school faith-based program of enrichment activities and a Bible program called Kids Club. We referred to this plan as the Lighthouse Initiative.

When we first considered partnering with Hellyer, Cindy Nardi and I discussed whether the high school should invest its student capital in the Junior University program at Hellyer if VCS could not lead a Bible club. Our conclusion? We should do all we could to help the school and the elementary students on whatever terms the Hellyer administration offered. "Just tell us how we can help," was our request.

After Jerry Merza began serving as Hellyer's principal, he spoke with Cindy Nardi about the lack of funds for any enrichment programs. Cindy shared with him the idea for the Lighthouse Initiative. He hesitated to green-light a Bible club, but was open to enrichment activities with a faith component as long as all participating students had signed parent permission slips. Starting in the 2010–11 school year, Valley Christian High School students launched after-school electives—including music, arts and crafts, sports, color guard, cheer, theater, and photography—in addition to their daytime mentoring through Junior University. Parent volunteers helped with adult supervision.

The new relationships greatly encouraged everyone involved. At the same time, we still wanted to launch a Bible-based Kids Club. But how could we pray with students and teach Bible stories in a secular public school environment and still obey the laws of the land?

While many of us had thought the Supreme Court rulings prohibited prayer and Bible reading in American public schools, we learned more accurately that the Supreme Court firmly ruled government schools may not teach religion, but must respect the beliefs of all families. Furthermore, the court decisions mandate that schools should protect the rights of parents to determine what religion should be taught to their children, if any at all. So where does this leave people of faith? Well, there's a silver lining: The Supreme Court does not deny public school students the right to pray *on their own initiative,* or to read the Bible as a self-initiated activity when class schedules allow.

We knew if students wanted to remain to pray after school with parent permission in adult-led or student-led groups, the Supreme Court defends their right to do so under the free exercise clause of the First Amendment to the U.S. Constitution. Up until then, Hellyer Elementary School simply did not allow VCS students to lead such an effort. So we continued to pray for God to open the door.

PRAYING IN THE CLASSROOM

Jerry Merza, a kind man, is well loved by the school community. I was a bit worried, however, about whether I might have overstepped my bounds by offering for our VCS students to pray for Lyn. It certainly was a pleasant surprise, then, when Jerry called to report Lyn *did* want to meet with Valley Christian students to pray for her healing.

Wanting to be sensitive to Jerry's situation, I made a proposal. "Given the Supreme Court rulings forbidding prayer in the public schools, we can meet with Lyn and the students at VCS if you think best."

But with a surprising firmness, Jerry replied, "No, I want to pray at my school."

Taken aback, I quickly concurred. "Great, that will be best."

Later I remembered the words of the man who came to Jesus wanting Him to heal his son: "Lord, I believe; help my unbelief!"[38] We had made the appeal to the Supreme Court of the Heavens and the Earth, but apparently I was still thinking as if the Supreme Court Judge of the Heavens and the Earth had not taken the case. Deep down inside, I knew something bigger and more significant was happening.

I gave considerable thought to whether such prayer in school is within the bounds of the U.S. Supreme Court's intent. Again, I wish I could report I finally started acting and thinking as though our Creator is indeed the Supreme Court Judge of the universe, leaving a wide door open to the public schools, well within the rulings of the U.S. Supreme Court, but I seemed to have a big blind spot. I did, however, begin to ponder if the real problem might be a misunderstanding of whether or not the Supreme Court rulings had actually forbidden prayer in public schools.

Thursday, April 19, 2012, between 2 and 3 p.m. was the appointed day and time for prayer for Lyn. Jerry wisely chose the schedule, since school was dismissed at 1 p.m. on Thursdays for teacher in-service training. In addition, by 2 p.m. Valley Christian High School students would have completed their volunteer Lighthouse Initiative duties with the Hellyer students immediately after school.

I was looking forward to meeting Lyn, but wondered how sick she might be when we met.

When I arrived at Hellyer, I walked into the school office to discover Jerry Merza's schedule for the next hour would be unavoidably preempted with urgent and unexpected principal duties. *Oh, no—what a shame,* I thought.

In a few moments, Lyn came into the office to meet her husband. Her glistening eyes and black pupils reflected compassion and thankfulness mixed with anxiety. A red scarf with white patterns covered her head where she had evidently lost hair as a result of her cancer therapies. I could see she was nervously hopeful, but clearly disappointed Jerry would not be able to join her for after-school prayer.

Jerry directed us to the classroom where we could pray. The room belonged to Liz Nandakumar, the Hellyer School teacher who helped initiate the Junior University program there. She is also the wife of the senior pastor of Crossroads Bible Church in San Jose.

As we entered the classroom, compassion flooded the atmosphere. A total of thirty-six people filled the room, including twenty-nine VCHS students and three VCS adult staff, as well as Lyn, her three-year-old son Brayden, Lyn's friend Mylene, and me.

Jesus said, "For where two or three are gathered together in My name, I am there in the midst of them."[39] With Jesus "in the midst," those present were thirty-seven persons. Students took turns praying for Lyn as she sat in a chair next to her son, who sat on her friend's lap.

It was a privilege for me to pray for Lyn as well. I asked God to heal Brayden's mom so he could grow up with all of her loving care. I prayed Lyn would be able to attend her children's weddings and to greet her grandchildren into the world. In closing, we implored God that our prayer in the Hellyer Elementary School classroom would open doors for a growing movement of prayer in public schools across the nation and to other parts of the world. We all agreed with a hearty amen!

Lyn Merza (center) after prayer in the Hellyer classroom

After prayer, little Brayden held his mother's hand as we walked back to the office. What a huge difference we believed our prayers would make for Brayden and Lyn as God answered our petition, enabling mother and son to walk together, hand in hand, forever.

Asking in Faith

Back in the school principal's office, I found Jerry wrapping up his unforeseen duties. It was time to pose the question God had prompted me to ask: "Jerry, I'm scheduled to do the educational keynote at the Global Transform Our World conference in Hawaii next October 1–5. Would you be willing to come and help me with this address? So many wonderful improvements are happening at Hellyer. Your school is becoming a model to help other schools improve. It would also be great if your whole family came. Let's all go to Hawaii to celebrate Lyn's healing. We will take care of the expenses."

Jerry looked surprised, yet he was quick to answer. "I'd be happy to help with the keynote. But Lyn and I will need to discuss whether we should take the whole family."

Accepting his answer, I bade the Merzas farewell and walked back to my car. Then a scary thought hit me: *What if Ed Silvoso, the conference sponsor, doesn't like the idea of Jerry sharing the keynote address?* I sent up a fast prayer. "Lord, I feel sure it was You who asked me to invite Jerry, so how should I handle this?"

The Lord's voice in my mind was unambiguous: "Tell Ed I assured you, Jerry will be a great model for educational transformation, and before the keynote Lyn will be cancer free."

His strong words sent a tingle of electricity up my spine. "Okay, Lord, I'll call Ed."

The next day, I made the call. "Ed, this is Cliff." After we greeted one another, I continued with a full description of all that had occurred and my invitation for Jerry to share the keynote.

Ed was pleased and replied, "God is in this, Cliff."

Before long, Jerry let me know Lyn and their whole family would plan to attend the Hawaii conference. My heart leaped. This would be a great celebration of Lyn's healing.

"THEREFORE I SAY TO YOU, WHATEVER THINGS YOU ASK WHEN YOU PRAY, BELIEVE THAT YOU RECEIVE THEM, AND YOU WILL HAVE THEM." —JESUS (MARK 11:24)

CHAPTER 5

ANSWERED PRAYER: AN
EXPANDED VISION

JUNIOR UNIVERSITY was a great success! Hellyer students were meeting or exceeding the overall API-score achievement goals, and we began adding enrichment programs, long ago removed by severe budget cuts. With hundreds of Valley Christian High School students eager to serve, Hellyer Principal Jerry Merza and VCS Outreach Coordinator Cindy Nardi plotted a course in late April and May 2012 to launch a sports, art, and music club (i.e., SAM Club) at the elementary school in the fall of the upcoming 2012–13 school year.

Under the umbrella of the after-school Lighthouse Initiative, the SAM Club would provide additional expanded student opportunities, including art, athletics, dance, choir, musical instrument lessons, robotics, and other enrichment programs. Moreover, God answered our prayers for permission to begin the Bible-based Kids Club at Hellyer Elementary that fall.

Enthusiastic VCHS students disembarked from their buses at the Hellyer campus multiple times each week. VCS provided bus transportation for our student volunteers without one dollar of expense to Hellyer School or the Franklin–McKinley School District. The

Junior University continued as a completely non-religious academic mentoring program during the school day, while the SAM Club, Kids Club, and other Lighthouse electives served students after school with parental permission.

Our faith continued to grow. Since my "It's not fair!" prayer on a January morning just a few months earlier, the Supreme Court Judge of the Heavens and the Earth had ruled in our favor and opened doors faster than I could have imagined.

As school began for the 2012–13 year, I sensed God was up to something special. Each fall our faculty and staff schedule a day at Mount Hermon Christian Conference Center for a VCS spiritual retreat. The retreat is a time to recharge our spiritual batteries and focus on VCS's ministry for the coming year. This year Ed Silvoso, the VCS board chaplain, agreed to speak, and I invited Jerry and Lyn Merza to join us.

On Friday, August 31, 2012, I received a wonderful call from Jerry. The good news thrilled my heart! Jerry told me Lyn's latest blood test showed the level of her cancer marker (CA-125) had plummeted—and after her doctors looked at her latest PET scan results, they had declared her cancer free! In addition, Lyn's white blood cell count, which had been dangerously low, was now in the normal range. What a huge answer to prayer!

"Cliff, we are so thankful for the prayers of everyone at VCS," Jerry told me. "We are really looking forward to coming to your spiritual retreat."

I agreed the Lord was arranging a special retreat, and it would be a wonderful celebration of Lyn's recovery. I told Jerry the entire VCS faculty and staff would pray for Lyn to remain cancer free.

On September 17, the morning of our retreat, I drove my gray Honda Odyssey into the Hellyer School parking lot at 7:30 a.m. to pick up Jerry and Lyn. We had a great forty-three-minute discussion as I drove the winding roads to Mount Hermon, in the middle of Sequoia Redwood country near the town of Felton.

The drive gave me a good opportunity to invite Jerry and Lyn to speak to our 300 or so faculty and staff. They carefully considered my offer.

"I'll be nervous," Lyn said, "but I'd like to thank everyone for praying for me."

"I would like to speak too," Jerry said. "We are so thankful for Lyn's healing and for everything Valley Christian has done to help our school improve. We will take only about five minutes to say what we want to share."

A TESTIMONY OF HEALING

It was my privilege to introduce the Merzas. Jerry spoke first. He described some of the learning challenges his Hellyer Elementary students and teachers face, including a large number of students who cannot learn English from their parents, and many whose families face difficult socioeconomic circumstances. He talked about the huge impact VCS Outreach Coordinator Cindy Nardi and the VCS students had made on the quality of education at Hellyer.

"Without the programs your students have brought to Hellyer this fall, our students wouldn't have choir, musical instrument instruction, athletic coaching, art, dance, robotics, or Valley Christian student tutors who help teach and inspire our students to learn. The connections your students make with our students truly inspire them, give them hope, and foster higher achievement. When your students come on campus, it's the most exciting time of the week for our students. Thank you for all you are doing. It's making a significant difference at Hellyer Elementary School.

"Lyn and I grew up in Catholic homes. We are thankful for what our parents and the Catholic Church taught us about God, but we kind of strayed from our faith. We really didn't talk about our faith to each other or to our children. Like most people, we focused on caring for our children and our careers.

"We seldom attended church. You might say we were Christmas and Easter Christians. After Lyn was diagnosed with cancer, we didn't have a solid faith to turn to for encouragement or strength to face the disastrous news. When Dr. Daugherty asked if we would like Valley Christian students to pray for Lyn's healing, we didn't know how to respond at first. Then we decided prayer is what we needed.

"We received news about three weeks ago from the doctor that Lyn is cancer free. We can't thank God enough! But I'll let Lyn tell her own story."

Jerry sat down in the front row as Lyn began to tell her story. "I'm not accustomed to standing in front of people and speaking," she said. "But I really wanted to let you know what the children you teach are doing and have done for me and my family, and to thank you personally.

"What Jerry said about our church attendance is actually an exaggeration. We weren't Christmas and Easter Christians; we were more like wedding and funeral Christians. But things have changed in a big way for our family. Because of your prayers, I'm cancer free and I know God is with me.

"When I agreed to go to school for the students to pray for me, I didn't know what to expect. No one had ever prayed for me that way, and honestly, I didn't understand why anyone would, let alone high school kids. I was nervous, not knowing what would happen. I brought my three-year-old son, Brayden, and a friend visiting from out of town, Mylene. I expected maybe five people to be present for the prayer, but when I walked into the room it was filled with more than thirty people! Dr. Daugherty invited us to sit in the middle of the room and everyone gathered around us, placing a hand on me while reaching to each other so we would all be connected. And then they started praying, one person at a time.

"I was deeply moved. I had never experienced anything like that before. I had never felt so much love around me in that way. It was truly amazing."

BELIEVING FOR TRANSFORMATION

When Lyn finished, lots of joyful tears filled the eyes of those in the room, including mine. Lyn too pushed back tears of gratitude as she spoke. Clearly Jesus was in our midst as we thanked God for all He was doing for Hellyer School students and for Jerry's wonderful family.

Ed Silvoso and I looked at each other and realized we had just gotten a test flight for the Hawaii keynote message from Jerry and Lyn—and what a flight it was!

After Jerry and Lyn finished sharing their amazing story at the spiritual retreat, Ed's message encouraged the VCS staff and faculty to believe God for transformation beyond our local community. Ed emphasized VCS's significant role as a Quest for Excellence model, and challenged faculty and staff to aspire to a more global reach as VCS excels to the next level.

Following the retreat, Jerry and I met several times to coordinate our keynote address for the conference in Hawaii the next month. I'll admit I was curious. "Lord," I had prayed, "I know it will be fine for Jerry to help me with my keynote, but speaking to more than a thousand delegates from all over the world is a daunting task."

God came through in a big way. The superb documentary video about Valley Christian Schools recorded the previous January, which Ed Silvoso gifted to the school, was shown at the conference before we spoke. Both Lyn and Jerry shared their story of what God was doing in their lives and in Hellyer School, and of course the wonderful testimony of Lyn's healing from Stage IIIC ovarian cancer. The delegates were deeply moved to faith and action.

The Global Transform Our World conference in Hawaii was a great inspiration and insightful experience for Jerry and Lyn as well as for me. Our passion grew to bring Light, Life, and Learning with God's goodness, peace, and joy to our nation's public schools.

THE BIGGEST MIRACLE

Before continuing the story of God's expanding work in our schools, I must jump ahead to continue the story of God's amazing work in the Merza family. On Tuesday, August 12, 2014, I delivered my annual VCS keynote address to the school's faculty, staff, administrators, and board members. Entitled "Remain in Me," the address centered on some of Christ's last words before His crucifixion. I also called upon a passage from Jesus' prayer in John 17:3–4: "And this is eternal life, that they may know You, the only true God, and Jesus Christ whom You have sent. I have glorified You on the earth. I have finished the work which You have given Me to do."

After the keynote, our board, their spouses, and friends of Valley Christian met to hear great reports of how the year was beginning and to celebrate all of God's goodness. Jerry and Lyn Merza were in attendance, and I felt prompted we should pray for Lyn.

She happily accepted the offer of prayer and told us she had something to say first. With grateful tears she explained, "We really appreciate your prayers, because we know they are heard. Earlier this year I had a recurrence of cancer—I did three rounds of chemo, and by God's grace all tests showed I was going into remission again. Jerry and I prayed for God's guidance whether to finish the treatment with three more rounds of chemo as recommended by my oncologist. The Lord told us, 'No, I have provided all you need to be healed.' So March 27th was my final chemo session."

Lyn took a deep breath as she continued. "This past week I learned that the tumor marker, CA-125, is up to thirty-five, the highest point of the normal range. It could be that the cancer is coming back. But now I know the Lord, and He will take care of me and my family. The biggest miracle is that although my body may not be healed, my faith is healed. It could be that my time on earth will be shorter than I hoped, but I know I will be with Him forever, and I have peace in that because of Him. Before we came to Christ Jesus, I was afraid to die, to leave my children and Jerry behind. But I'm not afraid anymore, and it all started when the students at Valley prayed over me [April 19, 2012]. For that, I will always be grateful."

Lyn's gracious testimony touched me deeply, and I knew others felt the same way. I was very impressed with her great faith and courage, and her clear understanding of the immeasurable, eternal value of faith in Jesus Christ. His loving rescue of each individual He brings out of darkness into His marvelous light is truly "the biggest miracle."

Once again, everyone in the room prayed for Lyn's complete healing—whether on earth or eventually in heaven with Jesus.

MOVED TO ACTION!

At the Global Transform Our World conference in October 2012, within minutes after I finished my portion of the keynote address, it seemed God dropped a simple but profound strategy into my mind and heart: The plan was for Jerry to ask Carla Haakma, principal of Los Arboles Elementary School, if she would like to have the same Junior University and Lighthouse Initiative at her school as Jerry had at Hellyer. If she did, I would call to meet the principal of Andrew P. Hill High School to ask for help in securing more volunteers from the local public high school to join Valley Christian High School student mentors.

It seemed like a great way to expand the perimeter of Light, Life, and Learning and extend to another school the culture of goodness, peace, and joy that had developed at Hellyer School. The idea burned in my heart, and as soon as Jerry heard the idea, he was on board.

When Jerry became enthused, I knew God was once again leading the way—as the Supreme Court Judge of the Heavens and the Earth!

On our first school day after returning from Hawaii, Jerry called Principal Carla Haakma at Los Arboles to ask if she had interest in bringing the programs to her school. Her answer was a resounding "Yes!" Not only that, she told him, "We have a sister school, Daniel Lairon Elementary, and we work side by side. It would be really great if we can also include them."

When Jerry gave me the news, I knew for sure we would need help providing mentorship for three elementary schools. Most of the students from these schools would eventually enter Andrew Hill High School.

That week I went to the Andrew Hill website. The principal's name, I learned, was Bettina Lopez. I called the number listed on the website, expecting to work my way through an automated phone tree. To my surprise, a pleasant voice answered the phone.

"Hello, I'm Clifford Daugherty, president of Valley Christian Schools," I quickly stated. "We have a wonderful community service program for students at Hellyer Elementary School, and now Principal Carla Haakma at Los Arboles Elementary would like to expand the program to her school. At Valley Christian High School we have stretched our volunteer students and resources as far as we can, so I'd like to arrange a meeting with Principal Bettina Lopez to ask for help from Andrew Hill High School in enlisting volunteer students to serve at Los Arboles."

The next words I heard shocked me. "Yes, we can meet; I am Bettina Lopez."

I'm not sure how often Bettina Lopez answers the phone while leading a high school of close to 2,200 students, but I had the distinct impression the "Supreme Court Judge" had arranged our call.

Principal Lopez was very interested in the program. I was

encouraged. And I imagined what a wonderful initiative Andrew Hill and Valley Christian could jointly develop for high school students to help bring Light, Life, and Learning to students at Hellyer, Los Arboles, Lairon, and perhaps even more elementary schools in our neighborhood.

THE PROMISE OF BLESSING

The events that followed are not explainable without what Thomas Jefferson referred to in the last paragraph of the Declaration of Independence as "a firm reliance on . . . divine Providence." I am convinced the same divine Providence that helped found and shape the United States is fully able to restore the Light, Life, and Learning rudder and Common Virtues to rekindle a culture of goodness, peace, and joy in America's struggling public schools.

We held our first Junior University expansion planning meeting in my office on Friday, October 19, 2012. In attendance were Carla Haakma (principal of Los Arboles Elementary) and Bettina Lopez (principal of Andrew Hill High School), along with Jerry Merza (principal of Hellyer Elementary), Mark Lodewyk (principal of Valley Christian High School), and Cindy Nardi (Valley Christian Outreach Coordinator). Dr. John Porter, superintendent of the Franklin–McKinley School District, and Maria Dehghanfard, principal of Daniel Lairon Elementary, attended their first meeting on November 16. Over the coming months we prepared to launch the expanded program of Junior University and the Lighthouse Initiative at Los Arboles and Lairon schools for the coming fall of 2013. Volunteer students from Andrew Hill High School would team with the Valley Christian High School students as tutors, mentors, and enrichment activity leaders.

On October 22, just two weeks and a day after returning from the Global Transform Our World conference in Hawaii, I looked out my office window to the north to see a beautiful rainbow. I grabbed my iPhone and took a picture through the window, hoping to get the shot.

The photo turned out remarkably well. I couldn't help but wonder if the rainbow was a sign from God that He would bless and prosper the plans Jerry Merza and I brought back from the conference to bring Light, Life, and Learning to our local schools. It seemed too coincidental.

Note: Daniel Lairon Elementary School became a "College Preparatory Academy" in 2014 serving grades 4–8, while Los Arboles turned to focus exclusively on grades K–3 as a "Literacy and Technology Academy." Sylvandale Middle School (grades 7–8), also part of the Franklin–McKinley School District, joined the Junior University movement in the fall of 2014 (see Chapter 23).

As I studied the photo, a thought began to form, and a Google Maps analysis confirmed my hunch. The rainbow provided a canopy over Andrew Hill High School and the Franklin–McKinley School District campuses that had joined the Junior University and Lighthouse Initiative. Furthermore, the rainbow touched earth at Hellyer Elementary School, where Junior University began in 2006–07. (Later, when Sylvandale Middle School joined the initiative, I saw how it too was covered by the rainbow and added its location to the photo.)

The photograph made me think about the various schools involved in the programs. While much more could be written regarding all that took place during our planning meetings over the course of the 2012–13 school year, a leadership team from the different schools enthusiastically began working together to expand the Junior University and Lighthouse Initiative.

Our partnership with Andrew P. Hill High School proved especially fruitful. A strategy emerged to blend high school mentoring students from both Andrew Hill and Valley Christian to launch the Junior University tutoring program at Lairon Elementary. The Christian Club at Andrew Hill High School would also help start a Kids Club at Lairon to include both components of the complete Junior University and Lighthouse Initiative. Since VCS already provided bus transportation each week, I agreed to transport Andrew Hill students as well, without cost to our new friends. (By the time this book went to press, more than 265 mentor bus trips were taking place each week to serve students in our neighborhood public elementary schools.)

Marquee at Andrew P. Hill High School saluting their collaboration with Valley Christian High School

Working in partnership with these educators was exhilarating. The boundaries normally separating schools and students, including economic differences, ethnic distinctions, district lines, public/private school boundaries, and religious/non-religious divisions—all completely evaporated. Everyone involved understood that every child is precious because all people "are created equal," as Thomas Jefferson wrote nearly two and a half centuries ago.

This "across all boundaries" cooperation enriched the lives of participants, while shared resources multiplied the impact of everyone's efforts. Who has benefited the most? Undoubtedly it is the students in every school, without exception. The elementary students have received tutoring and support, improving their academic performance, while the high school mentors discovered they could truly model success and transform lives by their volunteer service.

But we noticed another phenomenon we did not expect—perhaps the best part of the story. Some discouraged and disillusioned teachers rekindled their dreams to transform students' lives. They once again began to believe their efforts could make a difference. As their students blossomed in achievement and enthusiasm, the teachers' own reborn hopes and dreams became part of a transformation in the culture of their schools, a culture increasingly characterized by goodness, peace, and joy.

And we could hardly have imagined all that lay ahead.

CHAPTER 6

THE SECOND PHASE—
MUCH BIGGER

OUR LORD'S PRESENCE seemed to fill the room.
It was a regular Tuesday evening meeting with the VCS prayer intercessors, but I felt a special inspiration when we read Isaiah 19 together
that night, June 11, 2013. God, we sensed, was speaking to us about
what He would accomplish using Valley Christian Schools as a model
for public school transformation in America and possibly beyond.

I remembered the many confirming words I had received on a
similar theme starting more than a decade earlier. Chapter 16 of my first
book, *Quest for Excellence,* records the sequence of events, including
this message from Pastor Eduardo Lorenzo of Argentina in October
2002: "God has something on the horizon for you. It is not just about
the school or the educational training happening here, but it is about
something much bigger—something beyond Valley Christian Schools."
Then on February 5, 2005, the Lord woke me up in the middle of the
night speaking similar words in my thoughts: "I have a second phase
of work I will do through you and the team I am bringing to you. . . ."

At the time, I imagined the development of many Christian schools.

Gradually, however, the seed of a dream began to grow into a much larger, more ambitious initiative. I sensed God telling me Valley Christian Schools would in some way become a great help to public schools. I shared this passionate dream with our prayer intercessors, and we prayed fervently about this matter on several occasions. The earliest written note I scribbled in the margin of my Bible about this sense of God's calling to pray and help our public schools is dated June 23, 2006, and appears next to Isaiah 19. The dream involved God's intent for VCS and the Quest Institute for Quality Education to help transform our public schools.

In this chapter of Isaiah I saw similarities between Egypt and our nation's public schools. From my perspective, the economic and moral hardship being experienced by public schools stemmed from our failure to honor God, confounding the mission to educate. But these problems cried out for new hope and true transformation. My 2006 note next to this passage concluded, "VCS and the Quest Institute will have an important role."

More specifically, the key verse of Isaiah 19, which serves as a great encouragement to me, is verse 22: "The LORD will strike Egypt, striking but healing; so they will return to the LORD, and He will respond to them and will heal them" (NASB). While God has allowed this hardship (striking), His ultimate intent is to heal and restore. He will turn the situation for good.

Even before our first involvement with Hellyer Elementary School, before I had met Principal Sheilah Lane, before I even knew of Hellyer's existence, God had spoken clearly through Isaiah 19 about VCS and the Quest Institute's significant role in bringing healing to the public schools. And now the prayer intercessors and I were hearing Him speak through this same passage again.

We now better understood how God is not limited to bringing

His message of goodness, peace, and joy only to children in Christian schools. God was reaffirming how He loves all children in all schools and longs to bring His goodness, peace, and joy to children in schools everywhere. Our understanding grew as we prayed and pondered the scriptures. God was teaching us how He intends to use and is using VCS's Quest for Excellence prototype to help transform public schools also.

Read on for two stories illustrating God's work in each of these arenas. First, a Christian school example.

VALOR CHRISTIAN HIGH SCHOOL

The same week in 2005 when God spoke to me about "a second phase of work," VCS had hosted a group from the Denver, Colorado, area who visited the school with the intent to build a similar campus. Although Valley Christian has helped many schools to grow and mature dramatically, this Colorado school became the first Christian high school developed from its inception on the VCS model. In an email the team leader sent after their visit, he wrote, "All of us were so excited by what we saw; we hardly needed an airplane to fly home! . . . What you all have accomplished is awesome; truly excellent. We will certainly keep you posted regarding our progress in Denver."

Our guests flew back to Denver and got to work. Despite some twists and turns along the way, with God's leading and provision they purchased property on thirty-five acres, engaged Adele Willson of Slaterpaull Architects, and began construction at 3775 E. Grace Boulevard, Highlands Ranch, Colorado. Groundbreaking took place on September 12, 2006. Governor Bill Owens spoke at the groundbreaking ceremony and described the campus as the largest capital investment for a high school in Colorado history. Construction of world-class facilities carried on at a record pace despite one of the worst winters in Colorado history.

Valor Christian High School (see http://www.valorchristian.com/)

Exactly a year later, I attended the opening of Valor Christian High School. It is a beautiful campus—perhaps the most beautiful school in the United States—and expanding. Almost 900 students are now enrolled, and they are currently building the 83,000-square-foot Valor Center for Culture and Influence, which will allow them to grow toward a target enrollment of 1,200. The Valor Center will also serve as the home of their planned Conservatory of Music. Although Valor is a dedicated high school (not K–12 like Valley Christian Schools), they have taken the Valley Christian High School example to heart, patterning after us not only their "VCHS" initials but also their school colors and their motto: "Influence from Excellence." With dedicated supporters donating more than $100 million, the school remains debt free. We at VCS are excited to have a close relationship with Valor Christian High School as charter members of the Quest Institute for Quality Education.

As Valley Christian and Valor Christian High School have both declared during construction phases, "Unless the LORD builds the house, the builders labor in vain."[40] We view ourselves as stewards of God's intellectual properties in our schools, and we hope such great schools will migrate across the nations, whether in the form of private or public.

Construction of the Valor Center for Culture and Influence in November 2014

Most children in America, however, attend public schools, and every child deserves a quality education founded on the Common Virtues of our Founding Fathers. We are just as excited about the transformational programs taking place in our local public schools, which are also members of the Quest Institute. Here is one of them.

"SPLISH! SPLASH! LEARN TO SWIM"

As our Junior University and Lighthouse Initiative began to expand to added schools with discussions during the fall of 2012, Carla Haakma, then principal of Los Arboles Elementary School and now a Franklin–McKinley School District administrator, asked a pointed question.

"Why are you doing this?" She wondered what motivation was driving Valley Christian Schools, a successful private school on a flourishing hilltop campus, to make such efforts to help students in severely underfunded neighborhood public schools.

It was an easy question for me to answer without a moment of hesitation. "We want the same goodness, peace, and joy that our students enjoy on the hill to flow into the valley. The students in public schools are just as precious as our students in our private school. Your students deserve the same academic, artistic, and athletic advantages our students enjoy. It's a matter of justice."

Some time later, I learned that drowning is one of the leading causes of unintentional death among children in the United States, ranked second only to car crashes. I also learned that children from poorer families are more likely to drown because they do not have the same opportunities to learn to swim, and their parents do not have the same resources to afford private swimming lessons for their children.

The good news, however, is that participation in formal swim lessons can reduce the likelihood of childhood drowning by 88 percent!

Learning to stay afloat

Valley Christian Schools has one of the largest swimming pools in Northern California. We built the pool larger than an Olympic-size pool to accommodate the Valley Christian High School swimming, diving, and water polo programs and an extensive aquatic program for the broader community.

Children whose parents can afford fees amounting to several hundred dollars learn to swim and compete through Valley Splash, a competitive swimming club. Sadly, few parents of children living north of Valley Christian Schools in San Jose's Seven Trees community, an under-resourced area of the Franklin–McKinley School District, can afford to pay such fees for swimming lessons.

"How unfair," I thought. "The public school children from socio-economically disadvantaged homes down the hill from Valley Christian Schools should learn to swim too!" My mind began thinking of ways to offer affordable swim lessons to the children in the Seven Trees Community Schools group (Los Arboles and Daniel Lairon Elementary Schools) as well as nearby Hellyer Elementary in the same Seven Trees neighborhood.

I turned to Cathy Manthey, our VCS Aquatics Director, for help, and she had a great solution. We could offer eight swim lessons to the children from these three public schools by recruiting our Valley Christian High School divers, swimmers, and water polo athletes to donate their time in the form of community service to teach the children to swim.

Children from these three schools, we calculated, could pay dramatically lower fees of only $20 for eight lessons—two lessons a week for four weeks, amounting to only $2.50 per lesson. We qualified all students from these local public schools because of their approximately 90 percent participation rate in the federal free and reduced-fee lunch program, offered only to students from economically disadvantaged families. We scheduled two four-week sessions during the summer of 2013, under the name "Splish! Splash! Learn to Swim."

We planned the swimming lessons to come under the umbrella of our Lighthouse Initiative program, in order to include animated Bible lessons, prayer, and singing in a separate session parallel with the swimming lessons. Our staff, in partnership with the public school administrators, drafted a brochure describing the program for the elementary schools to distribute to their students. Plenty of excitement surrounded our planning, but a worrisome question emerged: Is it legal for a public school to distribute literature from a Christian organization offering a learn-to-swim program with Bible stories, prayer, and Christian songs?

THE FREE EXERCISE CLAUSE

We put our program planning on hold and sought legal counsel from John Mark Cooley, attorney and general counsel for Valley Christian Schools and the Quest Institute. I forwarded the information in the brochure as follows:

CLASS CONTENT

A comprehensive learn to swim program in a Christian faith setting. Two-thirds of each class will be in the swimming pool with one-third of the class devoted to Bible stories, prayer, and Christian faith. Snacks will be served. The entire program includes eight consecutive weeks.

Students will be assigned a mentor/coach. The coach to student ratio will be 1:5. Mentor coaches are both high school and college students with at least two years of aquatic instruction experience and have attended or are attending Valley Christian Schools. Mentor coaches will be earning community service hours to fulfill school requirements.

We were thrilled to receive a detailed email from John Mark Cooley with an opinion affirming our plans. (I am reproducing it in the endnotes in the hope it might be helpful for other organizations and schools facing a similar situation.[41]) Citing various legal cases prohibiting "viewpoint discrimination," John Mark's note said "the First Amendment requires neutrality toward, not hostility against, subject matter which merely happens to be addressed from a religious perspective." In one case very similar to ours, the flyer a faith-based non-profit sought to distribute through the public schools had to contain a disclaimer saying their program was offered as a community service and the school district was not sponsoring or endorsing the organization or activity.

Just twenty-nine minutes after receiving the good news in my email inbox, I enthusiastically forwarded John Mark Cooley's message to Carla Haakma at the Franklin–McKinley School District office. I gave her the exact language for the legal disclaimer so she could have the brochure translated into the languages of the students' families, including Spanish and Vietnamese. VCS then printed the brochures for the school principals to distribute.

We joyfully launched the swimming lessons that summer. It was such a success we repeated the offerings in 2014 and plan to continue the program into the foreseeable future.

Enjoying the "Splish! Splash! Learn to Swim" program

The "Splish! Splash! Learn to Swim" program is a great example of the free exercise clause of the First Amendment in action. Rather than lamenting our underperforming schools, the Christian community has the responsibility and the opportunity to offer faith-based programs to enrich the lives of our public school children while transforming our schools with the same Common Virtues that gave birth to our nation.

Since we began the "Splish! Splash! Learn to Swim" program, hundreds of children from our underfunded public schools have learned to swim and received lots of goodness, peace, and joy from our volunteer high school students who share not only their swimming skills but their love of God and their faith as well. No one knows if any of these precious children will be spared drowning because they learned to swim, but one fact is certain: The scales of equity are tipping a bit more toward "justice for all."

Having fun during a "Splish! Splash!" Bible lesson

LIGHT UP YOUR WORLD

With the launch of Junior University at Hellyer Elementary School during the 2006–07 school year, and the expansion of both Junior University and the Lighthouse Initiative to other public schools, our efforts began to see real results, making us even more committed to these two programs. Still, we longed for the elementary students to experience more deeply the transformative power of our Founding Fathers' legacy, including the self-evident truths found in the Declaration of Independence.

A huge stride forward occurred on May 28, 2013, during a key presentation to public school teachers. As mentioned in Chapter 4, we had invited the developers of a values-based curriculum program called Light Up Your World (LUYW) to come to Valley Christian High School the previous fall to train 180 VCHS students taking part in Junior University. According to the LUYW website, "Light Up Your World™ is an organization dedicated to envisioning, training, equipping and releasing young people to make a positive difference in their world. . . . LUYW™ helps the student to discern how to make choices that will affect their life and the world around them in a positive way. . . ."[42]

That spring day in 2013, about eighty public elementary school teachers, including those from four schools in our local Seven Trees community, gathered at Los Arboles Elementary School to hear about the Light Up Your World curriculum. Our Junior University and Lighthouse Initiative team of public and VCS school principals and I marveled at the overwhelmingly positive response the presentation received from public school educators.

Things seemed to be moving quickly. On June 7, following the excellent response to the LUYW presentation, the principals of Los Arboles, Lairon, and Hellyer Elementary Schools met in my office to discuss how to use the LUYW curriculum through VCS's Junior University program. The three principals gave enthusiastic reports of teacher requests for LUYW certification training wherein our Junior University student mentors and public school educators would use the curriculum to help adopt a school-wide vocabulary to bring Light, Life, and Learning and a culture of goodness, peace, and joy to their students.

The promise of a "second phase" of the Quest for Excellence movement was underway. It was not coincidental when Ed Silvoso asked to meet the following week.

CHAPTER 7

COMMON VIRTUES

"I tell you that virtue is not given by money, but that from
virtue comes money and every other good of man. . . ."[43]
—SOCRATES

BY THE TIME VCS Board Chaplain Ed Silvoso came by
my office the next Friday afternoon, June 14, 2013, I was convinced
our school was entering a new season. The dream God had whispered
to me seven years prior about the impact of Valley Christian Schools
and the Quest Institute on public schools was underway.

During Ed's visit, I described some details of the growing partnership developing between VCS and local public schools, including
Hellyer Elementary and more recently Andrew P. Hill High School,
Los Arboles Elementary, and Daniel Lairon Elementary. Ed and I
remembered the passages in my *Quest for Excellence* book predicting
VCS would enter into a new development involving "a second phase" of
the Quest for Excellence and the Excellence Brings Influence strategy.

I recalled the questions I had wrestled with: *Is it really possible*
for our nation's public schools to once again teach students, as part of
the daily instruction, to respect the same values our Founding Fathers
cherished to birth our nation? Could parents of children in all public schools

choose for their children to read and hear Bible stories, sing, and learn to
pray after school and at other parent-approved community programs?

In the wake of the recent presentation to the public school teachers about Light Up Your World, Ed and I discussed how we could build upon the foundation of the LUYW philosophy, which affirms the "immense incredible value" of every person and fosters mutual respect between students. We were inspired to align the Common Virtues Initiative, as described in Chapter 3, alongside the LUYW curriculum. Riding on the enthusiasm of the teachers, we felt growing excitement about partnering with the elementary schools to implement LUYW training to help develop a common, school-wide vocabulary that would foster a learning culture of kindness. In this respect, we aimed to use language consistent, once again, with a document every American child, regardless of religion, could embrace: the Declaration of Independence.

After our meeting, Ed asked for a description of my hopes and expectations for the interplay between Light, Life, and Learning; Junior University; the Lighthouse Initiative; and Valley Christian Schools. After prayerfully pondering his question, I developed the following response, which documents the development of these initiatives by our leadership team, comprised of participating public school principals, teachers, and our Valley Christian leaders.

THE FOUNDATION FOR EXCELLENCE

When we added the Lighthouse Initiative to Junior University, calling it the Junior University and Lighthouse Initiative (sometimes abbreviated as JULI), we wanted the program to help restore the "rudder" and "moral compass" to our public schools. To achieve our goal, we embraced the language of our nation's Founding Fathers. We agreed to call the values of our Founding Fathers Common Virtues. These Common Virtues became the "engine" to help propel the "vehicle" of the Junior University and Lighthouse Initiative forward. The combined programs, including Junior

University during school and the after-school Lighthouse Initiative, could help rebuild our schools on the strong foundational insights of our Founding Fathers that gave birth to our nation.

Junior University and Lighthouse Initiative programs are offered to all students as determined by each school's administration and faculty. Junior University's secular or non-religious mentoring activities take place during the school day, while the Lighthouse Initiative takes place after regular school hours. In the Lighthouse program, parental permission allows children to enjoy many co-curricular enrichment activities in a faith-based environment, as well as the voluntary Kids Club (by parent choice) with a focus on the Bible and prayer.

The Junior University and Lighthouse Initiative rests on the Common Virtues of our Founding Fathers. The Lighthouse Initiative also teaches the truths of the Christian faith through its after-school programs. Both combine to affirm a culture of goodness, peace, and joy as the backbone of the Light, Life, and Learning strategy, using the language from the Declaration of Independence. In this way, all the Junior University and Lighthouse programs are in legal compliance with both Supreme Court and federal court rulings regarding the establishment and free exercise clauses of the First Amendment. The programs are committed to uphold all First Amendment rights of students, educators, and parents in our public school community.

The Lighthouse Initiative, in the after-school Bible study Kids Clubs with parent permission, offers public school children the opportunity to learn more about the "truths" described by Jefferson when he wrote, "We hold these truths. . . ." Christian parents do not want public schools defining their children's faith, any more than do parents of another religion or those who want to avoid all religions. Nearly everyone would affirm the wisdom of official separation between government schools and the parents' important right to choose what their children learn about religious teachings. The Lighthouse Initiative offers parents the right to choose for their children to learn about Christian faith from the Bible in after-school programs.

The Lighthouse Initiative Kids Club after-school prayer and Bible study, with parent permission for attendance, is well received and a wonderful success in our neighborhood public schools. Since the after-school Kids Club began at Hayes (2008), Hellyer (2012), Los Arboles and Lairon (2013) elementary schools, about 500 children have expressed their personal faith in Jesus. To celebrate each student's faith journey, Bibles are awarded to children with their name and a date to memorialize their personal expression of faith.

The courts have ruled that parents can choose after-school faith-based programs for their children. Moreover, even during the school day schools can promote Common Virtues and values, which are widely shared by almost all Americans, including Christians and non-Christians. These virtues are crucial for developing good schools and good communities. In fact, such virtues are critical for building excellence in any arena, including good government and a good economy.

Confusion about good character development and Common Virtues in America's public schools has hamstrung efforts to provide an environment of excellence for American school students. Understanding and correctly interpreting the Supreme Court rulings can and will reverse this situation.

EXCELLENCE THROUGH A CHARACTER-BASED CURRICULUM

As we planned these initiatives, we broadly defined our goals. What is the ultimate purpose of investing Valley Christian Schools' time, talent, and treasure in our neighborhood public schools? In our brainstorming, we identified three domains of the Quest for Excellence philosophy, describing a comprehensive education. We call this A^3, or "A to the third power":

1. *Academic Achievement* (high-level success in the classroom),

2. *Artistic Beauty* (excellence in the arts), and

3. *Athletic Distinction* (sports programs emphasizing excellent sportsmanship and success on the field and court).

The Junior University and Lighthouse Initiative is a strategy to improve Academic Achievement, Artistic Beauty, and Athletic Distinction in our local public schools. Even the sky is *not* the limit for students when organizations and individuals such as high school community service volunteers, parents, corporate school partners, the faith community, and retirees offer their time, talent, and treasure to enable all students to discover and develop their God-given gifts.

In support of A^3, the Junior University and Lighthouse Initiative integrates Common Virtues, effectively communicated to children based on ideals of our nation's Founding Fathers as conveyed in the Declaration of Independence and other founding documents. Character development curriculum such as Light Up Your World helps communicate Common Virtues at each student's appropriate level of learning. The beauty of this approach is that teachers affirm a school culture of kindness and respect through a common vocabulary, integrated throughout all curricular and co-curricular school activities.

This common vocabulary articulates core "self-evident" truths not by teaching any particular religion but by relying on common, non-religious, secular language emanating from the Declaration of Independence—America's first founding document. These truths teach students about their right to be treated as equals, as well as their own responsibility to treat every person as having equal intrinsic value. Educators are encouraged to select appropriate character development curriculum of their own choosing, such as Light Up Your World, to teach Common Virtues.

Certainly, from a Christian's point of view, all truth is God's truth and consistent with the teachings of Jesus. From that perspective, and even without the Bible or prayer in the classroom, the Light of Christ *can* shine through the Declaration of Independence. Students will learn the truth through such fundamental tenets as: "We hold these truths to be self-evident, that all men are created equal, that they are endowed by their Creator with certain unalienable Rights, that among these are Life, Liberty, and the pursuit of Happiness."

The Junior University and Lighthouse Initiative fully respects and relies on the First Amendment's non-establishment clause and Supreme Court rulings. The Junior University program promotes Common Virtues alongside Academic Achievement, Artistic Beauty, and Athletic Distinction (the A^3 formula), while achieving two lofty goals: It does not conflict with Christian faith, and it remains secular in its presentation to students. The Lighthouse Initiative allows children, with parent permission, to learn about Christian faith after school in a variety of programs, including Kids Clubs and programs promoting the same A^3 goals. Both Junior University and the Lighthouse Initiative work together to help transform a school by cultivating a culture of goodness, peace, and joy.

The combined Junior University and Lighthouse Initiative provides or supplements programs the public school's budget may not afford but are important to offer as part of an A^3 quality education. Each public school principal determines which programs are most needed, and requests support in areas of preference and priority. For example, programs provided or supported in the public schools of Franklin–McKinley's Seven Trees community during the past few years include:

1. *Academic Achievement*

◇ *Academic Tutoring:* in subject areas where students may be struggling

- ❖ *Math Lab:* ALEX software installed on computers for individualized instruction
- ❖ *Reading Buddies:* mentors read with mentees (often English language learners)
- ❖ *Robotics Club:* design, development, and competitions

2. Artistic Beauty

- ❖ *Art:* portrait art and a variety of 2-D, 3-D, and/or multimedia forms
- ❖ *Choir:* two-part and three-part harmony
- ❖ *Dance:* lessons and team performance
- ❖ *Musical Instrument Lessons:* beginning in grade 4 or 5, including a jazz band concert

3. Athletic Distinction

- ❖ *Athletics:* sport-specific skill development
- ❖ *Swimming:* summer "Splish! Splash! Learn to Swim" program

The goal is to ensure all students are inspired and encouraged to develop the skills and knowledge for a college preparatory curriculum, giving them the option to attend college or an appropriate highly skilled career development program after high school. An effective character-based curriculum—combined with outstanding high school mentors serving as contagiously energized role models positive about Life and Learning—connects with elementary students to inspire accelcrated learning. All student mentors and mentees are motivated by their goals to help make the world a better place through their influence as world transformers.

The Common Virtues Initiative and the legacy of our Founding Fathers provide the critical components needed for students to understand the truth about their immense inherent worth. They learn all are "created equal," and that "they are endowed by their Creator with certain unalienable Rights, that among these are Life, Liberty, and the pursuit of Happiness. . . ."

While Christian and non-Christian students participate in the Junior University program during school, the rule for all Valley Christian volunteer student mentors is to "speak secularly but think and act as Christians," since the Junior University program does not require parent permission and is integrated throughout the school day.

A GRAPHIC OVERVIEW

Take a few minutes to review the following two charts, which capture the essence of this narrative description. The Quest for Excellence chart illustrates the Light, Life, and Learning continuum, as indicated by the arrows pointing right. Each of the Light, Life, and Learning columns describes the language and activities promoting that phase.

The Junior University and Lighthouse chart gives examples of the secular vocabulary of Junior University used during the school day in the first column, while the second column illustrates the parallel faith vocabulary for after-school Lighthouse Initiative enrichment programs requiring parental permission. Notice the themes and language common to both the Junior University and the Lighthouse initiatives. The commonalities shown in both columns include:

- ✦ Celebrating a Culture of Goodness, Peace, and Joy

- ✦ Light Up Your World curriculum

- ✦ Common Virtues found in the Declaration of Independence

- ✦ The same A^3 enrichment opportunities = Academic Achievement, Artistic Beauty, and Athletic Distinction

- ✦ Ten parallel values, with a distinct secular or Christian vocabulary

QUEST FOR EXCELLENCE™

» LIGHT	» LIFE	» LEARNING
We hold these truths to be self-evident . . . All men are created equal . . .	. . . Endowed by their Creator with certain unalienable Rights, that among these are Life, Liberty	. . . And the pursuit of Happiness
Illuminate the dawn with a great light warming the fertile soil of self-awareness and value with the understanding all students are gifted	Sprouting seeds of goodness, peace, and joy to cultivate emotional strength for every student's personal learning readiness to uncover God-given giftedness in every student	Develop premier schools through Academic Achievement, Artistic Beauty, and Athletic Distinction to develop the God-given talent of every student
Light Up Your World Curriculum*	Lighthouse After-School/ Summer Program Christian character development, with Bible stories, songs, musical instrument training, art, sports, cheer, and much more Summer "Splish! Splash! Learn to Swim"	Academic Tutoring, Robotics, Sports, Art, Music, STEM/STEAM, STMath, Breakthrough Silicon Valley, Project Lead the Way, and much more
LUYW-certified adult trainers teach students to discern their value and the value of others	JH & HS student mentors with LUYW training mentor elementary student mentees to grow academically to make positive personal choices to affirm their intrinsic value	To value and influence others in positive ways as positive world transformers
Every person has immense incredible value*	Bring goodness, peace, and joy to our community and the world	Ensure that all students develop the skills and knowledge to pursue a program preparing them for university and/or careers and lifelong learning
Imparting value to others*	Students learn strategies to make a positive difference in the world and to walk in their destiny*	Students are motivated learners to make this world a better place as world transformers*
Learning to value myself and others	Affirming a culture of kindness	A^3 = Academic Achievement, Artistic Beauty, and Athletic Distinction

*Light Up Your World™ — www.LightUpYourWorld.org — An adopted curriculum

JUNIOR UNIVERSITY	LIGHTHOUSE
Celebrating a Culture of Goodness, Peace, and Joy	Celebrating a Culture of Goodness, Peace, and Joy
All Students – During School	Parent Permission – After School
Public School – Secular Vocabulary	Public School – Faith Vocabulary
Light Up Your World™ Curriculum Adoption*	Christian Values & Light Up Your World
Founding Fathers' Values and Common Virtues in the Declaration of Independence	Bible Lessons, Prayer, Common Virtues & Values in the Declaration of Independence

A3

ACADEMIC ACHIEVEMENT ·	ARTISTIC BEAUTY ·	ATHLETIC DISTINCTION
1. Math Olympiad – SOAR	1. Art	1. Nutrition
2. Reading Buddies	2. Band – Instr. Lessons	2. Skill Development
3. Robotics	3. Choir	3. Splish Splash
4. Tutoring	4. Cheer, Dance – Flags	4. Team Sports

1. Teachers and high school students model respect for younger students in view of every person's immense, incredible value*

2. Students learn to respect themselves and others

3. Students learn that academic achievement empowers them to transform their community and the world through goodness, peace, and joy

4. Every student has unique gifts that emerge as gifted passions when discovered and developed

5. As mentors, high school students help offer comprehensive learning opportunities to enable elementary students to discover and develop their gifts and emerging passions

6. Mentors model goodness, peace, and joy to feed the hearts of young elementary student mentees to inspire accelerated student learning

7. Teachers challenge students to fly with their dreams to pass on goodness, peace, and joy to others and to transform the world into a better place by helping others

8. Parents are valued as the primary educators of their children

9. Good character is an expression of Common Virtues to others

10. The community celebrates the achievements of all students as they prepare themselves to serve as transformers with good character to transform their communities and the world

*www.LightUpYourWorld.org

1. High school student volunteers teach Bible stories, to emphasize God's love for all and that all people have infinite value

2. Students learn to love God and their neighbors as themselves

3. Students learn through prayer and academic achievement to transform their community and the world through God's love

4. Every student has God-given gifts that emerge as gifted passions when discovered and developed

5. As mentors, high school students help offer comprehensive learning opportunities to enable elementary students to discover and develop their God-given gifts and emerging passions

6. Mentors model faith, hope, and love, feeding the soul with goodness, peace, and joy to inspire and enrich the minds and hearts of students to learn

7. Mentors challenge students to share God's goodness, peace, and joy with others to positively transform the world because Jesus loves everyone

8. Parents are valued as the primary educators of their children under God

9. Christian character is an expression of God's goodness to others

10. The community celebrates the achievements of all students as they prepare themselves to serve as transformers with Christian character to transform their communities and the world

The sequence of Light, Life, and Learning is important for improved achievement. The "Light" warms the soil of the soul, bringing "Life" and a passion for "Learning." The Light also illuminates the truth (as proclaimed by our Founding Fathers) that our Creator made us with unchanging, equal, and infinite value, each with a unique purpose and destiny. That Light warms the soul emotionally, bringing to Life intrinsically motivated Learning, which is accomplished by many Junior University and Lighthouse enrichment opportunities. Light and Life create emotional readiness for Learning! Too often educators fail to achieve academic success because the preceding Light and Life have not sufficiently prepared students for Learning.

Although I initially developed the charts, the vocabulary on both charts was reviewed, modified, and agreed upon by our entire Junior University and Lighthouse Initiative team. The team included four public school principals (Hellyer, Los Arboles, Lairon, and Andrew Hill); two VCS principals (high school and junior high); Dr. John Porter, the Franklin–McKinley School District superintendent; and myself.

Repairing the Schoolhouse Door

Our Junior University and Lighthouse Initiative leadership team used two illustrations to help capture the power of these endeavors. The first image of the red schoolhouse (next page) represents our public schools. The two doorposts represent Junior University and the Lighthouse Initiative, and a yellow door of educational opportunity features three big hinges representing the legacy of Common Virtues of our Founding Fathers, as described in the Declaration of Independence.

I explained to our partnering public school principals, "I am *really* impressed with the quality of administrators I've had the privilege of getting to know personally and professionally. Your students, parents, teachers, and all of your employees are so fortunate to have such capable leadership in your district and schools. If your quality of leadership and teachers could control the learning outcomes of your schools, your students would be among the highest achieving in the world. We don't have better administrators or teachers in private schools or even at Valley Christian Schools. So what is the difference?"

One huge difference: In so many of our public schools, the doorway to learning has become disconnected at the hinges. Given our best intentions not to offend anyone in a pluralistic society with conflicting values among disparate groups, we have lost our moral compass and the Light, Life, and Learning rudder of our educational system. Our public schools have inadvertently neglected the Common Virtues all Americans share as a legacy—the values of our Founding Fathers.

The red schoolhouse, with the door of educational opportunity

The result? The hinges have come off the door of educational opportunity for too many students in our schools. Wonderfully talented teachers and dedicated administrators stand at the door propping it up so it doesn't fall on the children. They spend so much effort trying to hold the door open to opportunity and at times holding it shut to keep out negative influences that they lose their focus on building quality learning environments, great schools, and high-achieving students. Our school doors to opportunity should effortlessly open and shut without thought or huge amounts of effort.

Let's repair the door to opportunity by reconnecting it to the strong hinges of the Common Virtues contained in the Declaration of Independence given to all Americans as a legacy of our Founders. These Common Virtues will repair the rudder and recalibrate the moral compass of our American public schools to point them, once again, in the direction of true north.

Principal Jerry Merza at Hellyer Elementary School affirmed the transformational power of this approach when he said, "I can see the Lighthouse difference in students who attend the Kids Club. They are happier, more peaceful, and bring new life to our campus. It really is a culture of goodness, peace, and joy. It's amazingly evident and a huge positive influence in the lives of students who participate, and they significantly improve the school culture for all students."

In addition, we have discovered that the elements of both door posts (Junior University and the Lighthouse Initiative) are critically important. Many schools in the nation have one kind of program or the other: a tutoring/mentoring program during the school day, or an after-school Bible club. But one program working alone does not seem to have the same powerful results as both working together in a school to restore a culture of goodness, peace, and joy, along with improved achievement and Common Virtues. The Junior University program reinforces Common Virtues during the school day based on the legacy of our Founding Fathers, and the Lighthouse Initiative teaches Christian values after school, with parent permission, including many co-curricular enrichment opportunities.

One of the most important advantages Christian schools have

for developing serious-minded students and good character is our Christian worldview. Yes, it is our Christian foundation and worldview that serve as a moral compass and an educational rudder benefiting our quality of education. While public schools can't teach religious values, they can—and should—teach the commonly held American virtues of our Founding Fathers. Where the values of our Founders appear too religious, public schools should simply teach the fact that our Founding Fathers believed in a divine Creator (as mentioned in the Declaration of Independence) and leave religious choices to the guidance of parents and to the students as they mature.

OPENING THE FAUCET OF RESOURCES

Another discussion we had with our public school partners concerned the scarcity of community resources for our public schools. In many communities, finding support for public schools is like trying to get water from a faucet with the valve turned off.

Parents, I believe, are willing to spend money on private school tuition and to liberally donate resources because most private schools offer a quality education with a fully functioning navigational compass and a well-trimmed rudder. The schools' shared values give educators the navigational tools to steer a straight course toward quality education. And common values offer fertile ground for Light, Life, and Learning to cultivate school cultures of goodness, peace, and joy, inspiring financial participation by the community. I used the following faucet illustration to show how public school educators can open a flowing faucet of community resources by building upon the foundation of common American virtues.

The virtues of the Founding Fathers served to inspire Colonial Americans to declare their independence and freedom in establishing this nation. And just as certainly, these same time-proven virtues have the power to inspire communities to heap plentiful, badly needed resources upon our public schools today. When schools turn on this valve of "self-evident" truths—including that everyone is created, and all are created equal—resources will flow freely from people of faith and from patriotic Americans who may not profess any religious persuasion but who believe in education, including Common Virtues. These are people who long for our schools to revere and honor the legacy of our Founding Fathers, who boldly proclaimed through our Declaration of Independence that "all men are created equal. . . ." If all are created equal, then every child is a national treasure. It is our great privilege to uncover and harness our most precious treasure through quality education for the benefit of all people everywhere.

Turning the valve on the faucet of resources

VCS students, teachers, administrators, and the board of directors are very supportive of our nearby Seven Trees public schools because of how aggressively the administrators and teachers in these schools have embraced the Common Virtues legacy of our Founding Fathers. Such passionately shared virtues have tremendously inspired the high school students at both Valley Christian and Andrew Hill to volunteer their time, talent, and resources to our local elementary public school students. I estimate VCHS students each year invest about 20,540 voluntary hours in these students and their schools, in addition to significant funds they contribute through their fundraisers and outright donations. During the 2013–14 school year, VCHS's Race2Educate Club initiated and managed a 5K community race, and about $5,000 of the money raised went to the three elementary schools in our nearby Seven Trees community. In addition, the VCHS fashion show raised thousands of dollars to help build a new playground at Los Arboles Elementary School.

Faculty members at Valley Christian have committed nearly the equivalent of a full-time teacher to support VCS students as they mentor and coach elementary students from our local public schools. And our administration and board support a budget of multiple tens of thousands of dollars annually to transport VCHS and public school students to a wide variety of Junior University and Lighthouse Initiative programs.

Examples abound of how people will commit resources to support those who open the faucet of self-evident truths and Common Virtues. In the 2014–15 school year, Hellyer Elementary, where Junior University started, became the first (and only, as of this writing) school in the district to provide each one of its students an Apple iPad tablet.

Even more amazing, Cairn University heard about two Andrew Hill High School students who won mentor awards from their principal for their volunteer work in Junior University and the Lighthouse Initiative. Cairn administrators were so moved by the story they offered the young man and young woman full four-year scholarships to Cairn. Both of these hardworking students, with difficult life circumstances and scarce funds, were astonished by their scholarship offers and awakened with new college dreams. One has enrolled at Cairn University, and the other, having received her letter of acceptance, is weighing her options for this fall. Moreover, Cairn has now established two full-tuition scholarships each year for qualified Andrew Hill mentors in the Junior University and Lighthouse Initiative programs.

And that's not all: A second private foundation, inspired by the Junior University and Lighthouse Initiative to restore Common Virtues to American education, committed two annual full-tuition scholarships for hardworking, financially disadvantaged graduates of Sylvandale Middle School to attend Valley Christian High School and the four-year college of their choice. What an incredible way to turn on the faucet valve of community resources for students at our local public secondary schools!

The power of rekindled Common Virtues based on the legacy of our Founding Fathers knows no boundaries. If these ideals have sparked your imagination for how you might open the faucet of resources for your neighborhood schools, read on for more about the ultimate source of all goodness, peace, and joy.

CHAPTER 8

ACCESS TO THE OMNIS: THE ULTIMATE STANDARD OF EXCELLENCE

*"Commit your works to the LORD, and your
thoughts and plans will be established."*[44]
*"The steps of a good man are ordered by the
LORD, and He delights in his way."*[45]

FLASHBACK: FINDING A TRIANGLE . . .

The room was quiet, as was I. For several moments I looked at the plot plans and prayed for divine guidance. I felt certain there was something there we hadn't seen.

Stretching for possibilities, I asked, "Who owns that triangle of land jutting into the baseball field?"

Someone answered, "That's the end of San Ramon Drive, and it's county land. We can't get that from the county."

"Claude," I asked the VCS chancellor, "would you check out the title on the property? There is something we've missed here. We need ten more feet and I believe it's here someplace."

Claude agreed to make the inquiry, and the meeting ended.

A couple of days later my assistant interrupted me with what seemed like a routine call. "Claude Fletcher on line two."

"Okay, I have it," I answered.

Claude's voice sparkled. "I found your ten feet. In fact, I found fifteen feet! It turns out our neighbor Tom DeHart, not the county, owns the triangle of land—Tom didn't even know he owns it. I talked to Tom and he was very agreeable. He's willing to sell the triangle to us for $1,000 to make the baseball field work."

I was stunned. . . .

Those who have read *Quest for Excellence* will recognize this story. As I recall the scene, my initial reaction comes flooding back: *I was right! There was the answer we couldn't see!* Just as I was tempted to tell myself how smart I was, I stopped short. *No—there it is again: God's provision and Access to the Omnis! How did it work? Why me? What's really behind all of the amazing achievements of VCS's development and the power of the Quest for Excellence and the Excellence Brings Influence strategy?*

The stories in my first book illustrate how this sort of divine insight, power, and provision is nearly a daily occurrence in my personal life. But no matter whether it is Claude Fletcher, Cliff Daugherty, or someone else, I have come to believe God's principles involving the Quest for Excellence and the Excellence Brings Influence strategy are as reliable as God is unchanging.

What are the "Omnis"? The Bible describes God having omnipotence, omnipresence, and omniscience. His unique character qualities as all-powerful, everywhere-present, and all-knowing are comprehensive and limitless. He created and ultimately owns all the resources in the universe, and can release them according to His will. He knows where to find ten extra feet needed for the baseball field He promised, even when the engineers say it's impossible by virtue of "simple math"!

What's even more amazing is how God allows human beings access to His wisdom, miraculous power, and inexhaustible resources. All of this and more can become available wherever people who understand His nature, character, and ways are working to bring goodness, peace, and joy to the people in their world.

How did I come to this understanding? Here is the story of my journey of discovery.

THE ULTIMATE STANDARD OF EXCELLENCE

The power of the Quest for Excellence caused me to reflect more deeply on its meaning. Convinced the Quest for Excellence in some way is more than a catchy inspirational theme, I began to understand that somehow God was pouring Himself into the transformation of our lives and the development of His divine purposes involving Valley Christian Schools. We had received donations of more than $40 million to construct Valley Christian Schools, and more than $10 million was donated to enhance teacher salaries. Added resources totaled another $60 million to fund construction. Today, more than 2,800 students and staff appreciate receiving outstanding support in the form of training, equipment, materials, and facilities.

As the success of the Quest for Excellence begat more success, I became almost obsessed to discover the "mystery" explaining how to unlock the power of the Quest for Excellence phenomenon. I thought of the words in the Founding Purpose of VCS: "That the students might know that in Christ are hidden all the treasures of wisdom and knowledge. . . ."[46] We have certainly received great treasures at VCS! Deep in my heart I sensed the connection between God's treasure house and the Quest for Excellence. During my prayers I asked God to unlock His knowledge and wisdom as to the treasures. Why and how are the Quest for Excellence and the Excellence Brings Influence strategy so powerful at Valley Christian Schools?

As I prayed, scriptures came alive to me in new ways, and I set out to discover all the verses in the Bible speaking of *excellence* in relation to God's nature, character, or works. I found eleven verses in the New King James Version with nine different descriptions of God's excellence. At first I simply listed the eleven verses in nine rows describing nine references to excellence about God. In the following table, the nine descriptions of God's excellence are in the left column, their Bible verses are in the middle column, and the Bible verse references appear in the right column:

BIBLE VERSES PRESENTING NINE DESCRIPTIONS OF GOD'S EXCELLENCE—NKJV		
Excellent Greatness	The **greatness** of Your **excellence** …	Exodus 15:7
	Praise Him for His mighty acts; praise Him according to His **excellent greatness**!	Psalm 150:2
Excellent Name	O LORD, our Lord, how **excellent is Your name** in all the earth!	Psalm 8:1, 9
	Having become so much better than the angels, as He has by inheritance obtained a more **excellent name** than they.	Hebrews 1:4
Excellent Guidance	This also comes from the LORD of hosts, who is wonderful in counsel and **excellent in guidance**.	Isaiah 28:29
Excellent Way	But earnestly desire the best gifts. And yet I show you a more **excellent way**. [The way of love – God is love]	1 Corinthians 12:31
Excellent Power	But we have this treasure in earthen vessels, that the **excellence of the power** may be of God and not of us.	2 Corinthians 4:7
Excellent Things	Sing to the LORD, for He has done **excellent things**; this is known in all the earth.	Isaiah 12:5
Excellent Knowledge	Yet indeed I also count all things loss for the **excellence of the knowledge** of Christ Jesus my Lord, for whom I have suffered the loss of all things, and count them as rubbish, that I may gain Christ.	Philippians 3:8
Excellent Ministry	But now He has obtained a more **excellent ministry**, inasmuch as He is also Mediator of a better covenant, which was established on better promises.	Hebrews 8:6
Excellent Glory	For He received from God the Father honor and glory when such a voice came to Him from the **Excellent Glory**: "This is My beloved Son, in whom I am well pleased."	2 Peter 1:17

The final verse from 2 Peter 1:17 struck me in a big way. A study of the passage revealed that the capitalization of "Excellent Glory" and equivalent phrases in the NKJV, NIV, NASB, and other Bible versions is necessary because "Excellent Glory" is used by Peter as the name of our heavenly Father. Of course, it was God the Father who spoke the words quoted in the verse ("This is My beloved Son, in whom I am well pleased") at Christ's transfiguration.[47] This discovery led me to complete assurance of this foundational truth: God describes Himself as the ultimate standard of excellence through His name "Excellent Glory." I became more convinced that studying the Bible's revelation of God's nature, character, and works is the key to unlocking the pipeline of His excellent works through our lives.

"FOR HE RECEIVED FROM
GOD THE FATHER HONOR AND GLORY
WHEN SUCH A VOICE CAME TO HIM
FROM THE EXCELLENT GLORY:
'THIS IS MY BELOVED SON,
IN WHOM I AM WELL PLEASED.'"
—2 PETER 1:17

To better illustrate the Bible's insights on the idea of excellence as revealed in the nature, character, and works of God, I further developed the table by adding a fourth column on the far left side identifying these three excellence categories. The verses describing God's excellence are then redistributed to match the categories of God's nature, character, and works. The column listing the excellent attributes of God as named in the verses also adds descriptors corresponding to each attribute of excellence:

		BIBLE VERSES PRESENTING SEVEN CATEGORIES OF EXCELLENCE IN RELATION TO THE NATURE, CHARACTER, AND WORKS OF GOD (NKJV)	
GOD'S NATURE	**Omnipotence** Greatness Power Glory **Omnipresence**	The **greatness** of Your **excellence** ...	Exodus 15:7
		Praise Him for His mighty acts; praise Him according to His excellent **greatness**!	Psalm 150:2
		But we have this treasure in earthen vessels, that the **excellence of the power** may be of God and not of us.	2 Corinthians 4:7
		For He received from God the Father honor and glory when such a voice came to Him from the **Excellent Glory:** "This is My beloved Son, in whom I am well pleased."	2 Peter 1:17
	Omniscience Knowledge	Yet indeed I also count all things loss for the **excellence of the knowledge** of Christ Jesus my Lord, for whom I have suffered the loss of all things, and count them as rubbish, that I may gain Christ.	Philippians 3:8
GOD'S CHARACTER	**Holiness** Name	O LORD, our Lord, how **excellent is Your name** in all the earth!	Psalm 8:1, 9
		Having become so much better than the angels, as He has by inheritance obtained a more **excellent name** than they.	Hebrews 1:4
GOD'S WORKS	**Creator** Things	Sing to the LORD, for He has done **excellent things**; this is known in all the earth.	Isaiah 12:5
	Counselor Guidance	This also comes from the LORD of hosts, who is wonderful in counsel and **excellent in guidance.**	Isaiah 28:29
	Savior Way	But earnestly desire the best gifts. And yet I show you a more **excellent way.** [The way of love – Jesus is the Way]	1 Corinthians 12:31
	Mediator Ministry	But now He has obtained a more **excellent ministry,** inasmuch as He is also Mediator of a better covenant, which was established on better promises.	Hebrews 8:6

As I studied the Bible verses describing the three categories of excellence in relation to the nature, character, and works of God, I reflected on my own experience in learning the difference between *knowing of* God and getting to *really know* God. Memories of early struggles to work "for God" rather than allowing God to work through me also came to mind.

Yes, I thought. *This table is very insightful.* To even begin to approach excellence by God's standards, the journey must begin with learning about God's excellent nature. Then to really understand His excellence, we must learn how to know God personally. Then, by God's grace, we become a candidate for the divine Creator to perform His excellent works through our lives.

Jesus affirmed: "Most assuredly, I say to you, he who believes in Me, the works that I do he will do also; and greater works than these he will do, because I go to My Father. And whatever you ask in My name, that I will do, that the Father may be glorified in the Son. If you ask anything in My name, I will do it."[48]

"YET INDEED I ALSO
COUNT ALL THINGS LOSS
FOR THE EXCELLENCE
OF THE KNOWLEDGE OF
CHRIST JESUS MY LORD,
FOR WHOM I HAVE SUFFERED
THE LOSS OF ALL THINGS,
AND COUNT THEM AS RUBBISH,
THAT I MAY GAIN CHRIST."
—PHILIPPIANS 3:8

My study of Christ's teachings regarding asking for "anything in My name" brought me to the insight that "in My name" means according to the will and purposes of Jesus Christ as Lord, including His ultimate purposes for His creation of the universe and all of us.

Jesus, our Creator, further developed this idea that *His* works can become *our* works in His teaching about the vine and the branches. He said, "Abide in Me, and I in you. As the branch cannot bear fruit of itself, unless it abides in the vine, neither can you, unless you abide in Me. I am the vine, you are the branches. He who abides in Me, and I in him, bears much fruit; for without Me you can do nothing."[49]

Abiding in Christ Jesus is the best strategic position I can imagine to get to know Him and His Excellent Glory intimately! That would be like moving into the White House and Oval Office to learn about the nature and powers of the president. In such close quarters, I could observe the president's true character and have an insightful personal opinion about whether his word can be trusted. He, too, could observe me closely. If I were appointed as the Secretary of State, I could even speak and act with the power of the president when authorized.

Oh, but Jesus, the ultimate "Excellent Glory," is so much closer than a housemate or a trusted colleague! He proposes much more than a mere mortal appointment as Secretary of State. His invitation is to "Abide in Me, and I in you," and as He enters our lives, He brings all of Himself. His Excellent Glory inhabits our beings, and His Excellent Greatness then surrounds us. His transformation of our hearts, souls, and minds makes it possible to follow Christ's command to "love the Lord God with all your heart, with all your soul, and with all your mind"[50] and for God to do His great creative works through us.

To better represent this journey, I added arrows to the following table, pointing from the top of the cell denoting "God's nature" through "God's character" and finally past "God's works."

EXCELLENCE	EXCELLENCE: THE NATURE, CHARACTER, AND WORKS OF GOD THE QUEST FOR EXCELLENCE AND THE EXCELLENCE BRINGS INFLUENCE STRATEGY		
	EXCELLENT	**VERSES DESCRIBING EXCELLENCE**	**BIBLE REFERENCE**
GOD'S NATURE	**Omnipotence** Greatness Power Glory **Omnipresence**	The **greatness** of Your **excellence** …	Exodus 15:7
		Praise Him for His mighty acts; praise Him according to His excellent **greatness**!	Psalm 150:2
		But we have this treasure in earthen vessels, that the **excellence of the power** may be of God and not of us.	2 Corinthians 4:7
		For He received from God the Father honor and glory when such a voice came to Him from the **Excellent Glory:** "This is My beloved Son, in whom I am well pleased."	2 Peter 1:17
	Omniscience Knowledge	Yet indeed I also count all things loss for the **excellence of the knowledge** of Christ Jesus my Lord, for whom I have suffered the loss of all things, and count them as rubbish, that I may gain Christ.	Philippians 3:8
GOD'S CHARACTER	**Holiness** Name God is: Holy, Good, Peaceful, Loving, Kind, Faithful, Gracious, Just, Merciful, Truthful, Unchanging, and much more	O LORD, our Lord, how **excellent is Your name** in all the earth!	Psalm 8:1, 9
		Having become so much better than the angels, as He has by inheritance obtained a more **excellent name** than they.	Hebrews 1:4
GOD'S WORKS	**Creator** Things	Sing to the LORD, for He has done **excellent things**; this is known in all the earth.	Isaiah 12:5
	Counselor Guidance	This also comes from the LORD of hosts, who is wonderful in counsel and **excellent in guidance.**	Isaiah 28:29
	Savior Way	But earnestly desire the best gifts. And yet I show you a more **excellent way.** [The way of love – Jesus is the Way]	1 Corinthians 12:31
	Mediator Ministry	But now He has obtained a more **excellent ministry,** inasmuch as He is also Mediator of a better covenant, which was established on better promises.	Hebrews 8:6

Arrows Indicate Sequence to Learn of the Lord and to Personally Get to Know Him

The next chapter goes deeper on this same theme, with a wealth of very practical applications for anyone, in any sphere.

CHAPTER 9

YOUR PERSONAL GPS

"If you abide in Me, and My words abide in you,
you will ask what you desire, and it shall be done for you."[51]

MANY MODERN TRAVELERS think of their global positioning system (GPS) as nearly indispensable. I remember standing in front of my car headlights to read a map on a dark isolated road long before global positioning system devices were conceived. Kris and I laugh when recalling how a heavy fog set in while we attended a Sunday evening church service in Merced, California, before we were married. I was expected to have Kris home in Sonora by 10 p.m. Trying to comply with Kris's curfew, I jumped out of my yellow Volkswagen bug repeatedly while pointing its headlights at roadside mailboxes to identify the streets we traveled. These days, what could be better than having an on-phone or in-car device communicating with satellites to pinpoint your location, and give directions, to within a few feet!

Travelers on the journey of life need this kind of help even more urgently. From a spiritual perspective, all Christians have access to a divine GPS connecting to "the heavens" to track and direct our journey.

God admonished Joshua, "This Book of the Law shall not depart from your mouth, but you shall meditate in it day and night, that you may observe to do according to all that is written in it. For then you will make your way prosperous, and then you will have good success."[52]

God inspired David, the psalmist, to describe the person whose "delight is in the law of the LORD" and who "meditates" on God's law both "day and night." He said such a person "shall be like a tree planted by the rivers of water, that brings forth its fruit in its season, whose leaf ... shall not wither"; then, whatever that person "does shall prosper."[53]

Solomon described wisdom in personal terms when he declared, "Get wisdom! Get understanding! Do not forget, nor turn away from the words of my mouth. Do not forsake her, and she will preserve you; love her, and she will keep you. Wisdom is the principal thing; therefore get wisdom. And in all your getting, get understanding. Exalt her, and she will promote you; she will bring you honor, when you embrace her."[54]

God's Word does not hide the path to acquiring wisdom and understanding. It plainly says, "The fear [reverence] of the LORD is the beginning of wisdom, and the knowledge of the Holy One is understanding."[55] An absolutely critical component of the Quest for Excellence and the Excellence Brings Influence strategy is to make the Bible your personal GPS for life's mission to know God intimately.

Daily immersion in God's Word is crucial for personally knowing God. Meditating on God's law day and night, emphasized by both Joshua and David, is a requirement for success by God's standards. I practice meditation as the continuous comparison of how I am living my life in light of the God-given principles and practices of success and prosperity revealed in God's Word.

While only twenty-three years old, I was challenged to promise God I would read the Bible at least five minutes each day unless I am sick or otherwise unable. I was warned not to make the promise unless I really intended to keep it. When I made the commitment, I thought I was honoring God. But now, many years later, I understand how every moment of reading God's Word has brought me closer to thinking godly thoughts. In this process of transformation, God has honored the daily alignment with His Word by giving me the privilege of experiencing His excellent works through my life.

As Clifford Daugherty, I am far from excellent. But the presence of Excellent Glory *in* Clifford Daugherty is excellent, and His name is Jesus Christ. Paul the Apostle put it plainly: "Christ in you, the hope of glory."[56] To settle any question about whether Jesus Christ is God, he wrote, "For by Him [Jesus] all things were created that are in heaven and that are on earth, visible and invisible, whether thrones or dominions or principalities or powers. All things were created through Him and for Him. And He is before all things, and in Him all things consist."[57]

It seems absurd to think I could have God's thoughts. Again, Paul made a similar statement to the Corinthians: "For 'who has known the mind of the LORD that he may instruct Him?' But we have the mind of Christ."[58] Decades of gaining God's thoughts—"the mind of Christ"—have given me great advantages and huge personal benefits. The alignment of my thinking with God's Word through meditation on a daily basis helped me realize that true excellence is ultimately the nature, character, and works of God. Becoming more excellent is really becoming more like Jesus—instead of more like Cliff!

Speaking of Himself, Jesus told Nicodemus, "No one has ascended to heaven but He who came down from heaven. . . ."[59] Certainly, Jesus' teaching makes it clear, human beings cannot ascend to truly excellent heavenly thoughts or works or to heaven itself as mere mortals. But thanks to Jesus, in whom "dwells all the fullness of the Godhead bodily"[60] as our Creator, He Himself has come into the world to bring us His mind and His Word containing the profound thinking of God.[61]

"For as the heavens are higher than the earth, so are My ways higher than your ways, and My thoughts than your thoughts."[62] God has given us His own Spirit-empowered GPS: the Bible. It offers God's heavenly, omniscient insight on how to gain understanding, wisdom, prosperity, and success along life's journey. The divine wisdom in His Word offers insight for all.

To Know Jesus Intimately

Paul the Apostle was able to write, "I know whom I have believed and am persuaded that He is able to keep what I have committed to Him until that day."[63] After acknowledging Jesus as Lord, Paul entrusted his entire life to Jesus. Paul's knowledge of God's nature, His personal character, and great works provided the strong foundation for Paul's personal relationship with Jesus. This intimate personal relationship allowed God to work through Paul to write about one third of the New Testament. His close relationship with Jesus made Paul confident he would never hear the dreaded words of Jesus on judgment day: "I never knew you; depart from Me, you who practice lawlessness!"[64] Instead, Paul looked forward to hearing Christ say, "Well done, good and faithful servant; you were faithful over a few things, I will make you ruler over many things. Enter into the joy of your lord."[65]

Ultimately, the Quest for Excellence is the quest to know Jesus and become like Him so He can do His great and excellent works through us. In the process, His desires become our desires and we seek to do His will. Then it becomes possible for the power of the Excellence Brings Influence strategy to take root in and through our personal lives. At this point, the promises for prosperity and success found in Joshua 1:7–9 and Psalm 1:1–3, mentioned at the beginning of this chapter, become real.

As we learn of God's nature and character through His Word, prayer, and meditation, we can have a personal relationship with God leading to an amazing display of His supernatural works through our lives, including the power of His omnipotence, omnipresence, and omniscience. That's the power of the Omnis! Accessing God's wisdom and understanding ensures our true prosperity and success in accordance with His perfect will and plan for our lives. It is amazing to me how God changes our view of the true nature of prosperity and success to conform to His perspective. God's nature, character, and works are truly excellent, bringing us back full circle to the ultimate definition of excellence as the nature, character, and works of God.

GOD'S WORK IN AND THROUGH YOU

Before God works *through* you, He must do His great work *in* you. This idea is powerfully communicated by the writer of the book of Hebrews. "Now may the God of peace . . . make you complete in every good work to do His will, working in you what is well pleasing in His sight, through Jesus Christ."[66]

Someone once said, "the highest form of worship is work." Of course, this maxim must be qualified with "the work" being God's work, through us, by God's power. When we begin to understand the nature and character of God—including His infinite omnipotence, omnipresence, omniscience, holiness, love, and unending resources—a great truth becomes obvious. As God begins to work through a mere human being, instant transformation and transcendence is imparted to an otherwise finite mortal. As God inhabits our lives, His immortality transcends our mortality. Limitations of resources, intellect, space, time, and power no longer apply because, as Jesus said, "The things which are impossible with men are possible with God."[67] Truly, if God elects by His grace to create His works through us, our potential achievements are limited only by God's will, plans, and purposes. This is how ordinary people can have "Access to the Omnis" and to God's divine resources.

Even Jesus limited His great works to His Father's will. Such was the case when Jesus prayed to His Father in agony, "Not My will, but

Yours, be done" while facing the cross.[68] This truth was also evident when Jesus taught His disciples to pray, "Your will be done on earth as it is in heaven."[69] Jesus declared that He did only what was in harmony with His heavenly Father's purposes.[70]

Learning to know God personally by meditating upon His Word leads to a great opportunity to love God by keeping His commandments. Jesus said, "You shall love the LORD your God with all your heart, with all your soul, and with all your mind."[71] He also said, "If you love Me, keep My commandments" and "He who has My commandments and keeps them, it is he who loves Me. And he who loves Me will be loved by My Father, and I will love him and manifest Myself to him."[72]

How profound! We love Jesus by keeping His commands! The Father loves those who keep Jesus' commands. And Jesus promises to love and manifest Himself to those who keep His commands. There we have it: a personal disclosure of the Creator of the Universe to mere mortals of His own creation! Can you imagine what those ingenious creative manifestations involve? For me personally, I relish every disclosure, every supernatural provision, every miraculous insight, and every provision to achieve God's purposes through my life "according to His riches in glory by Christ Jesus."[73]

Dare I say it again? This is what the Quest for Excellence means. This is God's Excellence Brings Influence strategy to accomplish all of His purposes through our lives, and to fulfill the prayer Jesus taught us to pray: "Your kingdom come. Your will be done on earth as it is in heaven."[74]

Yes, for me to say I can do God's works is truly absurd, but for Jesus to say "I will do it" means it is possible for Him to do anything He wants through you and me.[75] We learn more of His nature and absorb His character through "the knowledge of God,"[76] then we better love Him by being obedient to His commands. In this way He can "fulfill all the good pleasure of His goodness and the work of faith with power,"[77] works that can be attributed only to God's love, power, and grace in and through our lives.

A PICTURE OF TWO OXEN

Jesus said, "Take My yoke upon you and learn from Me, for I am gentle and lowly in heart, and you will find rest for your souls."[78] Here He gives us a picture of two oxen working inside the yoke together, side by side. Thank God He is in the yoke beside me doing most of the hard pulling, so when I fail from exhaustion and weakness, omnipotent Jesus pulls with His power, and I find rest for my soul.

It is important to learn from Jesus about God's excellent greatness, power, omniscience, and love—for me and for every breathing thing He longs to redeem. What a privilege to let Jesus' all-powerful "pull" accomplish His great creative works while I cooperate and walk beside Him. This is how the Quest for Excellence is achieved supernaturally in our lives. We can attain great influence through the excellent greatness of Jesus. He is the one doing the hard pulling, alongside of us, enabling us to desire and achieve His purposes in all we do, "heartily, as to the Lord."[79] This strategy gives us great advantages both in our personal lives and through the careers God chooses for us, empowering us to bring His transforming influence to our family, community, and world. In this way, then, it is true—the highest form of worship is work. That's how Excellence Brings Influence!

There is no work too hard for Jesus, and there is no price He cannot afford. He is in all His ways infinitely powerful, loving, and holy, and He is determined to achieve His excellent works through those who will but take up His yoke and walk with Him. Experiencing God's good works is a normal way of life when every step with Jesus is directed and empowered by Him.

A study of the Bible references on the following table reveals that in every instance of "good works" involving Christians in the

New Testament, such works are of God—by His grace, through His power, according to His will—and are not described as the works of human beings.

THE VERSE	WHO IS WORKING, OR WHOSE ABILITY?	KIND OF WORK	REFERENCE
"This is the work of God, that you believe in Him whom He sent." (Jesus speaking)	God	Believe in Him whom He sent	John 6:29
Be steadfast, immovable, always abounding in the work of the Lord, knowing that your labor is not in vain in the Lord.	Work of the Lord	Labor in the Lord	1 Corinthians 15:58
God is able to make all grace abound toward you, that you, always having all sufficiency in all things, may have an abundance for every good work.	God is able God's grace God's sufficiency God's abundance	Good work	2 Corinthians 9:8
He who has begun a good work in you will complete it until the day of Jesus Christ.	"He": referring to God; God's ability to complete	A good work in you	Philippians 1:6
Walk worthy of the Lord, fully pleasing Him, being fruitful in every good work and increasing in the knowledge of God.	In the knowledge of God	Every good work (work of God)	Colossians 1:10
That our God would count you worthy of this calling, and fulfill all the good pleasure of His goodness and the work of faith with power . . .	Faith of Jesus Christ; Power of God	Fulfill the good pleasure of His goodness and the work of faith	2 Thessalonians 1:11
May our Lord Jesus Christ Himself, and our God and Father . . . establish you in every good word and work.	Our Lord Jesus Christ Himself, and our God and Father	Establish you in every good work	2 Thessalonians 2:16–17
That the man of God may be complete, thoroughly equipped for every good work.	Be complete and thoroughly equipped by God	For every good work	2 Timothy 3:17
Make you complete in every good work to do His will, working in you what is well pleasing in His sight, through Jesus Christ.	Through Jesus Christ	Every good work to do His will	Hebrews 13:21

The Quest for Excellence and the Excellence Brings Influence strategy rest entirely on knowing of or about God, personally knowing God, and loving God—experiencing God's supernatural plans, works, and power to achieve all of His purposes to and through our lives.

To complete the table introduced in the previous chapter, I added a column on the left to represent God's wisdom and understanding (as endorsed in Proverbs 4:5–8) and His excellent creative works through our lives.

> "JESUS REPLIED, 'THIS IS THE WORK
> OF GOD—THAT YOU BELIEVE IN THE
> ONE HE HAS SENT.'"
> —JOHN 6:29 (HCSB)

> "FOR IT IS GOD WHO IS WORKING
> IN YOU, ENABLING YOU BOTH
> TO DESIRE AND TO WORK OUT
> HIS GOOD PURPOSE."
> —PHILIPPIANS 2:13 (HCSB)

> "NOW MAY THE GOD OF PEACE . . . MAKE YOU
> COMPLETE IN EVERY GOOD WORK TO DO HIS
> WILL, WORKING IN YOU WHAT IS WELL PLEASING
> IN HIS SIGHT, THROUGH JESUS CHRIST."
> —HEBREWS 13:20–21

Inspired by the Holy Spirit, David penned this promise: "Delight yourself also in the LORD, and He shall give you the desires of your heart."[80]

"The Spirit of the LORD is upon Me, because He has anointed Me to preach the gospel to the poor; He has sent Me to heal the brokenhearted, to proclaim liberty to the captives and recovery of sight to the blind, to set at liberty those who are oppressed; to proclaim the acceptable year of the LORD." Luke 4:18–19; see also Isaiah 61:1–2a

		GOD'S EXCELLENCE	VERSES DESCRIBING EXCELLENCE	HELPFUL SCRIPTURE
INFLUENCE Prov 4:5-8 / Matt 11:29	**GOD'S NATURE**	**EXCELLENT POWER** Omnipotence God Almighty	"I know that You can do everything, and that no purpose of Yours can be withheld from You." Job 42:2 But we have this treasure in earthen vessels, that the **excellence of the power** may be of God and not of us. 2 Corinthians 4:7	Genesis 17:1 Mark 10:27 Luke 1:37 Revelation 15:3a
— LEARN OF ME — GET UNDERSTANDING & WISDOM		**EXCELLENT PRESENCE** Omnipresence Wonderful Mighty God	"Am I a God near at hand," says the LORD, "and not a God afar off? Can anyone hide himself in secret places, so I shall not see him?" says the LORD; "do I not fill heaven and earth?" says the LORD. Jeremiah 23:23–24	Psalm 139:7–10 Proverbs 15:3 Isaiah 9:6 Matthew 18:20
		EXCELLENT KNOWLEDGE Omniscience	Yet indeed I also count all things loss for the **excellence of the knowledge** of Christ Jesus my Lord, for whom I have suffered the loss of all things, and count them as rubbish, that I may gain Christ. Philippians 3:8	1 Samuel 2:3 Job 28:24 Psalm 139:4 Psalm 147:5 Colossians 2:2–3 1 John 3:19–20
		EXCELLENT GREATNESS & GLORY Most High God Everlasting Father From Everlasting Eternal Lord	The greatness of Your **excellence**. . . . Exodus 15:7 For He received from God the Father honor and glory when such a voice came to Him from the **Excellent Glory**: "This is My beloved Son, in whom I am well pleased." 2 Peter 1:17 Praise Him for His mighty acts; praise Him according to His **excellent greatness!** Psalm 150:2	Genesis 14:20 Deut. 10:14 Isaiah 9:6 Micah 5:2 Matthew 3:17 Revelation 22:13
— LOVE ME — HEART	**GOD'S CHARACTER**	**EXCELLENT NAME** God is: Holy, Good, Peaceful, Loving, Kind, Faithful, Gracious, Just, Merciful, Truthful, Unchanging, and much more	O LORD, our Lord, how **excellent is Your name** in all the earth! Psalm 8:1, 9 Having become so much better than the angels, as He has by inheritance obtained a more **excellent name** than they. Hebrews 1:4 The fruit of the Spirit is love, joy, peace, longsuffering, kindness, goodness, faithfulness, gentleness, self-control. Galatians 5:22–23	Exodus 34:6 Leviticus 20:26 1 Samuel 2:2 Psalm 99:3–5 Psalm 103:8 Malachi 3:6 Matthew 22:37 John 15:14 Luke 1:49 Romans 12:2
— YOUR WILL BE DONE — TO & THROUGH US	**GOD'S WORKS**	**EXCELLENT THINGS** Creator and Sustainer of all things and of all life Great and marvelous works	Sing to the LORD, for He has done **excellent things**; this is known in all the earth. Isaiah 12:5 That you may approve the **things that are excellent**, that you may be sincere and without offense till the day of Christ. Philippians 1:10	Genesis 1:1 Acts 17:24-28 Romans 11:33-36 Colossians 1:17 Revelation 15:3a
Arrows Indicate Sequence to Learn of the Lord and to Personally Get to Know Him		**EXCELLENT GUIDANCE** Counselor Prince of Peace	The LORD of hosts, who is wonderful in counsel and **excellent in guidance**. Isaiah 28:29	Proverbs 16:1-3, 9 Psalm 37:3-6, 23 Isaiah 9:6
		EXCELLENT WAY Redeemer and Savior	And yet I show you a more **excellent way**. [The way of love – Jesus is the Way] 1 Corinthians 12:31	Matthew 6:33 John 10:10 Revelation 15:3b
		EXCELLENT MINISTRY Mediator	But now He has obtained a more **excellent ministry**, inasmuch as He is also Mediator of a better covenant. Hebrews 8:6.	2 Corinthians 5:18 Philippians 2:13

Under the same Holy Spirit anointing, King Solomon concluded: "All the ways of a man are clean in his own sight, but the LORD weighs the motives. Commit your works to the LORD and your plans will be established. The LORD has made everything for its own purpose. . . ."[81] God's insight into correct motives reveals the key unlocking all of God's excellent power. This truth is better understood by comparing this verse in both the New King James Version as well as the New American Standard Bible. The NKJV says "The LORD has made all for Himself," and the NASB "The LORD has made everything for its own purpose." Taking both versions into account uncovers the more complete intent of God's message written in the original Hebrew language.

To the extent people commit their works to the Lord, their thoughts and plans are established in harmony with their gifts and passions and the goals they were created to achieve—and all of those thoughts and plans are perfectly aligned with God's purposes. When God, the Creator and Sustainer of the heavens and the earth, transplants His thoughts and plans into our minds, all of His divine power and resources are commanded to work through us to accomplish the passionate desires He and we long to fulfill.

What an exciting way to live! The great plans and purposes of Jesus Christ, our Creator, banish all room for boredom and aimlessness in a life dedicated to Him. God's thoughts and plans are tailored for each one of us. They are as unique and special as our fingerprints, and they are measured in waves of goodness, peace, and joy. "For the Kingdom of God is . . . living a life of goodness and peace and joy in the Holy Spirit."[82]

Ready for more inspiration? Part II features real-life stories of the Quest for Excellence principles in action. (A full list and discussion of "The Twenty Indispensable Principles" appears after the Conclusion.) These stories will take us around the world and even into outer space. Fasten your seat belts!

PART TWO

THE QUEST
FOR EXCELLENCE
IN ACTION:
THE INVISIBLE
HAND

CHAPTER 10

THE VIEW HALFWAY
AROUND THE WORLD

"Where there is no vision, the people perish."[83]

THE COFFEE SMELLED GOOD, and the pastries
invited company. Blue and white nametags waited to greet pastors
as they made their way toward the small gym at Valley Christian
Schools' Skyway campus. Linda Skovmand looked to greet guests.
Security golf carts dodged cars to locate pastors and offer them rides
to the building, while hurried parents delivered students for another
school day. In the gym, white folding chairs circled a vocalist and an
acoustic guitarist offering songs of praise. Another monthly pastors'
prayer meeting in Silicon Valley was about to begin.

While pastors gathered this brisk morning in late 2005, I went to
my office to greet Pam Watson, my executive assistant. She reminded me
of my meetings for the day and we took care of some correspondence.
Before long, I realized I was about thirty minutes late returning to the
pastors' prayer meeting. I slipped inside just in time to join a small
prayer group with familiar faces except for one with a bronze, dark

brown complexion. Following our usual pattern, we took turns around the small circle of four, exchanging prayer requests and praying for each pastor and ministry individually.

Pastor John Isaacs interrupted the prayer with an introduction. "This is my guest, Abraham Philip. He is from New Delhi, India. He launched a Christian school in the New Delhi slums and is here to raise support for the ministry. What are your prayer requests, Abraham?"

Abraham's gentle, accented voice ably projected his enthusiasm: "Please pray that the slum children in New Delhi and their families will come to know Jesus. We have a school where they are learning to read the Bible. Except for this mission school, these nearly 400 children could never escape the poverty in the slums. We feed them one meal a day and provide uniforms. The parents are poor and can't even afford good food and clothing for their children. The school is three stories tall and sits on only 900 square feet of land. There are no chairs or tables—the children sit on the floor. Pray for God's financial support to keep the school open. Several families have already come to know Christ. The people are mostly Hindu and Muslim."

We prayed, and my heart stirred.

What a contrast between their poverty and our beautiful campuses, I thought. *Nine hundred square feet of land for 400 children in New Delhi, compared to fifty-three acres or 2.4 million square feet of land for our 1,695 students at the Skyway campus.*

Later, I did some quick calculations. Comparisons revealed that the children in New Delhi had just over two square feet of land per student, with about seven square feet of building space per student. In comparison, VCS had more than 1,040 square feet of land per student with more than 110 square feet of building space per student.

After the prayer meeting, I invited Abraham to my office so

we could get acquainted. My mind raced as to how we might help. Because English is the official teaching medium in the New Delhi school—although their native language is Hindi—I offered curriculum and other learning materials that might help their children.

As we parted, I offered my hand. "Let's keep in touch, Abraham. I would like to learn more about your school in New Delhi."

GETTING A GLIMPSE OF WHAT GOD WANTS TO DO

Just after the first of the year in January 2006, I received a follow-up phone call from Abraham. "I know you are very busy." He apologized in his soft voice. "You mentioned about some help for the slum school in New Delhi. If you're still interested, I could meet you in your office to update you on what is happening at Grace Public School."

I agreed to meet, but was honest with him. "I want to help," I said. "But I'm thinking about practical help with materials and curriculum, *not* dollars. You are probably aware since Valley Christian Schools is a non-profit corporation, I am not permitted to donate VCS's tuition or contributions to another school. They are the school's only two sources of substantial revenue."

"Of course, I completely understand," Abraham assured me.

By the time he arrived in my office on Friday, January 6, just before noon, my appetite reminded me it was still looking for breakfast. We decided to take our meeting to one of my favorite restaurants, El Rancho Steakhouse, located on Monterey Avenue just down the hill from the Skyway campus. We call it "Conference Room L."

Abraham appeared meek and reserved. He clearly intended to honor my request to not expect anything other than practical, non-financial help. After ordering our lunches, we settled in to talk. "Abraham, do the children in your school speak and read English well enough to use some of our curriculum and materials?"

"They are learning to speak and to write English, but they speak Hindi at home with their parents."

Naively I asked, "Would an online learning-to-read-and-write program from Valley Christian Schools be helpful?"

"The children can learn like children in America, except they live in a slum and our school does not have computers."

"If we send a laptop and projector, could you connect it to the Internet?"

Abraham shifted in his seat. "This part of New Delhi is poor, and while other places have the Internet, it is unavailable where Grace Public School is located."

Not appreciating the magnitude of the problem, I wondered about a possible satellite connection, but decided to drop this line of inquiry for a more basic question. "What kinds of materials and curriculum would be most helpful?"

"Just about anything would be more than these children have," he replied without further comment.

I felt like I was trying to get water from a disconnected garden hose. Abraham, it seemed, was trying hard not to violate my boundaries to help with only curriculum and materials.

Sensing a tug from God to help Abraham, I began to question my decision to set boundaries. But I had to have more information. "Can you tell me more about what the school needs? How can we help the children?"

Abraham glanced down toward his place setting and hesitated. He seemed reluctant to answer, but finally looked up. "The school will close this June."

His unexpected words dropped like a bombshell. "Why?"

"Another school had a fire that killed about thirty-five children because of too few exits. The government is now requiring adequate safety exits for all schools. Schools that cannot comply must close at the end of this school year. Our school cannot comply because the building is surrounded by other buildings and has only one narrow front door."

"Do you have any possible solutions?"

"Yes, we have found a piece of land that would be ideal for a new school," Abraham continued. "But this is a slum area and the people have very little money. They could never afford to buy this property."

"What is the land like and how far away is it from your current location?"

"It's about a five-minute walk to this property from the current school. The land we have is 900 square feet with a building of three floors and 2,700 square feet of classroom space. The new land is 4,500 square feet and has one building with six small rooms to temporarily house all 400 students until construction is completed on a new school building. The city of New Delhi will approve the new school, but God must help us get all the money. First we need $80,000 to buy the land. The old structures on the land will house the school until we can raise funds to build a modern, three-story school with 10,000 square feet."

FLASHBACK MEMORIES

As I listened to Abraham, my heart connected with his crisis as an emotional image gripped my consciousness. My mind jumped back in time to when Valley Christian Schools, too, lost its high school campus on even shorter notice. My first book, *Quest for Excellence,* told the story.

Facing the end of two years of lease extensions on our high school's rented property, we had found no other options for adequate facilities, and in spring 1989 reluctantly signed a lease on a small, former public elementary school. The vacant campus adjoined a fifty-acre site we hoped to purchase. According to a clause in our contract, if anyone offered Union School District cash without contingencies to purchase the property, we would lose our lease immediately. The clause made me uncomfortable, yet VCS had no choice but to accept these terms if we hoped to open the high school that fall. Besides, such an offer, coming out of the blue, seemed unlikely.

That summer we moved the high school onto the elementary campus and shoehorned in everything we could. Kris and I left on a three-week vacation and were enjoying our last full day away when I received a phone call. The improbable—the unthinkable—had happened. A developer had offered the school district a no-contingency cash offer of $1 million per acre for the elementary school campus and the adjacent fifty acres, immediately displacing Valley Christian. With little more than two weeks before the first day of the fall semester, our high school had no home.

With one ear still tuned to Abraham, my body recalled the heart-stopping shock of that moment. In my flashback, however, I also remembered what I had told the colleague phoning with this bad news.

"Well, Steve," I said, *"we are now going to discover just how powerful God is and how much He cares for VCS. This is an impossible situation except for God's miraculous provision—so there's a big miracle on the way."*

"Hello, Mr. Cliff. Here is your food." Rabob, the restaurant owner, interrupted my memories as she delivered our lunch. Delectable eight-ounce rib-eye sandwiches greeted our eyes and olfactory senses.

After introducing Abraham to Rabob, I offered thanks for our lunch and asked Abraham for more details. "In addition to the cost of the land, what needs to be done to the building for your students to attend there?"

"The buildings are living spaces now, but after we buy the land we can clean and paint them and use them for classrooms until we build a new school. This is so much more land than where the school is now. If we get this property, we can care for our K–6 students and keep them from going back to the streets. With the additional room, we can also add junior high and keep our current sixth-grade students. Eventually, we hope to open a high school and have almost 1,600 students in grades

K–12 with two school sessions a day. Because of Grace Public School, many families are becoming Christians in a place usually closed to the gospel message. We are accepted by the community because we offer the only hope for these children to get an education."

A shot of adrenalin hit my pulse. It felt like a time warp. Abraham's school was at the crossroads. My own crossroads for Valley Christian Schools had been so similar. As we ate our mouth-watering sandwiches, my thoughts again raced back to our VCS journey. After God in the nick of time miraculously provided a new site for the high school in 1989, we faced another deadline ten years later at the end of yet another lease extension. God led us through numerous cliffhanging episodes toward the realization of our dream of our own new campus.

The parallels were eerie. I sensed God confronting me with a question: "Do you care as much about the children in New Delhi, India, as you care about the students at Valley Christian Schools?"

Our VCS board and I often remembered Jesus' statement, ". . . to whom much is given, from him much will be required."[84] I knew our board believed God had a mission for VCS beyond our community. In fact, VCS's mission statement ends with the words ". . . and the world."

I began to suspect the boundaries I had set—to offer only curriculum and materials for the school in India—were Cliff's boundaries and not God's. A realization gripped me: *Unless they get the new land, this school will no longer exist—and what good will curriculum and materials do then?*

DISCERNING GOD'S HEART

Rabob offered more coffee with a pleasant smile. I asked Abraham, "Do you have any money to put toward the $80,000 piece of land?"

"Yes, we have a $40,000 commitment from Pastor Bill Webb, senior pastor of Blondy Church of God in Blondy, Tennessee. Pastor Webb came to visit our school in India. His church will donate $40,000 if God provides the other half of the money in time to purchase the land."

"When do you need the money?"

"By February 15."

Less than six weeks away. A strong, deep-seated burden to help settled into my entire being. *Is this God talking to me? It certainly seems like God speaking loud and clear. I really need to know for sure.*

"Abraham, your situation is so similar to our VCS journey. It seems like God may be speaking to me to help you, but I'll need to learn more about your ministry by checking references. Can you get the phone number of Pastor Bill Webb for me? And do you have other American leaders I can contact for more information about your ministry?"

"Yes, of course. We have a California non-profit corporation called North India Christian Ministries USA, and its purpose is to support the ministry in India."

"Please give me all the details you can," I requested. "My heart trusts your heart, but if we are going to find a way to help get the land, I must do my 'due diligence' to inform and give confidence to our administrative team and our VCS board of directors."

"I'll send information to you via email attachment by tomorrow."

As we walked toward my van in the parking lot, I was shaken by the change in my heart. *Am I getting too involved?* I wondered. I had walked into the restaurant intending to explore the possibility of helping with curriculum and materials, and now I was reliving the burden of God's calling to build VCS. Only this time the burden was not for Valley Christian, but for a school I had never seen on the opposite side of the world. *This is either a huge distraction or a BIG surprise from God.*

On our way back to the VCS campus, I asked Abraham, "Would you be willing to come to our administrative meeting to share this opportunity with our team?" He readily agreed.

When we arrived at the office, we checked the calendar with my assistant, Pam, and scheduled Abraham's visit with the administrative team for Tuesday, January 17.

I asked Abraham if I could pray with him before he left. The burden was not letting up and I needed to bring it to the Lord. Afterwards, I sat alone still feeling shocked and awkward. *I am the president/ superintendent of Valley Christian Schools in San Jose, California, and I'm feeling a burden to build Grace Public School in New Delhi, India. That's scary!*

"Lord," I prayed, "if You want VCS to help get this land for the school in India, please speak to our administrative team and our board so I'm not alone on this. You know I can't use VCS's donations or tuition. Where can I find up to $40,000 in just over a month? Oh yes, and please speak to Kris and our prayer intercessors too."

As promised, Abraham emailed the attachment with the list of board members from North India Christian Ministries USA. He also added the names of several others who had visited Grace Public School in New Delhi. I made my first call to Pastor Bill Webb at Blondy Church of God. "Abraham Philip said your church is committed to giving $40,000 to purchase land for a new school in New Delhi. We at Valley Christian Schools may be interested in helping buy the land, but I need more information. What can you tell me about the school?"

"I've served as pastor here for many years," Pastor Webb began, "and during my time of ministry I've seen many foreign missions' needs. Without a doubt, this opportunity offers more results for the dollars invested than any other ministry opportunity I have come across. I personally visited the school and was impressed by how much they are accomplishing with so few resources. That's why our little church made such a big commitment. We're currently in a campaign to raise money to build our own church. But we couldn't pass up this opportunity. This $40,000 gift is by far the largest single gift our church has ever committed. That's how strongly we feel about this school. Pastor Abraham is a godly man who has proven himself over many years. He can be trusted."

Pastor Webb was very convincing. I hung up the phone with the thought, *If I was looking for an excuse to get out of this burden, that didn't help. I'd better call our prayer intercessors about building a school in the slums of New Delhi.*

Was the Holy Spirit birthing a new vision in me—a glimpse of what God wanted to do? After all, I wanted to believe the Quest for Excellence can become real to anyone, anywhere, at any time. This was the ultimate test, I reasoned: Can the Quest for Excellence work even on the other side of the world, for the poorest of the poor in the slums of New Delhi, India? I reflected again on the three big questions I had asked God at the beginning of this journey:

1. Can I confidently say God is willing and able to do the same miraculous works to build schools like VCS in any community where people are praying and working to bring His goodness, peace, and joy to the children in their schools?

2. Are there really enough resources to build great schools in every community, even during difficult economic times?

3. If the answers to the first two questions are yes, what can I say to help people find enough resources to build great schools like VCS? In other words, how can ordinary people with ordinary means get "Access to the Omnis" to accomplish the Quest for Excellence in their schools, their businesses, or their professional lives?

I suspected I was about to get some answers.

CHAPTER 11

WHERE YOUR TREASURE IS: FUNDRAISING 101

"For where your treasure is, there your heart will be also."[85]

THE FOLLOWING MONDAY at our weekly VCS intercessory prayer meeting, we sought God's direction regarding Grace Public School in New Delhi and its impending closure. "What would You have us do, Lord?"

As scheduled, Pastor Abraham shared his heart with our administrative team the next week on Tuesday morning, January 17, 2006. The team asked if he would come back for more discussions a week later. By that time, I had spoken with several others on Abraham's list of board members and those who had visited his school in India. All discussions brought confirmation to everything Abraham and Pastor Webb had expressed.

My executive assistant, Pam Watson, recognized the name of Eric Wilder, missions director at Silver Creek Church in San Jose. She has known Eric for many years. Pastor Stuart Nice from Santa Clara Christian School was one I recognized. He and Eric had visited Grace Public School in December 2005, just a month earlier.

By Monday evening, January 23, I found myself sharing my burden with our Valley Christian Schools board of directors. They were open and interested in continuing our "due diligence" as to how we might help Abraham and confirm the viability of Grace's relocation to the new property.

At 8:00 the next morning, I walked into a packed meeting room. About fifteen administrators and staff surrounded the conference table. Eric Wilder attended at Pam's request, as well as Melvin Johnson, president of North India Christian Ministries USA. Sheri Vavken, VCS's lead intercessor, came for information and to pray.

After introductions, Abraham gave a PowerPoint presentation about the ministry, and Eric and Melvin shared their hearts. Before they left, Eric handed videotapes from his December New Delhi visit to Werner Vavken, the VCS Faculty/Staff Chaplain and E-Learning Director at that time.

At the next administrative team meeting on Tuesday, January 31, Werner surprised us with a polished video of Grace Public School's ministry, complete with music, he created from Eric's videotapes. Tears filled many of our eyes as we saw the contrast between the poverty of the slums and the transformation of the children at Grace Public School.

FUNDRAISING 101

From the time I learned of the impending closure of Grace Public School, I could not escape the passion and calling God had given me to help with the remaining money needed to purchase the land for the school's relocation. I went to bed praying about the situation. I woke up during the night as I dreamed about the school. A continual warmth and heartfelt compassion filled my soul, and it seemed I could not help but discuss the school's plight with almost everyone. Unrelenting waves of compassion pushed on my heart from every side.

The VCS board of directors and I were in the process of establishing the Quest Institute to help develop quality education in schools across America, and perhaps around the world. While reflecting on the meaning of my burden for the India school, I considered one of the three big questions I had asked earlier: "Can I confidently say God is willing and able to do the same miraculous works to build schools like VCS in any community where people are praying and working to bring His goodness, peace, and joy to the children in their schools?"

Now I get it! I thought. God's answer came through loud and clear as He spoke to my mind: *Now you know why you do not have to worry about whether I can raise the money for the emerging Quest Institute schools. When I speak to someone to give millions to build a quality school, that person experiences the same unrelenting call to give* millions *of dollars that I put on your heart to give* thousands *of dollars. There is no escape. There is no release until the gift is given and I reward them with great joy!*

What a message. What a lesson! I felt assurance about God's call on my life and that He could and would call educational leaders to work with the Quest Institute and others to build great schools. I could confidently tell people: God is not only able but willing to do the same miraculous works to build excellent schools in any community where people are praying and working to bring His goodness, peace, and joy to the children in their schools.

No price tag is too big for God. Building a comprehensive K–12 school can cost $100 million or more for construction alone, not including the land. To be sure, quality schools come in different shapes and sizes, depending on the community. What it looks like to reflect God's excellence in one community will differ from the reflection of excellence offered by a school in a dissimilar place. But one fact is certain: God works through His people to build great schools. And people passionately committed to the principles of the Quest for Excellence will certainly have God's blessings to build one of the finest schools in their community—regardless of cost.

Yes, God can and will do this work any place where the Quest for Excellence is alive and well—where people are praying and working to bring His goodness, peace, and joy to the children in their schools. Even in the slums of New Delhi! What a lesson!

As my burden for the India school increased, God took me through a crash course on Fundraising 101. Now I understand how God speaks to potential donors about giving money and why people listen and passionately act, as I did when He spoke to me to fund Grace Public School in New Delhi. The best example I can use to describe what it felt like when God spoke to me to raise money for Grace Public School is this: It was like what I felt when I fell in love with Kris before we were married. I could not escape the call of love to marry Kris. I loved her and there was no logic to follow—only love. It didn't matter that she had just graduated from high school and I had completed only two years of college. We were in love and we were married with God's blessings. It's working, and has worked for more than forty years! We can't imagine having a better marriage.

Having learned my lesson firsthand as to how God can easily fund quality schools, I was determined to give any amount needed to finish raising the entire $80,000 to purchase the land in New Delhi. By February 3, a shortfall of only $9,700 remained, but the money had to be sent immediately in order to arrive in New Delhi by February 15 to fund the escrow closing.

On Friday, February 3, 2006, VCS wrote a check for $9,700, and I had the privilege of personally handing it to Abraham. We wired the money to New Delhi, and the land purchase for the new school closed on February 15. With funds committed to repay the $9,700, VCS's CFO, Don Shipley, wisely took steps to ensure no money came from

VCS's operational tuition funds or donations for educational programs. Personal contributions designated for the Grace Public School project secured the entire $9,700.

What joy! What fulfillment! What comfort. What proof of Jesus' teaching, "It is more blessed to give than to receive"![86]

WHERE YOUR TREASURE IS . . .

But God, it seemed, was leading VCS to do even more for the struggling Christian school in the New Delhi slums. The property we helped purchase did not provide adequate classrooms, and a new school still had to be built. I would need more firsthand information, however, before I could challenge our faculty, students, and VCS families to raise the funds for its construction.

Sheri and Werner Vavken, VCS intercessors for more than twenty years, responded to the call. They offered to take a major detour on their European vacation to visit Grace Public School in New Delhi during the first week of April.

The Vavkens' visit gave us all fresh vision. On Tuesday, April 4, our administrative team was privileged to meet the Grace Public School team via an Internet video conference. During their trip, Werner and Sheri saw the new school grounds and witnessed the relocation of students from the obsolete school to the new location. They brought back great pictures and fresh video of the students and the school.

A month later, Sheri and Werner came by my office and asked if I would like to go with them to an Indian restaurant in Santa Clara where Pastor John Isaacs, who had introduced me to Abraham at the pastors' prayer meeting, would speak about the prospects of building Grace Public School in New Delhi. I had a rare free evening, making it possible to attend.

The smell of curry tickled my nostrils as we walked through the door of the restaurant. Several pastors and their families had gathered to learn about Grace Public School. Abraham and his family greeted everyone warmly.

Before long, Sheri and Werner were enjoying Indian food while I drank water. I was hoping no one would notice I am not at all fond of curry. On the wall at the back of the room I saw large architectural drawings of the proposed three-story school. The Vavkens showed the group their most recent pictures and video and described what they saw on their trip. Pastor John Isaacs gave an insightful message. We learned the cost to construct the brick and steel school would come to about $15 per square foot. *What a contrast to VCS's construction costs,* I thought—$350 to $600 per square foot, depending on the building.

Just before we left the restaurant, a statement Jesus made during His Sermon on the Mount began repeating itself over and over in my mind: "Where your treasure is, there your heart will be also."[87]

The unresolved difficulty I had with this verse troubled me afresh. For many years I had suspected it was inaccurately translated. The verse seemed backward to me. I reasoned it should say, "Where your heart is, there your treasure will be also," since our money usually follows our interest. A good example: I love my wife so much I sometimes buy her illogically expensive gifts. My heart occasionally overcomes my financial logic, and now Kris has some fine jewelry! But I had studied the verse in the original Greek, and the translation "Where your treasure is, there your heart will be also" is consistent with the most reliable ancient Greek manuscripts.

At home that evening, I read the verse again from Matthew 6:21. "Kris," I confessed, "this is one of the most challenging verses in the Bible for me. The meaning of this verse has eluded me for many years."

Every time I turned around, the verse came to mind over and over. It continued like a broken record in my thoughts. Kris and I discussed it further without added insight.

For three nights I went to sleep without resolve. Finally, I prayed, "Lord, Your Word says, 'If any of you lacks wisdom, let him ask of God, who gives to all liberally and without reproach, and it will be given to him.'[88] Please give me the wisdom to understand this verse."

Then on the fourth day it hit me. *This teaching of Jesus is a strategy on how to shape and redirect our hearts after God's heart. Not a teaching about why people spend their money.*

Now it began to make sense! It became so obvious. If parents want to spark their children's interest in learning about investing in the stock market, opening a brokerage account in the child's name with a thousand dollars ensures for the child a steep learning curve about investments. If we want our students to have the heart of Jesus for the poor children at Grace Public School, we should challenge our students to invest their treasure in the lives of those children.

. . .THERE YOUR HEART WILL BE ALSO

The dots began to connect. The VCS staff consistently prays for God's Holy Spirit to bring His love and spiritual life to the hearts of our students. God was answering our prayers and showing us how to use Jesus' teaching in Matthew 6:21 to transform our students' hearts to have the heart of Jesus for the children in New Delhi. It dawned on me: Our students had what the children in New Delhi needed—and our students needed what the children in New Delhi had.

Before Werner and Sheri visited Grace Public School in New Delhi, they had asked the principal what gifts they could bring to the Indian children. Werner imagined taking a laptop computer or a projector.

"Just bring our children pencils and some chocolate candy."

As small as it seemed, the Vavkens honored the request. Werner and Sheri could hardly describe the children's delight as they received their personal pencils.

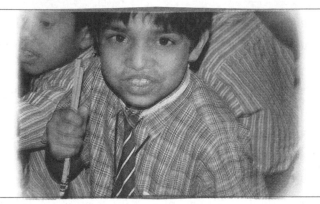

Children from Grace Public School receiving pencils

"They were so very thankful," Sheri said. "The children's smiles and joy overwhelmed both of us. We have seldom seen such joy and happiness in children."

Werner added, "The children at Grace Public School had more joy for receiving pencils than our students express when they are given laptop computers."

I remembered Jesus' words, "It is more blessed to give than to receive."[89] If pencils gave more joy to their children than laptops did for our students, what joy would our students discover, I wondered, if they helped build a new school in the New Delhi slums—if they saw how investing their treasure led students to Christ and helped the Indian children escape poverty?

All these thoughts reminded me of a reported interview with the late Mother Teresa. The interviewer asked, "Why are you visiting America when so many children are dying of poverty in the streets of Calcutta?"

"The poverty is much worse in America," Mother Teresa replied. "The poor children in India die in the arms of God. The poverty in America is a poverty of lonely and impoverished souls."

O God, I prayed, *May our students gain such a joy of the Lord in their giving that they become truly rich toward You.* I longed for our students to give the boys and girls in New Delhi what their parents could never afford—a quality Christian education to escape poverty.

I recalled how our intercessors and I had prayed for God to lead friends of VCS to donate the many tens of millions of dollars needed to build our Skyway and Leigh campuses. Most of our students could never afford tuition high enough to pay for the more than $100 million required to build Valley Christian Schools. Generous donors helped bring tuition within reach of our families.

God spoke to me as I pondered: *I sent major donors to help build Valley Christian Schools. Now I am asking you and VCS's students to be the major donors for the poor slum children in New Delhi. They cannot afford to build their school in their community without your help, any more than you could build Valley Christian Schools without the help of VCS's major donors. Tell your students they need to pass on to the poor children in New Delhi what I gave to them.*

With that divine directive, I began preparing for my annual keynote address to the VCS community on August 15, 2006. I also wanted to challenge our students during chapel to raise money and donate funds to help build Grace Public School, but I realized our faculty and staff needed to set the example for our students by their own giving. VCS teachers would need to plan creative ways to lead and encourage their students, in ways appropriate to each grade level, to contribute toward building the new Indian school. My challenge to our VCS faculty, staff, and students was to complete the construction of Grace Public School within the next four years, culminating in the Fifty-Year Golden Jubilee Anniversary of Valley Christian Schools during the 2009–10 school year.

Jesus Himself declared: "The Spirit of the Lord is on me, because he has anointed me to preach good news to the poor. He has sent me to proclaim freedom for the prisoners and recovery of sight for the blind, to release the oppressed, to proclaim the year of the Lord's favor."[90]

In renewing our determination to maintain Valley Christian Schools' commitment to Christian values, I realized, *There could be no better way for our students to gain the heart and mind of Jesus than to gift a new school to the needy children in New Delhi.* We had the opportunity to extend the gift of what God had done for us by becoming the "major donor" to build a Christian school for the Indian children who could not otherwise attend school because of the desperate poverty in their slum area. We prayed we and our students would give with the same thankfulness as we had when God graciously provided the multimillion-dollar donations for building our Skyway campus.

The new Grace Public School building in New Delhi, India,
with children in their newly furnished classrooms

SUCCESS!

Our dream became reality. The new Grace Public School opened on Monday, April 5, 2010—the day after Easter. How appropriate!

God used Valley Christian Schools' teachers and students to achieve the goal of building the school in the slums of New Delhi in time to celebrate VCS's Fifty-Year Anniversary. Well over half of the funds needed to build came from Valley Christian Schools students and staff. Additional gifts in March 2010 purchased seven classrooms of furniture, making it possible for Grace Public School to open the new facility.

In helping to build Grace Public School, Valley Christian students sent the Good News of Christ and His transformational power to some of the poorest children in the world. Jesus' words in Matthew 6:21, "For where your treasure is, there your heart will be also," helped launch the mission. As VCS students gave to the poor in accordance with the call of God, their hearts were transformed toward loving God and His wonderful children more deeply.

In an email I wrote to our team that month, I expressed appreciation as well as an ongoing challenge:

> Grace Public School students are sitting at desks and not on the floor for the first time in their lives! Continued chapel offerings and VCS student fundraisers are needed to furnish the remainder of the GPS classrooms. Continued VCS financial offerings are needed to expand with grades 9–12, so GPS students can graduate and attend college. Reaching this goal will help break the cycle of poverty for many students who would otherwise remain imprisoned by bleak conditions and a devastating caste system. As the verse says, "Shall the prey be taken from the mighty, or the captives of the righteous be delivered? But thus says the LORD: 'Even the captives of

the mighty shall be taken away, and the prey of the terrible be delivered; for I will contend with him who contends with you, and I will save your children'" (Isaiah 49:24–25). Let's rejoice and praise God for allowing VCS students and staff to help build and open the doors of Grace Public School to "save your children." In a very special way, the students of Grace Public School are our children!

What God did to build a quality Christian school in the slums of New Delhi underlined to me how His Quest for Excellence can happen anywhere and at any time. There is no escaping the power of the Quest for Excellence when God speaks, and there can be no true Quest for Excellence through our lives unless we listen, pray, and obey.

It is always scary when I get a glimpse of what God wants to do in and through my life. It's normal for me to doubt. How can I be even a small part of the Lord's truly supernatural, God-sized vision with my feeble abilities and means?

Divine prayer is the decision to align ourselves with God's purposes in the face of otherwise unscalable mountains of doubt. It's okay to doubt as long as doubt leads us to fervent prayer. That's the power of the Quest for Excellence!

And it remains forever true: God shows no partiality or favoritism from one person to the next.[91] He is not limited by time, place, or circumstances. He is able—and desires—to accomplish all His blessings through any person who seeks His purposes in accordance with His will to bring His goodness, peace, and joy to His children. "For it is God who works in you both to will and to do for His good pleasure."[92]

Sounds simple, doesn't it? Yet experience teaches that living these truths requires huge God-given faith and patience. The story in the next several chapters captures the agonies and the ecstasies of another amazing episode in our Quest for Excellence journey.

CHAPTER 12

A Beacon of Goodness, Peace, and Joy

"You are the light of the world. A city that
is set on a hill cannot be hidden."[93]

IT STARTED AS AN ORDINARY summer
day in late August 2005. The campus was gearing up for the start of
school. Pam's voice reached through the open doorway to my office.

"There is a family you need to meet. Rick and I really like them.
The father is a board member of Achiever Christian School. They're
looking toward junior high and are interested in VCS for their two girls."

"Sounds great," I replied through the open door. "Let's do it."

Later that day, visibly excited Bob and Ronnie Rubino talked with
Pam in her office. I joined the conversation. Bob's dark suit and red
tie matched his pristine smile, insightful eyes, and dark hair. Ronnie
echoed his cheerful greeting with the same kind of joyful, unas-
suming demeanor. Bob's business card announced his position with
a Fortune 500 company: "Vice President and Chief Technical Officer,
KLA–Tencor." Subsequent dialog revealed Bob had held the post for

more than nine years. His service tenure seemed incongruous with his young 30s appearance.

Ronnie and Pam agreed to continue their conversation while Bob and I toured the campus. My heart stirred warmly and told me the Holy Spirit was orchestrating something special.

Thirty minutes into the tour, as we made our way up the long stairs from the baseball stadium, Bob blurted out an astonishing offer.

"This is an amazing place! What can I do to help? Let me know how I can help and I'll do it." I could sense awe and determination in his voice.

It was my turn to be awestruck. His words stunned me into silence for the moment. (My friends would say any silence from me is a miracle.) I couldn't get my thoughts around an appropriate response except to say, "What an amazing offer! I'm not sure how to answer, but I'll pray about your question." I began praying silently as we continued to walk.

School had yet to get underway, but Dave Gregoric, director of the VCS jazz programs, was already practicing with one of the jazz bands as we passed the pool and headed toward the music rooms. Bob's eyes brightened, his smile growing as the sounds of jazz drew us through the band room door.

He fired questions almost faster than I could field them. As we talked, Bob told me how he had earned a full ride to the Berklee College of Music upon high school graduation. A world-class music conservatory in Boston, Berklee is known for its jazz. Bob described his tough decision to decline his trumpet scholarship in favor of a computer technology and business degree. Thus he became Chief Technical Officer at KLA–Tencor rather than a professional musician.

The wheels began turning in my head. "I'm getting an idea about what to ask you to do. Troy Gunter is VCS's Director of Visual and Performing Arts, K–12. Last year we started adopting his vision for developing our performing arts program. It's a conservatory model.

Troy's vision includes hiring specialized instructors for every part of the arts program to give each student the very best expert training. We talked about actually launching a true conservatory. Your career success tells me you are a great developer of ideas and programs, and you must know how to positively connect and work with talented people."

I studied Bob's facial expression for clues to whether I should continue. His eyes focused. With permission granted, I floated the key question: "Would you work with Troy to strategically assess, plan, and launch a conservatory of the arts at Valley Christian High School?"

Bob's mental computer must have calculated at warp speed, as he kicked out a one-word answer: "Yes."

"Let's go meet Troy Gunter."

We found Troy standing in front of a long line of students and parents in the small gym, helping students get enrolled into their correct music courses. We observed until he had a short break, and I moved to speak with Troy before the next parents approached.

"Troy, I want you to meet Bob Rubino. He has two beautiful young ladies enrolling in the junior high. He's a successful Chief Technical Officer for KLA–Tencor and a great musician. Bob wants to help you launch the conservatory. Would the two of you plan some time together?"

Troy's face registered a cloud of confusion, and I quickly added, "Bob just wants to help, not interfere with your great leadership."

"Okay." Troy crunched his eyebrows as they traded contact information.

When Bob and I headed back to my office, he reassured me. "Don't worry, after we meet, Troy will be fine."

Two weeks later I heard from Troy. "Bob is a great guy! We're working on a strategic planning analysis."

Six months later, Troy had his strategic plan ready to present to me. It was amazing! Bob sat toward the back of my office as Troy described the conservatory vision in tandem with beautiful PowerPoint visuals. What a great team. God was working through Troy and Bob to take Valley Christian High School's performing arts program into the future.

Their presentation was so impressive I immediately asked if we could place their launch proposal on the agenda for the March 2006 meeting of the VCS board of directors. They happily agreed. The coming fall, I sensed in my heart, was about to witness the launch of a remarkable conservatory of the arts.

ENTER STAGE RIGHT

One indication of the magnitude of God's next steps can often be discerned in the quality of people He brings to the task. I have often said, "God is an efficient Commander-in-Chief. He doesn't send big guns to small skirmishes. And when He plans to take more turf for His kingdom, He always brings adequate firepower."

Bob Rubino's involvement with the conservatory qualified him, I felt, as one of God's "big guns." Then I got a call from Mike Ainslie, a VCS director, with a request to meet.

Seeking a quality Christian high school, Mike and his wife, Karen, had actually moved from Los Angeles to enroll their two children, Joshua and Alisan, at VCS. They made their decision after conducting what Mike called an extensive academic audit on schools across the state. As a principal at Deloitte & Touche, Mike had the freedom to move his office to the San Jose Deloitte location. Within a year, Mike was serving on our VCS board.

Just over six feet tall, Mike is an impressive guy. He earned a full Division I swimming scholarship while still in high school. His demeanor revealed the wisdom garnered from more than a dozen years as an international corporate finance specialist for Deloitte in Hong Kong. Mike exuded energy oozing from his entire being.

"I'm not sure why I'm here," Mike said when we met in my office. "I'm going to Hong Kong and I strongly sense God is telling me I have some duty to perform for VCS while I'm there. Do you have any idea what that might be?"

My mind raced through possible needs, but I couldn't make a connection with Hong Kong. We decided to ask God to help Mike understand what He planned to accomplish during this trip. We prayed together and committed the entire matter into God's hands.

After prayer, I felt inspired to share the exciting news about Bob and Troy's strategic planning toward the launch of a VCHS conservatory. As a board member, Mike was happy to get advance notice about the upcoming presentation. Moreover, Mike's amazing strategic mind began its analysis, and I quickly became the beneficiary of his thinking about the development of a conservatory.

Within a week I received an email from Mike in Hong Kong. He had made what he thought was a divine connection for the conservatory. Mike told me he had led a Bible study at the home of Lily and Scott Homer in Hong Kong. As guests left, the Homers asked if Mike might remain for a personal visit and prayer. During the visit, Lily and Scott described a nagging sense of what they suspected might be God's call to leave their impressive positions in the Hong Kong professional music scene. Scott played first violin with the Hong Kong Philharmonic Orchestra, acknowledged as one of the top symphonies in Asia, and served occasionally as its Acting Concertmaster. Lily served as Concertmaster for the Hong Kong Sinfonietta and taught violin at all levels, including university positions. Scott, I learned, is distinguished as having been one of the youngest Concertmasters in the United States to hold this post for a professional symphony orchestra, when he became Concertmaster of the Sacramento Symphony in California at age 22.

The story later recounted by Mike, Lily, and Scott painted the scene for me. As they chatted, an inspiration hit Mike, and he found himself saying to the Homers, "I can't tell you what God might be directing you to do, but I have a crazy idea that could be totally out of line—you can be the judge." Mike plunged on. "Just before I left San Jose, I met with Dr. Clifford Daugherty, president of Valley Christian Schools. It's the wonderful school where Joshua and Alisan attend. The school has a good music program, but it's on its way to becoming a great program. Plans are underway to develop a conservatory of music. Could it be God is preparing and calling you to help launch the conservatory program at Valley Christian High School in San Jose, California?"

Lily and Scott looked at one another as the question landed on their minds and hearts. "Certainly, our hearts are unsettled. It may be that God is preparing us to accept such an assignment," Lily said. "We need to pray and get more information."

They agreed to send their résumés to my attention, and then they prayed. The idea already seemed to be taking root in fertile soil. By the time I received Lily's email and attachments, Mike had put me on the alert. "They are amazing musicians and godly Christians who are simply seeking the Lord's leading."

When I saw their résumés, even I, certainly not a musician, was impressed. Scott and Lily had soloed in most of the great musical halls of the world. Lily was born in mainland China and successfully auditioned to earn a full scholarship to Juilliard, where she met Scott, who is Caucasian and American born. While she lived in mainland China, Lily later told me, she had never even heard of Jesus Christ. In America she heard the gospel message and received Christ as her personal Savior. Both Scott and Lily attended music conservatories.

Before long I was on the phone with Mike Ainslie, who suggested we offer an all-expense-paid "look-see" tour of Valley Christian and the

San Jose area. I forwarded the Homers' résumés to Troy Gunter, and his first comments were, "Not a chance. Even if they came, I doubt we could keep them. They are too talented and accomplished to remain at Valley Christian Schools." But he added, "Miracles still happen, and we are praying for the Lord to help us build a conservatory."

The Homers accepted our offer. Their daughter, Hanna, soon to be a kindergartner, remained in Hong Kong with friends for the week. When they arrived, Troy and I met Scott and Lily in my office overlooking the San Jose skyline. As we sat at the twelve-foot conference table, a sense of awe seemed to circle the room.

After some discussion, I asked the looming question: "You two have professional positions in two of the finest orchestras in the world. You have taught on the college level, and your options for prestigious positions around the world are broad. Why would you even consider coming to Valley Christian High School?"

Troy chimed in with his concerns. "And even if you come to VCHS, would you remain?"

Scott and Lily took turns answering. "When I went to a music conservatory in high school," Scott began, "the musical training was very fine, but the moral peer pressure, educational quality, and spiritual influences were really poor. The high school conservatory dorms were located in the university setting. Unfortunately, high school students generally don't have the maturity to successfully navigate the negative moral influences of college life. The academic education was also poor. The conservatory mindset was that you are a musician, and you will be a professional musician, so the academic quality outside of music education suffered.

"In addition," he went on, "the spiritual climate was very non-supportive of students who may have hoped to live a Christian life. When we learned from Mike Ainslie that Valley Christian High School planned to launch a conservatory, we decided we wanted to help make it happen. We don't know of even one high school conservatory in the world offering all three elements: including strong musical instruction, well-rounded academic quality, supported by strong Christian values and faith. We can't imagine a more important achievement than to help launch the world's first quality conservatory of music in a Christian school."

Lily explained further. "It's true, we've attained many professional achievements, including instruction at the university level. But by the time students arrive at the university, their techniques are fully formed, for better or for worse. Many gifted and talented musicians never overcome the poor techniques they acquired as children. Bad techniques seldom change. We would like to shape good techniques at the elementary level and continue to train those same students through high school. That would be a dream."

It quickly became obvious God was calling Scott and Lily to come to VCS. With that settled, our attention turned to the upcoming VCS board of directors meeting on March 13, 2006, where we planned to make a conservatory launch presentation. Lily and Scott, we realized, could be very helpful with the presentation. They happily joined our final strategic planning sessions in preparation for the meeting. Troy would make the presentation with the support of our executive team and the Homers.

Providentially, the Homers brought added meaning and substance to the board presentation. Their enthusiasm and commitment to join the faculty made a huge impact on all of us. As I listened, the thought came to me again: *God doesn't send big guns to small skirmishes.* The conservatory represented a huge kingdom advance, and God had sent the best.

As before, Bob Rubino sat back and enjoyed Troy's proposal to launch the conservatory. The SWOT (Strengths, Weaknesses,

PAGE 31

PAGE 91

Andrew P. Hill
Warmly welcomes
Valley Christian H.S. students
in the Spirit of Collaboration!!

Together, we'll build our tutoring
program at
Lairon Elementary!!

ANDREW P. HILL
HIGH SCHOOL

VCHS

VCHS

PAGE 78

PAGE 90

Andrew Hill 9-12

Los Arboles K-3

Lairon 4-8

Sylvandale 7-8

Hellyer K-6

PAGE 166

PAGE 166

PAGE 222

PAGE 243

PAGE 249

PAGE 273

Ten Commandments

I   Thou shalt have no other Gods before me

II   Thou shalt not make unto thee any graven image

III   Thou shalt not take the name of the Lord thy God in vain

IV   Remember the Sabbath day to keep it holy

V   Honor thy father and thy mother

VI   Thou shalt not kill

VII   Thou shalt not commit adultery

VIII   Thou shalt not steal

IX   Thou shalt not bear false witness against thy neighbor

PAGE 247

PAGE 250

PAGE 296

PAGE
314

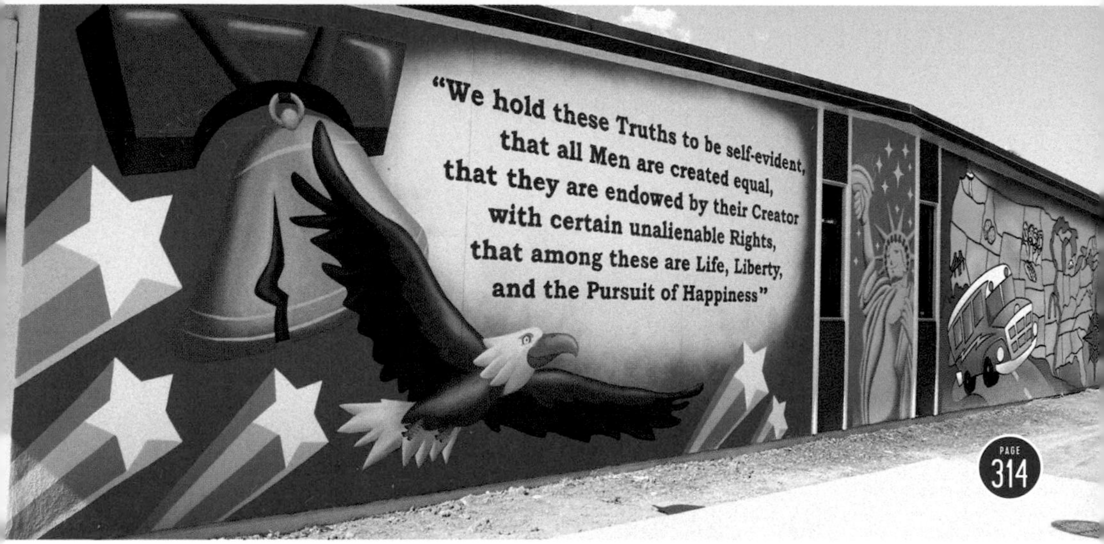

"We hold these Truths to be self-evident, that all Men are created equal, that they are endowed by their Creator with certain unalienable Rights, that among these are Life, Liberty, and the Pursuit of Happiness"

PAGE
306

PAGE
318

Opportunities, and Threats) analysis worked, and it all made sense to the VCS board. After prayer and contemplative discussion, the board moved to launch what Scott Homer had described as the first Christian high school conservatory in the world.

By the time the Homers boarded their return flight to Hong Kong, two major decisions were made: 1) The conservatory would launch in the fall of 2006; 2) the Homers would move from Hong Kong with Hanna, who would join Valley Christian Schools as a kindergartner in the fall.

The efforts of Troy and his conservatory launch team met with great success. Articles and beautiful pictures appeared in *San Jose Magazine,* officially announcing the faculty, course offerings, application process, and graduation requirements.

The conservatory's vision statement was initially heralded: "To advance the first world-class scholastic conservatory of music founded on Christian faith and values as reflected in the life and teachings of Jesus Christ." Music offerings were later expanded to dance, theater, fine art, and other performing arts. The mission statement was proudly displayed on the new conservatory website and in various Silicon Valley media: "To discover and develop the extraordinary God-given talent of young artists, and to reclaim the arts as an expression of God's love among the varied cultures of the world."

With physical space at a premium, Troy creatively transformed his band storage room into a music performance area, which successfully served the conservatory's first twenty-six declared major and minor students who enrolled for the 2006–07 school year. The conservatory dream had become a reality.

STAIR STEPS TO GROWTH?

It's always a good day when your bankers are happy. On January 27, 2007, our Bank of America client managers, Marianna Pisano and

Daniel Dryzin, had big smiles on their faces after completing their quarterly review of VCS financials, ratios, and enrollment trends. They liked the innovative conservatory launch and VCS's steady tuition and enrollment growth. The VCS cash-to-debt ratio had grown from 15 percent in 2003, when we took out our first Bank of America loan of $38 million, to about 40 percent.

Our CFO Don Shipley, a CPA with a Wharton MBA, had once again impressed our guests. Don is a man of few words and lots of wisdom. He and I are about the same height—around five feet five or six inches. We both have dark hair and mustaches. Don is the kind of CFO bankers love: He hadn't missed a financial projection since arriving at VCS from the business district of New York City in 2002.

Of course, whenever I mentioned Don's one-hundred-percent track record on financial projections, he was always quick to say, "I need to thank God for our projections. No human being can make accurate projections one hundred percent of the time."

Just when I thought the bankers were ready to leave, Marianna asked, "So what does your vision look like going into the future?"

Eagerly I seized on this opportunity to test my thoughts on our business-savvy bankers. More cautious by nature, Don eyed me as though he wondered what I was about to say. Maintaining the confidence of bankers in the senior management team is critical to a healthy banking relationship, and Don is not an off-the-cuff kind of CFO.

As I reached for pen and paper, I felt inspired. All eyes watched while I extemporaneously drew four stair steps, from the bottom left to the top right of the paper. I labeled the first step 2006–07, the second 2007–08, the third 2008–09, and the fourth 2009 and beyond. Each step showed growing enrollment goals for the conservatory, both annual and cumulative.

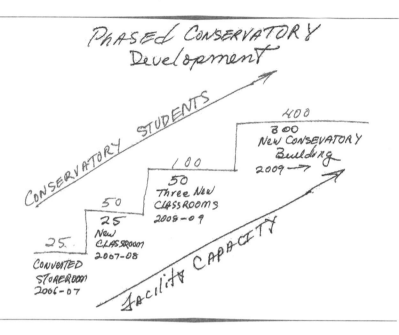

Stair-step drawing with conservatory enrollment goals

The first facility acquisition step for the fall of 2006 had been simple enough. Troy had converted the band storage room into a classroom, and the conservatory met our first enrollment goal with twenty-six students enrolled. We envisioned a phased approach to test our strong inclinations that building a conservatory would attract more students. We wanted to "turn up the rheostat" on Artistic Beauty in our A^3 model (Academic Achievement, Artistic Beauty, and Athletic Distinction). This Excellence Brings Influence approach, we believed, would prove our "build quality and they will enroll" theory.

I told the bankers about my spring 2006 agreement with Troy to enroll twenty-five conservatory students in the fall of that year, and then build another classroom for the second year. Assuming we enrolled another twenty-five in the fall of 2007, we would build three more classrooms for fifty more students to enroll in the fall of 2008. We had agreed, "If the rheostat strategy pans out and the conservatory enrollment magnet attracts a total of 100 students by the fall of 2008, we will plan to build a large Conservatory of the Arts building to take the entire program to the highest levels imaginable." I believed this plan would attract a minimum of 400 new students, increasing the total high school enrollment to about 1,528 students. (VCHS enrollment that spring of 2007 was 1,128 students.)

Improved quality, experience had taught us, always strengthens the marketing magnet to attract more and higher-quality students. In the music field alone, VCS already had growing vocal programs, great jazz bands, a Western States Championship award-winning field show competition marching band, and a spring concert band that had just taken top prizes at the national Disney band competition in Orlando, Florida.

But we still saw lots of room for improvement. Our high school scheduling structure limited the number of music courses to one performing arts course per semester, at best. The school orchestra was weak, and hopes to develop a full symphony orchestra seemed out of reach unless we could provide more scheduled periods in a student's day for strings and other specialized conservatory courses. Troy Gunter described his goal to work with the high school administration to design a new scheduling approach, allowing music major and minor students to take two, or possibly even three, performing arts courses per semester and still meet all graduation and college admission requirements.

After hearing the conservatory vision, our bankers became excited. They eagerly offered a tour of a recent Bank of America–funded project for the Colburn School's Conservatory of Music, located across the street from the Walt Disney Concert Hall in Los Angeles.

Don and I agreed to tour the Colburn campus. As a bonus, the bank provided complimentary tickets to enjoy the Los Angeles Philharmonic Orchestra at Disney Hall, which had opened only three and a half years earlier. Bob Rubino and Sheri and Werner Vavken joined us as we traveled to Los Angeles in March 2007. In addition to touring both the Colburn School and the Disney Concert Hall, we enjoyed Jean-Yves Thibaudet's performance of Ravel's Piano Concerto for the Left Hand, and marveled at the Los Angeles Philharmonic, conducted by Esa-Pekka Salonen.

Between events, we learned more about the bank's enthusiasm for using tax-exempt bonds to fund the next phase of VCS's development to build the Conservatory of the Arts and Student Life Center (the eventual building name). It was reassuring to know our bank was interested in helping to finance the project.

The big unanswered question still loomed large, with no guarantees: Would expanded conservatory offerings and facilities attract increased numbers of students, with even more talent, enabling us to afford to build the facility with increased revenue to service and repay the bank's loan? The formula had always worked before. But would we now run into an invisible glass ceiling that would cap student growth, preventing the addition of improved facilities and programs? No one could say for sure. The stair-stepped, phased growth approach we hoped would help answer this question.

"IF WE BUILD QUALITY, THEY WILL ENROLL"

We had met the conservatory's initial enrollment goal of twenty-five, with twenty-six students enrolled for the first year. Immediately we launched plans to construct a new classroom to accommodate the next twenty-five conservatory students for fall 2007.

Our hilltop Skyway campus had often presented architectural challenges. As I walked the campus, I saw open space under a cantilevered portion on the east side of the education building, nearest the football stadium. *We should be able to use open space for construction,* I reasoned.

Not so fast. At first, the architect and builders said the difficult conditions and the dramatic slope under the education building would not allow construction of a classroom in that space.

I found their answer hard to accept. Pressing the issue further fostered a resolution not immediately evident. Engineers designed a solution by reinforcing the steel beams above the new classroom and actually hanging the classroom rather than placing all its weight on the inaccessible foundation footings. We came to call this space "the hanging classroom." Its cost of about $650,000 proved well justified, as the added tuition from the increased capacity of twenty-five newly enrolled students paid for the construction expense within a few years.

By the fall of 2007, actual conservatory enrollment exceeded our fifty-student strategic goal with a total of fifty-six students. The hanging classroom filled to capacity, and we committed to building classroom space for the next fifty conservatory students we expected to enroll in fall 2008. Eric Scharrenberg, VP of Athletics and Physical Education, and Mike Machado, head football coach and high school dean, were already busy planning a two-story weight-training facility at the east side of the football stadium. The VCS board's building committee chair, Mike Sprauve, suggested we add a third story with three classrooms. Those classrooms would give us exactly what we needed to accommodate the third conservatory growth phase with fifty added students.

Setbacks and difficulties delayed completion of the $3 million three-story weight-training/classroom building. As a stopgap measure for the 2008–09 academic year, the mat room was temporarily modified to provide two makeshift classrooms. The situation was not pleasant, and both the wrestling program and the English Department endured less than ideal facility accommodations. In spite of the challenges, VCS exceeded its enrollment goals in the fall of 2008 with a total of 106 students declaring a conservatory major or minor. Our "build quality and they will enroll" theory proved as reliable for the conservatory as we had experienced for all previous VCS program developments.

Given that all evidence pointed to the viability of the fourth phase of the plan, serious prayer and planning to develop the Conservatory of the Arts and Student Life Center commenced. We imagined a building of 40,000 to 50,000 square feet would accommodate specialized music and arts programs and approximately 300 added students.

My hand-sketched stair-step drawing later became a formal chart presented to our board, as shown below, illustrating how God provided above and beyond our goals.

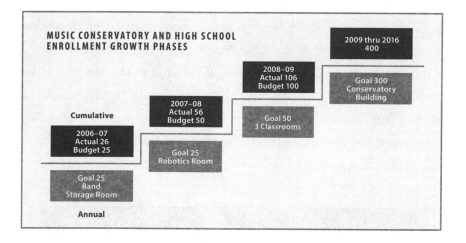

A DESIGN EMERGES

The next door God opened shows the wonderful way He rewards those who follow Him. In 2006 and 2007, VCHS was privileged to serve as a model for the development of Valor Christian High School in Highlands Ranch, Colorado (a story recapped in Chapter 6). I first met Adele Willson, Valor's architect, when she made a couple of trips to survey VCS's campus. Valor Christian High School opened in September 2007, and Bob Rubino and I were pleased to attend the new campus dedication.

While speaking with Adele Willson at the ceremony, I learned to my amazement she specialized in designing performing arts buildings. She agreed to come to VCS and help develop a conceptual design for the Conservatory of the Arts and Student Life Center. A couple of months later she and her colleague, Lyn Eller, came from Colorado for two days to create artistic and conceptual renderings of the proposed building. I explained the conservatory's mission to glorify God as the ultimate Creator, to reflect His continued creative works through His people, and to reclaim the arts for the cause of Christ as an expression of God's love, goodness, peace, joy, and light to the world.

Perhaps these words proved inspirational. When I saw the renderings, my heart soared. The design dramatically announced the loving goodness of God, shining through transparent heavenward-cantilevered canopies, and translucent windows of the soul to the heart of all of humanity. The daytime rendering spoke of the purifying light of Jesus shining from above into the hearts of all people. The nighttime rendering illustrated the light of Jesus shining from within Holy Spirit–filled Christians to a darkened and needy world.

Nighttime conceptual design rendering of the conservatory

I imagined young artists committing their hearts, lives, and talents to extend God's kingdom of "goodness, peace, and joy" as a beacon of light to shine around the world—beckoning all to open the windows of their souls to the transforming light of Jesus.

But would members of our VCS board and executive team have the same reaction? I well recognized the faint likelihood that all would universally accept first renderings. My heart even grieved a bit thinking how possible iterations of renderings might follow in response to everyone's comments. The end result, I hoped, would not detract from my own positive view of the first renderings.

Daytime conceptual design rendering of the conservatory

At the January board meeting, I watched the expressions on directors' faces as they evaluated the renderings. For a time no one said a word, undoubtedly out of polite respect for unknown opinions around the table. I waited for first comments and observed as eyes scanned the room to survey fellow board members' perspectives.

The tension subsided as the power of consensus emerged. No one objected. No one had any comments on how the design might improve.

Without even one design discussion, a board consensus of approval became immediately evident. They liked it! I had no doubt our Creator Himself inspired the creative work for our new Conservatory of the Arts and Student Life Center.

The unanimous, immediate approval of everyone who saw the conceptual renderings seemed to me almost miraculous—a testimony that the creative design of the conservatory was inspired by our Ultimate Creator. The building itself would serve as a place for building lives to reflect and continue God's creative works. True "Artistic Beauty" (the second component of our A^3 formula) comes from above, extending God's kingdom of "goodness, peace, and joy in the Holy Spirit"[94] to "whoever calls on the name of the Lord. . . ."[95] Hmm—this means *anyone* and *anywhere!*

At that board meeting in January 2008, I could not have been more excited about prospects for the new conservatory building. Yet the crucial matter of funding remained. Little did I know what the coming year would hold.

CHAPTER 13

WHOSE ECONOMY
IS IT, ANYWAY?

"I will . . . make a roadway in the wilderness."[96]

ALMOST A YEAR AFTER our Bank of America–
sponsored trip to Los Angeles, Marianna Pisano and her colleague at
the bank, Anna Jenkins, made a return visit to my office on Wednesday,
February 27, 2008, to review our investments. Valley Christian's CFO
Don Shipley joined us. I was excited to show Marianna and Anna our
Conservatory of the Arts and Student Life Center renderings hot off
the press. They too were captivated by the beauty of the design.

After discussing the school's financials and enrollment projections,
the issue of our tax-exempt bond financing arose, and our conversation
turned toward the letter of credit.

I popped the question. "Interest rates are relatively low. Is there
any way for VCS to get some sort of an option with today's rates to
construct the Conservatory of the Arts and Student Life Center? We
don't need the money now, but we expect to fund the project after
about one to two years."

Marianna was quick to answer. "Yes, if all the ratios work, we have a vehicle called a forward swap that could meet your needs."

A forward swap was a new concept to me, and Marianna's answer caught me off guard.

"How much money do you need to build the conservatory?" she asked.

Don spoke up. "About twenty million."

"We need to get you in touch with our Derivatives Group," Marianna said. "What are some good dates for you?"

Before long we set a follow-up meeting with Marianna Pisano, Mike Moss, and Doug Brown from Bank of America for Thursday, March 13, at 10 a.m.

On March 12, the evening before meeting with our bankers, a strong sense of God's presence came over me as I read Isaiah chapter 43, especially verses 1–6, 13, and 19–21, in my New American Standard Bible. Extraordinary warmth filled my being as adrenalin sped up my heart rate. *What is God saying?* I read the verses over and over:

". . . Do not fear, for I have redeemed you; I have called you by name; you are Mine!

"When you pass through the waters, I will be with you; and through the rivers, they will not overflow you. When you walk through the fire, you will not be scorched, nor will the flame burn you. For I am the LORD your God, the Holy One of Israel, your Savior. . . . Since you are precious in My sight, since you are honored and I love you. . . . Do not fear, for I am with you; I will bring your offspring from the east, and gather you from the west. I will say to the north, 'Give them up!' And to the south, 'Do not hold them back.' Bring My sons from afar and My daughters from the ends of the earth. . . . So you are My witnesses," declares the LORD, "and I am God" (Isaiah 43:1–6, 12).

"Even from eternity I am He, and there is none who can deliver out of My hand; I act and who can reverse it?" (Isaiah 43:13).

"Behold, I will do something new, now it will spring forth; will you not be aware of it? I will even make a roadway in the wilderness, rivers in the desert . . . to give drink to My chosen people. The people whom I formed for Myself will declare My praise" (Isaiah 43:19–21).

As I read these verses I felt certain God was speaking to me about the Conservatory of the Arts and Student Life Center through this passage. The message I so clearly heard related to God's direction to go forward with the conservatory construction. From these verses I understood:

1. VCS will go through some fiery, troubled waters, but we should not fear, because God loves us and is with us. He who is "from eternity" will protect VCS, the board, and the school's leadership as we go forward to build in obedience to Him.

2. The construction of the Conservatory of the Arts and Student Life Center is an "act" of God to bring His sons and daughters to the truth as His witnesses, "and who can reverse it?"

3. God is about to "do something new, now it will spring forth"; I sensed this "something new" referred to what Scott Homer called "the world's first Christian high school conservatory of music and the arts."

4. Success is guaranteed even in troubled times, because
it is God who says, "Behold, I will do something new,
now it will spring forth; will you not be aware of it?
I will even make a roadway in the wilderness, rivers
in the desert."

As I drove to campus the next morning, my mind was still mulling
over the verses from the night before. Don Shipley and I greeted Mike
Moss and Mark Slater from the bank as they arrived at my office for
our meeting. Providentially, Vera Shantz, VCS board chair, was able
to join us.

We had lots of questions. What is a one-year forward swap? How
does it work? What happens if we have difficulty getting building
permits? Is the forward swap a commitment by the bank to loan $20
million? What are the advantages and the risks? We expected to work
through lunch, since we needed every moment for our crash course on
derivatives and the bank's forward-swap offer. Mike Moss and Mark
Slater affirmed the bank's positive disposition toward the $20 million
forward swap, but we had to understand what we would be getting
into if we moved ahead.

We learned a forward swap provides three huge advantages:

1. Secured funding to give the project life: With the stabil-
ity of secure funding, we could confidently negotiate
all architectural, engineering, and building contracts.
The city would more likely work through the difficult
issues involving traffic and school capacity knowing
VCS had the money in hand to begin construction.

2. Fixed interest rate: Securing a historically low interest
rate, at about 3.5 percent, to build the Conservatory

of the Arts and Student Life Center gave reassurance
as to the affordability of the project.

3. No loan payments for a year: Our one-year forward
    swap would provide for the loan commencement to
    take effect on March 1, 2009, allowing the school time
    to get the project underway.

Don carefully noted all the points, and then spoke up. "All right,
but what are the risks?"

"A risk comes in if you don't build the conservatory," Mike replied.
"If you end up selling the swap because you don't need the loan funds
after all, VCS could have a loss on your $20 million principal." Mike
explained how falling (or rising) interest rates could diminish (or
increase) the value of our principal if we had to sell our fixed-rate
swap. We mulled over his words.

"Here's the bottom line," Mike emphasized. "You should not
take the swap unless you plan to build the Conservatory of the Arts
and Student Life Center. If you use the money to build, there is no
principal risk. As soon as you take the swap, the money is set aside
for construction."

The discussion continued. Other technical issues included fee
pricing for the bank's letter of credit (that is, the bank's credit rating
in exchange for a fee priced on the cash-to-debt ratio of the school).

The issues were complex, but the opportunity to borrow $20
million at a low interest rate to fund the conservatory could not
be ignored. With a VCS board of directors meeting scheduled for
the next Monday, we asked Mike and Mark if they would meet
with our board to describe and discuss the bank's offer to fund the
project. They agreed. After lunch they returned to their San Francisco
offices.

God Speaks in the Night

I woke up at 3 a.m. the next morning—my birthday, March 14, 2008—with a verse racing through my mind: "Behold, the former things have come to pass, now I declare new things; before they spring forth I proclaim them to you." I opened my New American Standard Bible, and found the verse in Isaiah 42:9. Next to it, I made the notation "3-14-08, 3:00 a.m."

Also, as I awoke, the word "after" came to mind, resonating like a bell. Since I grew up reading the King James Version, that's the text I often remember and hear when God speaks His Word to me. I found the word and its associated verse in Jeremiah 29:10. It says, "After seventy years are completed . . . I will visit you and perform My good work toward you. . . ."

In the margin next to Jeremiah 29:10, I wrote again "3-14-08, 3:00 a.m."

The significance of the word "after" had to do with the concept of the first year after the completion of a set of years on God's timeline. Specifically, the Bible counts seven years as one Sabbath of years.[97] The VCS Skyway campus opened in January 2000, so 2008 was our eighth year at that site. In the Bible, the numeral 8 signifies new beginnings.

My birthday visitation from the Lord continued. Next, at 3:35 a.m. (according to my Bible margin notes), penetrating thoughts took me on a tour of Isaiah 49:17–26. Adrenalin again sped my heart rate, and I continued sensing an extraordinary warmth within as I endeavored to hear what God was saying. Alongside these verses 17–26 I wrote the words "Yesterday B of A committed to conservatory loan":

> "Your builders hurry. . . . The children . . . will yet say in
> your ears, 'The place is too cramped for me; make room for
> me that I may live.' . . ." Thus says the Lord God, "Behold,
> I will . . . set up My standard to the peoples; and they will
> bring your sons in their bosom, and your daughters will be

carried on their shoulders. . . . Can the prey be taken from the mighty man, or the captives of a tyrant be rescued?" Surely, thus says the LORD, "Even the captives of the mighty man will be taken away, and the prey of the tyrant will be rescued; for I will contend with the one who contends with you, and I will save your children.[98] . . . And all flesh will know that I, the LORD, am your Savior and your Redeemer, the Mighty One of Jacob."

Next, at 4:38 a.m. (according to my notes), I was moved to open Chapter 5 of my first book, *Quest for Excellence,* to review the story of when God met the entire Valley Christian High School student body in a supernatural encounter during our chapel time. That spiritual revival at our rented Branham campus marked the most pivotal point in the history of VCS's transformation from a struggling institution into one of the finest Christian school systems in the world. The revival took place on March 12, 1993—almost exactly fifteen years before this early morning visitation on March 14, 2008.

The fifteenth year is the first year "after" two sets of seven-year periods. As I pondered all of this, I realized we had met with Mike Moss and Mark Slater from Bank of America on March 13, 2008—exactly one year "after" and one day "after" two Sabbaths of years had passed since March 12, 1993, the date of the spiritual revival. I made another notation in my Bible below Isaiah 43:19 when God spoke to me again: "Behold, I will do something new, now it will spring forth."

Through prayer, His Word, and reflection, God gave me plenty of evidence and faith He was orchestrating the Bank of America funding events. God had scheduled our Bank of America meeting the day before. I had no doubt He wanted the VCS board to approve the Bank of America $20 million swap resolution at our next board meeting on Monday, March 17.

Our intercessors agreed and prayed God would speak to each member of our board as He had spoken to me. I had concerns about the complexity of the deal, and the cautious nature of our board could make it difficult for our bankers to answer all of the board's questions for the board to become confident in accepting the $20 million forward swap. The timeframe was short—the idea had been presented to Don and me just the day before, on Thursday. Our board meeting was scheduled for Monday, when the board would first learn of the funding details. What we didn't know and couldn't have predicted: Sunday, March 16, 2008, the day before our board meeting, would mark the start of our nation's gravest financial crisis since the Great Depression.

On the Brink

Later on Friday, after my session with God in the wee hours of the morning, Bank of America's Mike Moss confirmed they were prepared to execute the swap Monday night, if our board approved. Mike's concluding comment sounded portentous: "By the way, rates are down today on some bad news about Bear Stearns. We'll keep our fingers crossed for next week!"

Bad news indeed! This one-line comment was my first omen of the Great Recession, which began in earnest on Sunday, two days later, with the sudden collapse of Bear Stearns, the nation's fifth largest banking institution. We had no idea what lay ahead: Virtually all business credit would suddenly disappear during the most devastating economy since the 1930s.

By Monday, the economic news had turned grim. *The New York Times*[99] reported, "In a shocking deal reached on Sunday to save Bear Stearns, JPMorgan Chase agreed to pay a mere $2 a share to buy all of Bear—less than one-tenth the firm's market price on Friday. . . . Only a year ago, Bear's shares sold for $170."

The Wall Street Journal[100] reported, "Meanwhile, worries persist that other . . . firms might be on shaky ground." The article said Richard Fuld, chief executive of Lehman Brothers Holdings Inc., in concern about the markets, had ". . . cut short a trip to India and returned home Sunday, ahead of schedule. . . ."

USA Today[101] warned, "If the U.S. economy were a car, all of its warning lights would be flashing red. . . . 'It's going to go from bad to worse . . .' says Kenneth Rogoff, a former chief economist at the International Monetary Fund and now an economics professor at Harvard." The report concluded by quoting Steve East, chief economist for FBR Capital Markets: "But the financial system is what provides the funding for all the other sectors of the economy, and if you have a broken financial system, you have a broken economy."

This news hung over us as our VCS board met with Mike Moss and Mark Slater on Monday evening, March 17. Sheri Vavken, our lead intercessor, kept in touch with our prayer intercessory team to support the board in prayer.

As guests, Mike and Mark were placed at the top of the agenda. After an opening prayer, Don and I introduced Mike and Mark at about 7:10 p.m. with a brief summary of what we had learned at our meeting the previous Thursday. Mike then began describing the bank's $20 million tax-exempt forward swap to fund the Conservatory of the Arts and Student Life Center.

It all seemed like such a rush of events. Only two months had passed since the board first saw a conceptual drawing of the building. Ordinarily, our VCS board would not begin efforts to obtain funding for construction until formal architectural plans were underway and we had started the process of obtaining building permits from the city.

By the time the Bank of America team made their presentation, the forward-swap rate had dropped to 3.30 percent, an amazingly low rate. Historic ten-year U.S. Treasury rates had been lower for only nine of 11,699 resets since 1962. (For comparison, the highest rate of 15.84 percent occurred in September 1981, and the average rate was 6.99 percent.)

Our VCS board of directors faced a challenging decision. Moving ahead took the risk that the apparent failure of Bear Stearns Bank might be the first of more large banks to follow. Steve McMinn, chair of the board finance committee, said, "The Bear Stearns collapse is a likely indicator signaling a serious economic crisis that could significantly affect VCS enrollment due to unemployment." He added, "Lehman could be next. This probably isn't the time to take on more debt."

CFO Don Shipley did his usual masterful job of preparing accurate financial projections. He remained positive. "We can afford the loan if enrollment projections hold firm."

Claude Fletcher, VCS chancellor, then spoke up. He and I both serve on the board in non-voting ex officio roles. Claude explained the dangers of becoming overconfident. He described two previously strong Christian ministries no longer in existence because of "overreaching." On the other hand, the opportunity to secure a 3.30 percent interest rate, clearly one of the lowest rates in the past forty-six years, seemed like it might be God's miraculous provision.

After almost three hours of discussion, the board asked the Bank of America team to step out of the room for private deliberation. The board prayed and asked for God's direction.

Following about a half-hour conversation, the board decided to forgo the loan until the economy was less volatile, giving VCS time to better assess the possibility of getting building permits for the conservatory project.

Mike and Mark returned to the meeting, learned of the board's decision, and politely gathered their materials to leave while assuring the board of the bank's continued interest in funding the conservatory. Before they departed, they checked interest rates one more time. The rate for our forward swap had already dropped to 3.28 percent, they announced, and if the board passed the swap resolution, VCS could exercise the $20 million transaction with a call to Mike's cell phone from Dr. Daugherty.

The bankers left, but uneasiness remained in the room. I felt strongly conflicted. On one hand, I sensed God's assurances for us to approve the forward-swap resolution. At the same time, I also held deep respect for the wisdom of the board's appropriately conservative governing decision.

With a pause, I posed a question. "Before we move forward on the agenda, can we pray and ask for God's wisdom?"

Everyone agreed. One by one each board member prayed aloud. As prayer concluded, I was impressed in my spirit to make a short comment. "I definitely honor and respect the board's decision, but it is certain that if the board were to approve the funding for the conservatory, hundreds—if not thousands—of students will come to Christ."

The room was quiet. For several moments, no one spoke. Before the meeting I had asked our intercessors to pray God would speak to our board members, because I knew I personally could not convince them to accept the loan given the grim economic outlook. Now I wondered: *Could it be the room is quiet because board members are hearing from God?*

Rick Watson was the first to speak. Rick had served as chair of the VCS board for seven years when the school had experienced its greatest growth. During those years, Rick and I often met weekly. His godly wisdom and prayer for the school, and for me, was seasoned during his entire career of impressive business success.

Rick looked to his left and then to his right, studying the faces of board members. He seemed to discern the need for a change of direction. I watched as what looked to be a nervous and compassion-driven smile graced his face. "What if we take the forward swap to give the opportunity to go forward as God leads? These are very good interest rates. Then we will put the school in position to advance as God leads. If we decide not to go ahead with construction, we simply won't take the funding a year from now—we can let the one-year forward swap 'unwind.' I'd like to hear from other board members."

Board Chair Vera Shantz spoke up. "This is a major decision, and I'd like to hear every board member's thoughts."

Around the room each director spoke. The thoughts they expressed were similar to Rick's. I sat in quiet awe as I observed this transformation. Within a few minutes, a motion was made and seconded to approve the resolution authorizing Bank of America to execute the one-year forward swap for $20 million. The motion passed unanimously. The board seemed a bit shocked, but very much relieved, having the confidence they had acted as the Holy Spirit led.

Susan Bagley, who with her husband, Craig, had turned around a failed church in Modesto, California, voiced a message from her heart. "I know what I'm about to say will seem illogical and strange. But I'm sensing we should wait about ten minutes before authorizing Cliff to call Mike Moss and Mark Slater to make the deal."

At this point, simple human logic was not ruling the board's proceedings. Everyone concurred and we waited.

After ten minutes, Vera Shantz, Don Shipley, and I used my conference office phone to call Mike Moss. As we listened to his phone ring, I wondered if he would pick up at such a late hour.

When the call connected, we heard what sounded like road noise before his voice answered. "Mike Moss."

"Hi, Mike," I replied. "Vera, Don, and Cliff here. Is it too late to do the swap?"

"No. Did the board approve the resolution?"

"Yes," I told him. "After further prayer and deliberation, the board unanimously passed the resolution."

"Wow! We're headed back to San Francisco, but we will pull off at the next off-ramp and call the Bank of America trading desk in Tokyo, Japan, to make the deal."

The timing was great! The swap consummated at about 10:25 p.m. at a historically low rate of 3.27 percent—well worth a ten-minute wait.

Timing.... This brings me back to the second of my three big questions that launched this journey: the question of resources. Can Valley Christian Schools' success during the dot-com era be explained as the result of our being in the right place at the right time? Did resources come to us because of the luck of our circumstances?

God was answering in a big way. In this instance as in so many others, He was showing us the Quest for Excellence is not limited by place or time. Any time is the right time for God when it is His time and in harmony with His will. God's vision is never lacking His provision—in good times or bad, in the boom of Silicon Valley or the gloom of the Great Recession. His promise stands firm: "My God shall supply all your need according to His riches in glory by Christ Jesus."[102]

I remain grateful for Claude Fletcher's admonitions of caution to the board. God used them to inspire the board unanimously to trust God in full view of what prudent people would normally view as unacceptably horrific risks. Then when the board members individually heard God's go-ahead, they faithfully followed His leading rather than their fears.

Each of us would desperately need to hear God's assurance again—more than once.

CHAPTER 14

THE INVISIBLE HAND

"He shall direct your paths. . . ."[103]

THE TRAFFIC LIGHT TURNED RED as we approached Market Street in the busy financial district of San Francisco. I could not believe my eyes: A determined toddler furiously pedaled his red tricycle right in front of my gray Odyssey minivan. With black hair pointed down and brave eyes focused ahead, his little legs pumped the pedals at warp speed.

I gasped. What kind of mother would allow her toddler to ride his trike in the busy San Francisco financial district? Adrenalin revved my body to instinctively jump out of the van and protect the child.

But then I saw it—Mom's hand holding tight on what looked like the top end of a small wagon tongue, securely attached to the back of the tricycle.

Relieved, my heart rate began to recover as I settled in to await the green light. My thoughts, meanwhile, flashed back to the economy's financial turmoil of the past year and the appointment immediately ahead. Claude Fletcher, Don Shipley, and I were on our way to Bank of

America on Tuesday, June 30, 2009, the last day of VCS's fiscal year, to sign loan documents for the $20 million forward swap. According to our original swap contract with the bank, the loan was to be funded by March 1, 2009. But an agreement on February 27 had extended the one-year forward swap to a two-year swap, stretching our window of time to get the loan funded. Now, like the toddler, we were making a momentous crossing in the financial district of San Francisco—heads down and eyes looking forward to building a 55,000-square-foot Conservatory of the Arts and Student Life Center. No doubt, ours too was a dangerous crossing, given an economy now in its fifteenth month of crippling recession.

Although I didn't know it then, by the end of 2009, Silicon Valley would lose 90,000 jobs, at a faster rate than the national average. Emmett Carlson, CEO of the Silicon Valley Community Foundation, reported: "On the heels of the worst economic year since the Great Depression, our region has entered a new era of uncertainty in which our ability to attract top talent, fund innovation, and preserve a decent quality of life is no longer guaranteed."[104]

Claude, I knew, had especially worrisome concerns. His life experience and wisdom gave him caution about overconfident leaders who sometimes overreach, pulling down otherwise successful ministries—or even huge corporations, such as Bear Stearns.

Don had made more than forty financial projections with all kinds of plausible assumptions. At times he was determined to move forward. At other times, depending on the assumptions, he wanted to hold up and protect the school from added risk.

I, too, wavered back and forth on whether taking the loan to build was the right decision. When praying with the VCS board and intercessors, and while reading God's Word, I felt especially faith filled, confident, and secure. Yet when I reflected on the economy, the loss of VCS parents' jobs, and other factors, my insides trembled.

As well, VCS faced its own financial challenges trying to cross the Great Recession's chasm. About 20 percent or more of VCS parents had either lost their jobs or suffered severely reduced incomes. Our Bank of America loan covenants required the school to maintain a 30 percent cash-to-debt ratio to avoid a technical default. VCS cash reserves had grown to $19 million, so with the school's current $38 million debt, cash reserves stood at 50 percent. Taking the added $20 million loan, however, would plunge our cash-to-debt ratio down to only 32 percent—a meager two-percent margin. Still, our conservative projections convinced Bank of America our ratios would hold—if the Great Recession did not become the Second Great Depression.

As I waited for the light to change, I recalled the steps VCS had taken in the past year. To help unemployed and underemployed parents cope with their struggles, we took a million-dollar expense right out of VCS's operational budget to fund additional financial aid. To make matters more challenging, the final donation of a ten-year annual $1 million gift concluded that very month—June 2009—and the annual payments on the $20 million loan would cost another million dollars per year. Everything added up to a $3 million annual budget hit—in the middle of the Great Recession.

All these factors contributed to our decision to raise VCS's tuition by six percent. It was justified, but risky: Would personal financial hardships and higher tuition push families out of the school? Our budget assumptions required an increased enrollment of fifty students per year to meet our bank-covenanted ratios for the Conservatory of the Arts and Student Life Center loan. But what if the recession put the brakes on growth?

We had to have a plan to control costs, and the plan was not pretty. Only a day earlier I had met with all VCS employees to share the following announcement (as finalized in a later memo):

In the event of enrollments below 2,275, our VCS Board and senior management team have elected to cut costs through salary reductions rather than through layoffs and larger class sizes. Beginning with our first 2009–10 fiscal year payroll this July, our senior administrators will receive a compensation reduction of ten percent, and all other employees will receive a five percent reduction. Senior administrative compensation is decreased by ten percent to help avoid added decreases for staff beyond five percent later this school year.

To the extent enrollment goals are met before school begins, compensation reductions will be reimbursed and full salaries will be restored. Conversely, if we have an added loss of tuition revenue during the school year, we may need to further decrease staff compensation beyond five percent.

On top of everything, we had to suspend matching contributions to employees' retirement accounts. Of course, all this news was ominous. The very first payroll reduction would come the third week of July. My concern about staff response weighed on me during planning for my annual keynote address in August to about 300 faculty, staff, board members, and friends of VCS.

Thankfully, the night before the signing of the loan documents, I had a serious talk with the Lord about these matters. God gave me a fresh infusion of His faith that Monday night, June 29, as I read these words in Isaiah 57:13b–19 (NASB):

"But he who takes refuge in Me will inherit the land and will possess My holy mountain."
And it will be said, "Build up, build up, prepare the way, remove every obstacle out of the way of My people." For thus says the high and exalted One who lives forever, whose name is Holy, "I dwell on a high and holy place, and also with the

contrite and lowly of spirit in order to revive the spirit of the lowly and to revive the heart of the contrite. . . . I have seen his ways, but I will heal him; I will lead him and restore comfort to him and to his mourners, creating the praise of the lips. Peace, peace to him who is far and to him who is near," says the LORD, "and I will heal him."

The toddler completed his tricycle journey across the street. The light turned green, and my foot hit the accelerator with confidence. As we proceeded, the eyes of my heart saw it: God's hand holding tight as He guided us toward Bank of America's $20 million funding of the conservatory construction.

WHAT HAVE I DONE?

That day, as we signed the loan, I felt fine. I was full of faith. Then, when I arrived home, a truckload of doubt crashed down on me. *What have I done? And in this economy!*

My spirit became troubled. Worry began to overwhelm me. As I prayed about the burden of responsibility for the $20 million loan documents I had signed earlier in the day, a battle raged in my heart.

"Lord!" I cried out, recounting the cold, hard facts. "We just received the last of ten $1 million annual gifts to support our faculty salaries. We added $1 million in financial aid to help the 20 percent of our families with severely reduced incomes or who are unemployed. Job losses continue to mount. The new annual payment on the conservatory loan will cost us over $1 million per year. It all adds up to a $3 million budget flip-flop."

A sudden fear gripped me: What if the "messages from God" I had heard to accept the loan and build the conservatory were, after all, not really from God? What if Cliff, rather than God, was speaking to Cliff's heart? Could I be deluded?

In spite of all God had orchestrated to build the conservatory, again I trembled and asked myself, *What were we thinking?*

Over the past fifteen and a half months, we had wondered if we should "unwind" (get out of) our $20 million Bank of America swap. But now it looked like we were locked in to our position. On top of the growing economic gloom, after we took the forward swap in March 2008, the interest rates went down even more. If we unwound the swap, it would have cost us between $3 and $4.2 million in lost principal, depending on the date. Eliminating the unwind option seemed like the Lord's way of saying, "I promised to not allow you to be tempted more than you can bear."[105]

Earnest prayer to follow God's direction was our saving grace. But for the grace of God, we might have taken the exit doors in the face of such a terrible economy. I don't know for certain, but I do know we gathered the data and considered all options.

The sober reality of signing the loan documents that day weighed on me heavily. I kept trying to have faith. I knew God had spoken to me, but I still struggled.

As I prayed, God moved on me in a very special way. He reminded me of the verses He had given me the night before. I returned to Isaiah 57 where the passage was marked in my Bible. As I read, several of the words spoke powerfully to me.

My conversation with God went something like this:

"But he who takes refuge in Me will inherit the land."

Yeah, Lord, we have some land we are trying to buy.

"And will possess My holy mountain."

Yeah, we are on a mountain, all right.

"And it will be said, 'Build up, build up.'"

I know, Lord; it's what You told me to do. But I am a mere mortal and I sometimes wonder whether it's God talking to Cliff or Cliff talking to Cliff. I don't doubt You, Lord, but I wonder if I get so excited I convince myself. I've been accused of being such a good salesman I can even sell the board of directors and think it's You speaking.

"Prepare the way, remove every obstacle out of the way of My people. For thus says the high and exalted One. . . ."

I hear You saying, "In case you are wondering, I'm the one doing the talking here!"

". . . who lives forever, whose name is Holy, 'I dwell on a high and holy place.'"

Lord, I want to be with You on that hill!

"And also with the contrite and lowly of spirit."

I want to have a holy and a contrite spirit!

"In order to revive the spirit of the lowly, and to revive the heart of the contrite."

I want to revive the spirit of the lowly. There are people all around us who need VCS. They need the conservatory building. They need our Christian teachers. They need the gospel. They need the Christian worldview. They need the Word of God. They need prayer. Hardly any other place around here has all of that available. That's what I want to do.

"I will not contend forever, nor will I always be angry. . . ."

This verse troubles me, Lord. Are You angry with us?

In my mind God replied, "No! I am angry with the way this world is going. I am angry with the greed. I am angry with the wickedness of people's hearts. But I am not always going to be angry."

He continued: ". . . I have seen his ways, but I will heal him."

Please heal us, Lord.

"I will lead him and restore comfort to him and to his mourners."

Who are the mourners, Lord?

I heard Him answer, "They are parents of children, who are mourning because of the loss of their children. They mourn just as Rachel mourned for the loss of her children, when all boys under age two were murdered as Herod tried to kill the baby Jesus. Children are being lost spiritually, and I want to intervene. 'Creating the praise of the lips. . . .'"

What do You want to do to save these children?

"I am going to create the praise of the lips on these children from their hearts. 'Peace, peace to him who is far and to him who is near. . . .'"

I want peace to students who come from far and to students who are near.

". . . and I will heal—I will heal multitudes. It really is Me speaking to you, so remain confident in Me and BUILD!"

"Lord, I Believe; Help My Unbelief!"

That is a conversation I will never forget. Afterward, I looked hard at the scripture and circled the verbs. Those words called me to action:

- **Inherit** the land
- **Possess** My holy mountain
- **Build** up
- **Prepare** the way
- **Remove** every obstacle
- **Dwell** on a high and holy place (our mountain)
- **Revive** the heart of the contrite
- **Heal**
- **Lead**
- **Restore** comfort
- **Creating** praise (to God)

"I want you to tell everyone," God directed me, "these verbs represent what I want to do in the second fifty years of this school. I'm going to continue to build and I'm going to continue to develop Valley Christian Schools."

I pondered, "If we are to lay the groundwork for the second fifty years of VCS, we must be determined to obey the Lord sacrificially. There is no recession in God's economy, and there has never been a depression in heaven; nor is His provision or arm shortened because of circumstances on earth. To successfully found the second fifty years of Valley Christian Schools, we must be willing to face difficult circumstances with the same faith-filled sacrificial determination David and Edie Wallace (VCS's original founders) possessed fifty years ago."

Comfort returned to my heart, and those words gave me a renewed holy boldness. I went to sleep after the signing on Tuesday, June 30, 2009, at peace with God and filled with fresh determination to make all of those words real in the lives of students for many generations.

After that, I was fine. When people talked with me, they would be certain I was on top of the situation with plenty of faith. Following this particular discussion with God, I didn't have any more doubts—for almost two whole weeks!

On July 13 that creeping feeling of anxiety returned. *Oh, no! Here it comes again—those doubts.* Even worse, I would soon need to give my annual keynote address, this one launching VCS's fiftieth school year. The August 18 date loomed large on my calendar. *What am I going to say?*

I felt like Gideon—struggling back and forth between waves of faith and then doubt. When God spoke peace to my heart, I believed and moved forward with confidence. But as time passed, doubts crept back into my reasoning. (Reasoning is what usually gets me in trouble.)

I thought about the recession. I thought about the possible lower enrollment and the reduction of staff salaries. I thought about the staff reaction to suspension of the employees' matching retirement program. And I thought about the main question: "Why are you borrowing $20 million to build a Conservatory of the Arts and Student Life Center in the middle of the Great Recession?"

O Lord, You are going to have to help me, because I still wonder whether I get excited and become my own best salesman.

I asked God question after question. *What if the recession becomes a depression? What if our enrollment strategy fears are realized? What if VCS loses enrollment going forward when we need growing enrollment to pay for the conservatory building?*

I knew Don Shipley, our CFO, asked these questions too, as did Claude Fletcher, our chancellor. Don said, "We have a great plan. As long as we grow the enrollment, everything will be fine."

I prayed for God's mercy. Like Gideon, I needed a strong faith from God that would settle my doubts forever. I read Judges 6:36–40, a passage in the midst of the account of Gideon being called by God to go against the great army of 135,000 Midianites with only 300 men.

I am like Gideon, I prayed, *because Gideon was afraid and doubted repeatedly. Lord, please help me have firm faith.* Gideon was afraid to ask God for more proof that He had spoken, but God accommodated his request for more proof because Gideon had honest doubts.

My prayers also echoed the father who took his sick son to Jesus and confessed, "Lord, I believe; help my unbelief!" Jesus had challenged him, "If you can believe, all things are possible to him who believes." Two miracles took place that day. The father gained unwavering belief, and his tortured son was healed.[106]

I wrote a note in my Bible next to Gideon's story in Judges 6: "I needed a confirming sign from God to settle my heart and to be certain that it was God moving the conservatory (building) forward, and not misguided Cliff."[107]

God's amazing answer came that very week. But for the whole story, we have to take a trip back in time.

CHAPTER 15

MY MOTHER'S LEGACY

"Each of you must show great respect
for your mother. . . ."[108]

I'M STILL AMAZED at how God answered my prayers for unwavering faith. It's a very personal and special story.

After my first year in college, I was privileged to visit my parents during the summer of 1968 at Lakenheath Air Force Base in Suffolk, England. My father, who served as a Chief Master Sergeant in the Air Force, was stationed there at Lakenheath. I had set aside about $73 in hopes of buying some great Bible reference books in England, where much of the Reformation occurred. Seventy-three dollars in 1968 would equal about $500 in today's inflated currency.

My parents and I took weekend trips. While they went "antiquing," I looked for good books. As we traveled, we kept an eye out for "Bed and Breakfast" signs in the windows of homes. By evening we would settle in for a visit and a night's sleep, with an English breakfast the next morning.

As we browsed in one of the antique stores, a leather-bound book on a shelf about ten feet high caught my eye. The shopkeeper described it as an old Bible and scaled a ladder to retrieve it for viewing.

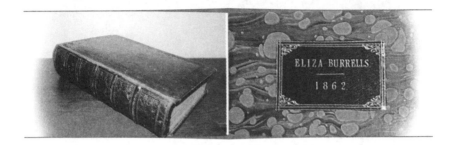

Bible with 1862 nameplate found in an antique store in England

It was big: about seventeen and a half inches tall, almost twelve inches wide, and four inches thick. It weighed about thirty pounds. The inside cover had the date 1862 engraved below the name of Eliza Burrells.

I immediately fell in love with this beautiful Bible. The trouble was, my mother loved the Bible too! I paid for it and wanted to take it home, but my heart got the better of me and I gave it to my mother. She cherished it dearly.

Almost three decades later, on Sunday, August 3, 1997, when Kris, the children, and I were visiting Mom and Dad at my childhood home in Merced, California, my mother called me into her bedroom. "Cliff, I've got something I want you to take home with you. I'm gifting this Bible back to you. I love it, but it belongs with you as our family Bible."

So the Bible came back to me after twenty-nine years of safekeeping with my mother. This life lesson proved, once again, it is more blessed to give than to receive, since the Bible became a gift from my mother to me. Over the years, we have recorded our family history in the Bible, including written messages from my departed grandmother,

mother, and father challenging successive generations of Daugherty descendants to serve the Lord.

In 2001, four years after Mom re-gifted her Bible to me, Mom was brushing her hair when an excruciating pain ran through her upper arm. A trip to the hospital emergency room revealed her arm's humerus bone had snapped in two. The diagnosis was ominous. X-rays showed her arm's bone marrow riddled with holes.

In a cold, sterile Stanford University Hospital office, Dad and I waited with Mom to hear whether the doctor would bring hope of a treatment for her recovery. Mom was all of 120 pounds and stood an erect five feet two, with brown eyes radiating insightful wisdom. She was full of life and loved to travel the country with Dad in their motor home.

Somehow she looked smaller, with her arm in a sling, as we waited for good news in the doctor's office. Time seemed to pass slowly. The tension was interrupted by a knock on the door. Two white coats entered the room.

One of them spoke bluntly. "You have osteosarcoma, a cancer in your bones that is incurable. You can expect to live for up to two years. . . . Any questions?"

I scrambled for an intelligent query but was abruptly interrupted. The doctor's tone exposed his aggravation. "Did you hear me? I said incurable. There is no known effective treatment. All I can do is to try and make her comfortable by relieving the pain."

The news came with a simply-stated, matter-of-fact finality, as if he were saying the hospital cafeteria had just run out of coffee, or meatloaf. It was shocking, to say the least. The medical intern, less seasoned, conveyed more sadness and compassion. But the older doctor explained the diagnosis the way an auto mechanic would describe your car's motor sputtering beyond repair.

After the white coats left, Mom spoke up. "I'm really surprised. I expected to live a long life, but God knows what's best."

Disregarding his bluntness, the doctor was right. All of my dad's research, treatment options, and special cleansing diets did not slow the cancer's ravaging effects. My mother died on February 12, 2003, just under two years after her diagnosis, as predicted by her "matter-of-fact" Stanford doctor.

As we prepared for Mom's funeral, I found her prayer list. I have a vivid image of Mom faithfully praying daily for her children, grandchildren, and everyone in the family, with her open Bible and her prayer list in front of her. As I viewed Mom's prayer list, I was moved to discover my name at the top, since I am the oldest child.

I treasured Mom's prayer list. But later I lost it! I felt terrible. I lost Mother's prayer list! Thankfully, the copy I made for my mother's funeral lay secure in my safe. But hopes to find the original vanished completely as the years passed.

THE FAMILY BIBLE

On Thursday, July 16, 2009, Rick and Pam Watson hosted a fundraising event for Mayor Chuck Reed at their beautiful Willow Glen home. Chuck served as our VCS attorney from 1988, when we bought the Skyway property, until he became mayor of San Jose in January 2007.

The misery of my conservatory funding doubts, which had returned that week, continued to torment me. With my annual VCS keynote address just a month and two days away, I asked God to give me the unwavering faith and confidence I severely lacked. Yet even with such an unsettled heart, I thought it best to attend Rick and Pam's fundraiser for our mayor and friend.

As Kris and I entered the Watsons' home, we noticed a large Bible. Prominently displayed at the entry of their home, open for all to see, was their beautiful leather-bound 19th-century family Bible. It made such a godly statement about their home. Immediately I knew: *That's what I want to do with our family Bible!*

Kris went home before I did and went to bed. When I arrived home later, I retrieved our family Bible. In the entry of our home sits a 19th-century hand-carved credenza, which my parents acquired in England on one of our bed-and-breakfast trips. After Mom died, Dad had asked if I would take it and care for it in our home. Moving a vase from the credenza (and hoping Kris would agree), I laid our family Bible open on it.

Kris awoke and came to the balcony to be certain it was I who had entered the house. She saw the family Bible on the credenza and exclaimed, "How did you know I wanted to put the Bible there?" She had had the same idea after seeing Rick and Pam's Bible earlier that evening.

The next day, I walked past the credenza and noticed the Bible didn't look balanced. I decided to open the pages closer to the middle. I turned some pages—and found my mother's original handwritten prayer list, right near the middle of the Bible! My heart leaped with fond memories of my praying mother.

At long last the list reappeared. *Well,* I thought, *at least I put Mom's prayer list in a safe place!* What could be safer than in our family Bible? I promised not to forget again, and left Mom's prayer list on the pages where I found it.

I was as happy as I could be. I couldn't wait for Kris to see Mom's prayer list on the open Bible as I moved to the stairs to tell her.

Suddenly I sensed the Lord addressing the issue I still carried continuously, the nagging doubts about whether we were doing the right thing moving forward with construction of the conservatory. As I got halfway up the stairs, the Lord brought this question to mind:

Now what do you think the odds are the Bible is open on the exact passage where I have spoken to you from Isaiah 57:13b–19?

The question arrested my thoughts. *Now that would be a miracle— I've got to go see.*

My heart throbbed with huge suspicion: *Mom's prayer list and the open Bible will be on Isaiah 57:13b–19.*

I bounded down the stairs more quickly than I had ascended. Then I stood stunned and in awe as I began reading from Isaiah 57:13b–19 on the open page:

> ". . . but he that putteth his trust in me shall possess the land, and shall inherit my holy mountain; and shall say, Cast ye up, cast ye up, prepare the way, take up the stumbling block out of the way of my people."

I knew the King James language "Cast ye up, cast ye up" is translated "Build up, build up" in my New American Standard Bible where I had marked the verses. As I continued gazing on the pages of our old family Bible, I remembered the NASB equivalent:

> "But he who takes refuge in Me will inherit the land and will possess My holy mountain. And it will be said, 'Build up, build up, prepare the way, remove every obstacle out of the way of My people.'"

Wow, I thought, *what are the odds that five and a half years earlier I would accidentally place Mom's prayer list in our family Bible on the exact passage God would use to confirm VCS's move forward with the building of the Conservatory of the Arts and Student Life Center? Furthermore, what are the chances I "just happened" to open the family Bible to the same passage where I circled the verbs and wrote "June 30, 2009" in the top margin sixteen days earlier, with my handwritten note next to the Isaiah 57 verses:*

"Last day of fiscal 2008–09 year — Went to San Francisco to sign docs for $20M loan to build the conservatory — On 6-29-09 God gave these verses, Is 57:13b to v. 19 as an assurance that we are doing God's will. . . . God wants to 'possess My holy mountain' — Fully build it out to 'revive the spirit of the lowly' and to 'revive the heart of the contrite' v. 15. 'God will heal His people' v. 19 — Those who are 'far and near' . . . He will use them for His purposes to 'inherit the land' and to 'possess His holy mountain' to 'Build up, build up' to 'prepare the way of My people to dwell with God in a high and holy place.'"

As I saw Mother's prayer list lying alongside Isaiah 57:13b–19, the Lord took me immediately into a state of holy awe. Now I had no doubt: God truly was the one who had spoken—and not Cliff!

TESTING THE STORY

For a moment I imagined myself sharing this incredible story with our VCS board of directors, administrators, faculty, and staff during my keynote address. But then it hit me: They might think I'm loony or, worse, that I concocted the entire tale. I decided to test the telling of the story with my wife, Kris, to discover her reaction. *She is safe,* I thought.

At my first opportunity, I walked Kris to the open family Bible and rehearsed the entire miraculous story. Kris too was amazed. She believed God really did this miracle of placing Mom's prayer list on the exact Isaiah 57 passage God had impressed on me both the night before we signed the loan documents and the evening of that same day.

Kris's response was comforting. *But she loves me and wants to believe,* I surmised.

For another relatively safe test, I ran the story past my daughter, Kristin, and my son, Zane. Children can be more objective than spouses, and if they thought the story sounded a bit "made up" or loony, I wanted to know. They too saw the hand of God in these events.

My son-in-law, Mike Annab, was my next and most challenging test case. In his role as IT director at technology-rich Valley Christian Schools, he usually identifies every possible problem before taking on a new project. He has a reputation for being extremely intelligent, logical, and at times brutally honest in search of the truth.

He will give me the real indication, I concluded, *as to how the faculty and staff at the school would respond.* His healthy skepticism, analytical and strategic mind, and intimate knowledge of Valley Christian's personnel would help ensure an acid test for how others might react.

The perfect time to ask Mike his opinion about whether God was really speaking to me came while we waited to share a meal at our home. "Mike, I want to tell you the amazing way God spoke to me about moving forward to build the conservatory. I need your honest assessment as to whether my experience is really of God."

His dark eyes signaled he was ready to listen and assess. As I retold the story, I watched Mike's body language and saw his jaw drop with wonder. *I hope he's pondering God's miraculous way of confirming His message, and not my seeming loss of reason!*

Finally I posed my question. "Do you think this really could be God speaking?"

"No doubt," he quickly answered. "There is no doubt." Mike paused, then flashed a wry smile. "It's not so amazing God did this—it's more amazing that you are listening."

"True!" I chuckled.

While Kris, Kristin, and Zane were quick to believe God had really spoken, Mike Annab's agreement was the clincher for me. I thanked God for speaking in such a convincing way that even Mike, with his incisive logic and engineering mind, was immediately convinced. I had my message for the keynote address just weeks away.

KEYS TO THE KEYNOTE

Excitement filled me as I looked forward to passing on God's message to everyone at Valley Christian Schools. Because this keynote would launch VCS's fiftieth year, I went through my address with David Wallace, our Valley Christian Schools' founder. He too gave me confirmation and encouragement, saying, "Cliff, this message is from God." I looked forward to having the privilege of Dave's presence at the keynote as we looked ahead to the schools' second fifty years.

In my preparation, I reflected on the comment I had heard years before at the administrators' conference: "You just happened to be in the right place at the right time to build Valley Christian Schools." It's true that God built Valley Christian Schools campuses in the middle of Silicon Valley's dot-com prosperity. Now God was proving His power to build what would become a $25 million Conservatory of the Arts and Student Life Center in the midst of economic austerity and the Great Recession. This truth underscored how the highest standard of excellence is the nature, character, and works of God, and how the Quest for Excellence is driven by our Lord Jesus, who moves forward in any and every economic circumstance.

I was learning important answers to two of my three big questions: 1) Can I confidently say God is willing and able to do the same miraculous works to build schools like VCS in any community where people are praying and working to bring His goodness, peace, and joy to the children in their schools? and 2) Are there really enough resources to build great schools in every community, even during difficult economic times?

Finding Mom's prayer list gave me confident answers: Any place is the right place and any time is the right time for those who catch a vision of what God wants to do and join Him by obeying His voice!

As Jesus promised, "If you ask anything in My name, I will do it." "Access to the Omnis" is a divine gift to those who ask and believe in Jesus![109]

For me, my journey of wavering between faith and doubt mirrored Gideon's experience in chapters 6–7 of the book of Judges. Gideon had many proofs of God speaking to him (6:12, 14, 16), and yet he still wavered in his confidence. He asked God for a sign the messages really came from Him (v. 17). God responded to Gideon's request with multiple signs, including:

1. The sign of fire from the rock consuming the meat and the unleavened bread (v. 21).

2. The sign of the dry ground and the dew-soaked fleece (vv. 37–38).

3. The sign of the dry fleece with dew on all the ground around the fleece (vv. 39–40).

Even though Gideon was afraid and still doubtful, he obeyed God and narrowed his army to only 300 men. Then "the LORD said to him, 'Arise, go down against the camp, for I have given it into your hands. But if you are afraid to go down, go with Purah your servant down to the camp, and you will hear what they say; and afterward your hands will be strengthened that you may go down against the camp'" (7:9–11, NASB). God acknowledged Gideon's fear and gave him one more confirmation—from the mouths of his enemies. Gideon eavesdropped while one of them described a dream and the man's comrade gave the interpretation: "This is nothing less than the sword of Gideon the son of Joash, a man of Israel; God has given Midian and all the camp into his hand" (v. 14).

Verse 15 tells the result: "When Gideon heard the account of the dream and its interpretation, he bowed in worship. He returned to the camp of Israel and said, 'Arise, for the LORD has given the camp of Midian into your hands.'"

Finally! Gideon believed and obeyed God fearlessly with unwavering faith! God was faithful to Gideon because Gideon wanted to believe without wavering, and he obeyed God even when he fearfully doubted. The way God repeatedly spoke to Gideon and graciously gave him numerous signs and wonders comforted me. Yes, I concluded, *I and our VCS board and executive team have doubted and wavered, but we have obeyed.*

Like Gideon, I too had a worship moment. Mine came with this amazing miracle of finding my mother's prayer list next to the open Bible passage of Isaiah 57:13b–19. With this sign, my confidence grew strong and my heart remained determined. I can truly say, since the experience with my mother's Bible, I had no further doubts as we moved into the construction phase to complete the Conservatory of the Arts and Student Life Center.

I took a picture of my NASB study Bible in front of our family Bible, with Mom's prayer list resting on it, to share with the board, administration, faculty, and staff during my August 2009 VCS keynote address to begin the school year. God used His signs to give them confidence and faith. Even though the Great Recession might have become the Second Great Depression, we were determined to take refuge in the Lord, to "inherit the land" and "build up" the Conservatory of the Arts and Student Life Center, and to "possess" God's "holy mountain," according to the verses in Isaiah 57.

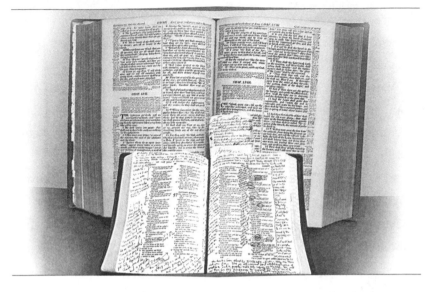

My NASB study Bible in front of our family Bible, with Mom's prayer list

I ended the keynote with a set of verses VCS founder Dave Wallace and I had agreed upon to summarize the message:

> "Fear not, for I have redeemed you.[110] Bring My sons from afar, and My daughters from the ends of the earth.[111] I will do a new thing.[112] The children will say, 'The place is too small for me; give me a place where I may dwell.'"[113]
>
> And if we do as God directs, God's Word promises, "I will save your children."[114]

Prayer for God's guidance, I reminded my listeners, served as the bedrock foundation for the VCS board of directors, and our faithful group of prayer intercessors took everything to the Lord on multiple levels. In difficult economic circumstances, "We are tempted to hold back to protect reserves and to protect what we have," I acknowledged. "But the Lord has told me, 'If you hold back to protect it, you will lose it. You succeed only if you follow Me.'"

The Quest for Excellence—the passionate pursuit to know the nature, character, and works of God—ensures success, but it never ends in this life! Our quest to follow Jesus continued with more gripping adventures to follow, as we would soon learn.

CHAPTER 16

A Troubling Impasse,
and a One–Two Punch

"Count it all joy when you fall into various trials. . . ."[115]

WHILE THE DRAMA surrounding the $20 million loan unfolded, another story was taking place. Meanwhile, back at the ranch . . . er, the hilltop . . .

The amazing account of how Valley Christian Schools acquired and built on the hilltop land for our Skyway campus appears in my first book, *Quest for Excellence.* Most of the approximately fifty-three acres of land on the hill in San Jose were purchased with a jointly-held title-purchase agreement with South Valley Christian Church. VCS began construction in August 1998 and moved onto the Skyway campus in January 2000. By December 2005, the church officially announced they had decided not to build on their portion of this land. They offered to sell to VCS their eleven acres, which VCS was using for parking, as provided in the 1989 joint-use agreement. South Valley Church and Valley Christian Schools obtained separate appraisals for this property at about $3 million each.

South Valley Church made an application to the City of San Jose to rezone the eleven acres for development of townhomes. The church believed the land could be sold for about $17 million after rezoning. From VCS's point of view, construction of townhomes would bring serious harm to the school's prospects for future construction, since parking and traffic flow through the Skyway campus would worsen. As a solution, the church offered to sell the property to Valley Christian Schools for $17 million.

Our prayer intercessors and the VCS board of directors prayed fervently about this matter. God gave us confidence we would be able to settle, based on the current appraisal. The board was willing to offer up to $500,000 more than the appraised value of $3 million to purchase the property, in order to be very fair with the church given added expenses they had incurred. Although VCS had the $3.5 million in hand, the church's desire to rezone the acreage for townhomes left the property in limbo. Meanwhile, VCS prayerfully opposed the rezoning application, as the school badly needed to retain the lot for daily traffic flow requirements and could not afford a $17 million purchase.

Unsuccessful attempts to purchase the church property gave us the sense negotiations would be futile into the foreseeable future. As it turned out, the church eventually withdrew its rezoning application, thankfully preserving parking and traffic flow for VCS. By 2007, however, VCS's priorities shifted.

The successful launch of the Conservatory of the Arts, along with God's leading, resulted in decisions to reallocate cash resources to construct the "hanging classroom" (as described in Chapter 12) for use beginning in fall 2007. As well, we decided to expand the planned two-story weight-training facility into a three-story, 5,300-square-foot Human Performance Building, adding three classrooms as well as athletic training facilities. These four additional classrooms provided increased capacity for a growing number of conservatory students. The hanging classroom was used for math classes during the day and hosted a co-curricular robotics program after school.

Then, as the conservatory program burgeoned, we confirmed the need to build the 55,000-square-foot Conservatory of the Arts building. Once VCS entered into the forward swap agreement with Bank of America, keeping a healthy cash-to-debt ratio became crucial, because taking the bank's $20 million loan would push that ratio close to its limits. Moreover, the new annual payment on the conservatory loan would cost more than $1 million per year. With this financial reality facing us, purchasing the eleven acres from the church—even if South Valley agreed to sell for the appraised $3 million—now seemed untimely. Land purchase discussions took a back seat while we pushed forward to fund and build the conservatory.

The growing strategic priority for the development of the conservatory became clear. The formation of the conservatory, which successfully rebranded our music department, had generated tremendous interest and enthusiasm from the community at large. Students were coming to VCS because of our music program in greater numbers than ever before. Across the board, all of VCS's music performance disciplines were experiencing a greater depth of talent from top to bottom.

Troy Gunter, director of the conservatory, and the rest of the Visual and Performing Arts (VPA) leadership team had a vision to expand the conservatory to include all VPA disciplines, including visual art, theater, and dance with the music programs. The team wanted to put even more emphasis on promoting the special relationship between spiritual formation and artistic talent. As Troy wrote in an email, "We don't merely want to create great artists; we want to produce great artists who are called to use their God-given talents to bring about Kingdom-building change." In the same way, I like to remind everyone that God's kingdom is "goodness, peace, and joy."[116]

Troy and his team relished "the tremendous task of building a world-class conservatory committed to equipping students with the tools necessary to positively change our culture for the cause of Christ." The conservatory development became a keen focus in the strategic planning of Valley Christian Schools.

Twists and Turns

CFO Don Shipley and I shared the news of the conservatory's great progress with Marianna Pisano, VCS's banker at Bank of America, during our 2008 fourth-quarter review meeting. She reminded us of the outstanding joint-title issue with the church and the need for a subordination agreement in relation to our forward swap of $20 million to fund the conservatory. With a signed subordination agreement, in case of a VCS default, proceeds from the sale of the property would go first to pay off VCS's Bank of America loan and second to pay off the church mortgage.

Because of the recession and other factors, South Valley Christian Church owed more money on the land than the $3 million appraisal or the school's $3.5 million offer. Selling the property used as collateral for their loan would not pay off what they owed.

But circumstances for South Valley had changed. On September 17, 2007, South Valley Christian Church merged with Los Gatos Christian Church to create the new Venture Christian Church. Pastor Glen Call of Los Gatos Christian and Pastor Dave Sawkins of South Valley Church, both nearing retirement, strategically designed the merger to benefit both churches. South Valley had grown to about 1,500 members but lacked a church facility, while Los Gatos Church had dwindled to about 700 members but owned twenty-eight acres and a beautiful church campus. It made sense to merge.

Pastor Dave Sawkins agreed to meet me for coffee on December 1, 2008. Our intercessors prayed in advance for the meeting. I arrived early at Pete's Coffee Shop and took the extra time to pray for God's guidance and direction for both the church and the school. Dave arrived about fifteen minutes later, and we greeted each other warmly. Dave's daughter, Susan, had attended Valley Christian Elementary and graduated from Valley Christian High School in 2005. Dave expressed how happy he and his wife, Sheila, were with their VCS experience for Susan.

"We had a lot of choices," Dave said, "but we chose Valley because we like how well you do what you do."

"Dave," I said, "Valley Christian Schools is growing. The conservatory program is really attracting students, and we have Bank of America's commitment for a $20 million loan to begin construction of a conservatory building. We strongly sense God's leading us to build. The school is completely packed without capacity for more students. We have hurdles with the city to overcome, but to take the Bank of America loan for construction, we need the church to sign a subordination agreement. You will recall how our last agreement provides for a signed subordination agreement by the school or church when needed."

Dave looked a bit stunned. He quickly recovered, however, with the question, "Do you still want to buy the church property at $3.5 million?"

It was my turn to be stunned.

"We'd like to buy it, Dave. When we offered $3.5 million, the school had the money. Our priorities changed after we didn't get an agreement and it became obvious we needed to build. I don't think the bank will make the loan for construction if we spend $3.5 million of our cash on the land. The ratios are strict."

"Cliff," Dave replied, "if God wants the school to build, He'll provide the money."

"God's been faithful," I agreed, "but money is tight for our donors. This recession is the biggest economic setback our nation has suffered since the Great Depression."

"More churches were built during the Great Depression than during almost any other time," Dave pointed out. "God will make it happen."

Before we parted, Dave prayed for God's blessings on the school and for His direction in these matters. I agreed to talk with our board and our bankers to see what might be done to buy the church's property.

It was an intense but pleasant meeting. Dave couldn't refuse to sign the subordination agreement given our last written pact, but he didn't consent to sign either. I wondered how we would enforce our agreement in those circumstances. The church dropping their asking price from $17 million to our offering price of $3.5 million was certainly good news. But making the conservatory and the church land deals happen concurrently seemed like a difficult or impossible prospect.

On Friday, February 27, 2009, Bank of America and VCS came to an agreement on the line of credit term sheet for the $20 million loan to build the conservatory, although the architectural plans, the environmental impact report, and city building approvals wouldn't materialize for some time yet. The agreement extended the one-year forward swap to a two-year swap, giving us more time to resolve such issues. But problems with the church property seemed endless.

Our executive team and I, including Claude Fletcher and Don Shipley, felt uneasy about funding the loan while the purchase of the church property remained unresolved. *Should we go forward with a construction contract before God answers our prayers to resolve issues related to the church property?* Given the bank's cash reserve requirements for the conservatory loan, the school asked the church for the opportunity to pay for the land over a five-year period. We prayed and we waited.

THREE SOVEREIGN SIGNS

If anyone doubted God was leading us to build the conservatory, the next events, including three sovereign signs, gave strong evidence God was, indeed, directing our way.

Even though we were determined not to allow the $20 million swap to expire—at a cost of about $2.8 million (at that time)—we heard God telling us to hold off on signing a construction contract. In late May, I shared my decision with Don Shipley. That night I wrote in the margin of my Bible on page 894, "On Friday, May 29, 2009, I told Don Shipley I don't want to go forward with the South Bay Construction contract until we get resolution on the impasse with Venture Church [formerly South Valley Christian Church]. It's been 22 years since acquiring the land. . . ."

I underlined the promises in Isaiah 60:17 and 21: "And I will make peace your administrators and righteousness your overseers. . . . Then all your people will be righteous; they will possess the land forever" (NASB).

Over the years I had learned from God's faithful provision that He would make a way. Even though the long and tedious negotiations made a fast resolution seem hopeless, I was confident God had a solution in the making.

On Monday, June 1, 2009, the brand new pastor of Venture Church, Chip Ingram, dropped by the VCS campus unannounced and met with Chancellor Claude Fletcher. Because I was taking care of an out-of-office responsibility, Claude filled me in later.

"Pastor Ingram came by to settle the land issue on his first day of full-time ministry as pastor at Venture," Claude told me. "He really has a wonderful heart to resolve the difficulties."

Wow! Who could have imagined a new pastor neither Claude nor I had met would come by unannounced—on the first work day after I had decided not to go forward on the construction contract until God resolved the land impasse? I told God I wouldn't move ahead without a resolution, and within one business day He brought a commitment from Pastor Chip Ingram to find one! With this sovereign sign, God was certainly at work answering our prayers.

It seemed we were on the verge of an agreement. The church's price was $3.5 million, exactly what VCS had offered to cover the appraised value of the land plus $500,000 for added improvements. Given Pastor Ingram's determination to find a resolution, I felt a release to move ahead and pursue signing the contract with South Bay Construction to build the conservatory.

But the second of the three sovereign signs confirming God's direction to build the conservatory would be no less amazing.

The process of getting a contractual agreement with the church to purchase the property lingered on, in spite of Chip Ingram's and our efforts. The devil is in the details, as they say. Our attorneys drew up multiple drafts without success. Given the collateral joint tenancy and environmental issues, a resolution of the challenges proved difficult.

On Tuesday, August 4, 2009, the VCS prayer intercessors met in my office as usual. Although our prayer intercessors had met almost every week since the 1990–91 school year, that evening was the only time during those nearly two decades when Chancellor Claude Fletcher and CFO Don Shipley attended with a specific joint prayer request. Both men had felt led to come to the weekly intercessory prayer time together.

Claude was troubled about one delay after another hindering the close of the VCS land agreement with Venture Church. The issues seemed to linger interminably. Our intercessors prayed fervently for God to confirm His provision of the land with the release of obstructions. I remembered the scriptural promise, "The effective, fervent prayer of a righteous man avails much."[117]

As has occurred many times in the development of Valley Christian Schools (stories documented in *Quest for Excellence*), God miraculously answered in immediate fashion. What seemed so gloomy the day before our intercession turned to bright sky the very next day. Venture Church and VCS, with the help of intermediary friends and our legal counsel, resolved the seemingly insoluble issues within twenty-four hours of our prayer meeting.

It was difficult to believe, and I had to check and double-check the contract date and the signatures to verify the facts. It was true: We met for fervent prayer on Tuesday, and the contracts for purchase of the land were delivered for signature on Wednesday. Don immediately signed and dated the contract in his own handwriting, "8/5/09."[118]

I would call these two sovereign signs a one–two punch by our Lord to make a point: The conservatory is His great work. But again, a third punch was yet to follow.

CHAPTER 17

A GROUNDBREAKING
SEASON

THE THIRD SOVEREIGN SIGN leading us
toward the completion of the conservatory makes a trilogy. The number
three signifies completion, perfection, and unity in the Bible.

If you wonder whether all of this is a random occurrence or simply
timing controlled by Venture Church or Valley Christian Schools, pay
close attention to what happened next.

On Friday, October 2, 2009, VCS celebrated Homecoming Weekend
and the start of our "Golden Jubilee" fiftieth year with a dedication of
the site for the Conservatory of the Arts building. The event featured
musical performances and speeches as well as prayer for the land and
symbolic groundbreaking. We went ahead with this groundbreaking
in faith, believing the Lord would soon resolve all the remaining issues
surrounding the start of construction.

Then God orchestrated a third and final sign. The following
sequence of events could be controlled and arranged only by a sovereign God:

- ❖ The close of escrow on VCS's purchase of the church's land took place Thursday, October 15, 2009, after more than two months of complicated and seemingly unresolvable delays. The transfer of title recorded the next day, on Friday, October 16.

- ❖ On the next business day after the transfer of title recorded, the contract with South Bay Construction to build the conservatory providentially arrived in my office for signature on Monday, October 19, 2009. CFO Don Shipley and I signed the building contract that same day.

Once again I was awestruck by God's perfect timing regarding all three major events, as the one–two punch became a one–two–three punch. God had directed me not to sign the conservatory construction contract until the church land purchase was resolved. I felt I had obeyed God by not moving ahead with the construction contract until getting the church's commitment to settle the property purchase issue with acceptable terms. But God allowed the delay of the South Bay construction contract signing for four months and 18 days after I had agreed to sign. I am convinced He timed the arrival of the South Bay contract for my signature only one business day after transfer of title for the church land purchase in order to make a point: He is REALLY in complete control.

The trilogy of God's sovereignly timed events, presented on the table that follows, are summarized here:

1. Only one business day after I announced on Friday, May 29, 2009, that God led me not to sign the conservatory construction contract until VCS and Venture Church came to terms on purchase of the church

property, Pastor Chip Ingram visited the VCS offices on Monday, June 1, his first full day as Venture Church pastor, to express his desire to settle the land issue and resolve the multi-year impasse by selling their land under terms the school could afford.

2. Within twenty-four hours after Don Shipley and Claude Fletcher joined our prayer intercessor meeting on Tuesday, August 4, 2009, to pray for a resolution to seemingly unresolvable contract issues for VCS's purchase of the church property, the contract for the school's purchase of the land unexpectedly arrived for signature on Wednesday, August 5.

3. Within one business day after the purchase of the church property was recorded by the title company on Friday, October 16, 2009, the South Bay Construction contract arrived at my office for signing on Monday, October 19, 2009—after a contract delay of four months and eighteen days.

"AND WE KNOW THAT GOD CAUSES ALL THINGS TO WORK TOGETHER FOR GOOD TO THOSE WHO LOVE GOD, TO THOSE WHO ARE CALLED ACCORDING TO HIS PURPOSE." —ROMANS 8:28, NASB

"THE MIND OF MAN PLANS HIS WAY, BUT THE LORD DIRECTS HIS STEPS." —PROVERBS 16:9, NASB

	EVENT	DATE	NOTES
1	I shared my decision with Don Shipley to hold off on signing the South Bay construction contract until VCS and Venture Church came to terms on the purchase of the church land.	Friday, May 29, 2009	God led me not to sign the construction contract until VCS and Venture Church resolved the land purchase issues.
	On his first full day as pastor at Venture Church, Pastor Chip Ingram came by the VCS offices unannounced to resolve the impasse regarding the school's purchase of the church land.	Monday, June 1, 2009	The next business day, Pastor Ingram came by announcing his desire to settle the land issue as one of his important priorities.
2	Don Shipley and Claude Fletcher joined the prayer intercessors for fervent prayer about the "interminable issues" related to closing the deal to purchase the church property.	Tuesday, August 4, 2009	Claude was troubled about multiple delays hindering close of the land agreement due to escrow difficulties out of our control.
	The contract for purchase of Venture Church land for $3.5 million was unexpectedly delivered for signature. Don Shipley immediately signed and dated the purchase contract in his own handwriting, "8/5/09."	Wednesday, August 5, 2009	We met on Tuesday for fervent prayer for a resolution to the property purchase impasse, and within twenty-four hours God answered prayer. What had seemed a bleak situation before prayer was miraculously resolved the following day.
3	Escrow closed on VCS's purchase of Venture Church land. Transfer of title for VCS's purchase of the church land was recorded by the title company.	Thursday, October 15, 2009 Friday, October 16, 2009	Two months of seemingly catastrophic delays in escrow closing had ensued after signing the land purchase agreement.
	The South Bay construction contract to build the conservatory unexpectedly arrived at my office for signature. I signed it the same day.	Monday, October 19, 2009	The construction contract arrived one business day after purchase of the church property was recorded by the title company. I signed the construction contract four months and eighteen days after I had agreed to sign, due to unavoidable delays.

Perhaps some might suspect we timed the agreements for the land purchase and the construction contract—especially in light of how I had determined not to sign the construction contract until we could purchase the land.

But in fact, we were very much *not* in control of the events or the timing. Even if someone wanted to dictate all the timing in these matters, there were simply too many uncontrollable variables to manage, with multiple attorneys, banks, and boards all vying for the best outcome from their point of view. Difficult and frustrating negotiations had dragged on for years. Even after Pastor Chip Ingram took the initiative to visit the school on his first day as pastor of Venture Church, problems persisted. In the end, the neat and tidy sequence of events spoke strongly of God's perfect timing. It was awe-inspiring to realize how closely God paid attention and controlled every detail—especially when we felt so frustrated and obstructed with what seemed to be unmanageable circumstances.

ANOTHER ROADBLOCK

Full speed ahead! I was ready to shout. But another roadblock still stood in our way. This obstruction arose from the City of San Jose.

Gerry DeYoung, our project planning consultant, has worked with VCS since 1987 and managed all of the school's engineering and city planning issues. Many of us believe he and his firm, Ruth and Going, are the best consultants in all of Silicon Valley for moving projects forward. Gerry is not easily frustrated. But in spite of his best efforts, for over a year we had had no success toward getting city approvals for the conservatory building permits. Problems cropped up associated with the original 1998 rezoning allowing only 1,300 students on the Skyway campus. If the city insisted on requiring a complete rezoning, the process could take two years or longer.

The clock was ticking. We had signed the $20 million loan documents on June 30, 2009, after getting Pastor Ingram's commitment to work out the purchase of the church's land. Our forward swap and interest payments of over $1 million per year would present a huge hardship without the added capacity of the conservatory building to increase student enrollment and revenue. Even worse, selling the

$20 million forward swap would result in a loss of principal in the multiple millions of dollars.

On Tuesday, November 3, 2009, our prayer intercessors took this problem to the Lord and seriously prayed for a resolution in heavenly places. Within a week, a breakthrough came.

The next Monday, on November 9, I wrote in my Bible at 8:02 p.m. on page 900: *"Met with Board Building Committee and Gerry DeYoung—We had seeming consternation and obstruction for over a year trying to get building permits [for the Conservatory of the Arts building]. Last Tuesday, 11-3-09, our intercessors prayed that God would send His heavenly host to push back dark forces of the 'author of confusion' and give Gerry new and fresh ideas on how to proceed. Gerry announced today that after getting legal counsel, the city agreed with Gerry's new idea on how to get permits on the previously approved 1998 rezoning. We expect permits in 3–4 months and construction to begin September 1, 2010. PTL!"*[119]

These are the two key verses God used in our prayers:

"'For My hand made all these things, thus all these things came into being,' declares the LORD. 'But to this one I will look, to him who is humble and contrite of spirit, and who trembles at My word.'"[120]

"For we do not wrestle against flesh and blood, but against principalities, against powers, against the rulers of the darkness of this age, against spiritual hosts of wickedness in the heavenly places."[121]

Again, God turned the tide in miraculous ways to move an otherwise seemingly irresolvable obstruction. The process took some time to work out, however. On April 12, 2010, Gerry DeYoung explained to the VCS board how Joe Horwedel, planning director for the City of San Jose, had determined the solution adopted in November 2009 would not work. But Joe then suggested another idea for a resolution and said he would work with us toward city council approval of our building permits at the June 15, 2010, council meeting.

As a sign of answered prayer, God had opened the door to a solution to break the gridlock in November 2009. The November "solution" became the stepping stone for the final answer worked out in April 2010 with Joe Horwedel's help, opening the floodwaters of God's provision.

CONSERVATORY CONSTRUCTION BEGINS!

On Tuesday, June 15, 2010, at 9:35 p.m.—after years of dreaming, praying, and planning, including repeated traffic and other environmental studies costing about $500,000—we rejoiced as the San Jose City Council approved permits to build Valley Christian Schools' proposed 55,000-square-foot Conservatory of the Arts and Student Life Center. The building would fill the space between the Education/Theater Building and the edge of the football stadium. South Bay Construction moved onto the campus and set up their trailers and fences as they prepared to break ground. Then on Monday, July 12, 2010, the city issued grading permits to launch construction of the conservatory.

July 14, 2010: VCS board members, senior management team, and prayer intercessors praying to thank God for the start of conservatory construction

On Wednesday, July 14, 2010, members of the Valley Christian Schools board, prayer intercessor team, and senior management team met to pray and thank God for the successful launch of the project.

During this long and often difficult journey, the VCS board of directors often paused during meetings to pray for God's direction. The change in economic climate had challenged the board and the executive team during its careful deliberation as to God's will and timing regarding this project. As with all of Valley Christian Schools' construction projects, Chancellor Claude Fletcher and Gerry DeYoung of Ruth and Going successfully championed the entire city planning and city council approval process.

Praying at the conservatory construction site

Don Shipley, our CFO, repeatedly offered detailed financial projections, giving the VCS board a prudent balance of faith and reason during their analysis and discussion. We thank God for His leading, for our amazing board and executive team, and for the prayerful support of VCS's intercessory prayer team, led by Sheri Vavken.

Troy Gunter, Director of the Conservatory of the Arts,
and Dr. Clifford Daugherty, VCS President

We had another reason to rejoice: Although average enrollment for the 2009–2010 school year still lagged a bit below our budget target, in January 2010 we had reached 2,280 students enrolled—enough of a rebound for us to reimburse almost all of that year's staff salary reductions by June.

Mike Schmidt, Prayer Intercessor; Claude Fletcher, VCS Chancellor;
Michael Sprauve, VCS Board Member; Kathy Hughes, Administrative Support;
Jihan Burridge, Library/Prayer Intercessor; Dan Burford, VCS Board Member;
Mark Skovmand, Prayer Intercessor; Werner Vavken, Prayer Intercessor, Faculty/Staff
Chaplain, VP AMSE; Don Shipley, CFO; Troy Gunter, Conservatory Director;
Vera Shantz, VCS Board Chair; Dr. Clifford Daugherty, VCS President

New Beginnings

As we prayed to thank God for the launch of construction, I recalled the "night visitation" on my birthday in 2008, the day after we met with the bankers about the potential forward swap, when God woke me up at 3 a.m. speaking to me through verses from Isaiah and Jeremiah. As mentioned when I told the story in Chapter 13, in the Bible the numeral 8 signifies new beginnings, because the Bible counts seven years as one "Sabbath" of years. Not only did the Bank of America's offer to fund our $20 million loan occur in the year two thousand *eight,* but 2008 was also the eighth year VCS had occupied the Skyway campus. Providentially, in 2008 Gabe Guven accepted the position of principal of the VCS elementary campus, and Shirley Hitchcock stepped into the role of directing K–12 accreditation and curriculum.

As I pondered, another curious timing occurred to me. There were exactly seven sets of seven years (or seven Sabbaths of years) from the opening of Valley Christian Schools in the fall of 1960 until the end of the 2008–09 fiscal year (June 30, 2009). Our Bank of America swap contract originally stipulated the $20 million loan was to be funded by March 1, 2009. Due to unavoidable delays, however, the bank extended the one-year swap and rescheduled the actual contract signing and loan funding for June 30, 2009—exactly the last day of the last fiscal year of the school's forty-nine completed years, making a perfect set of seven seven-year periods.

Is this just another coincidence? In the Old Testament, the fiftieth year marked the "Year of Jubilee," intended by God as a year of emancipation for slaves. The construction of the Conservatory of the Arts and Student Life Center began in June/July 2010, during VCS's fiftieth anniversary celebration, at the completion of the "Year of Jubilee." The fiftieth year was the year "after" the seven Sabbaths of years and the beginning of the eighth set of seven years. Again, the number 8 in the Bible symbolizes "new beginnings."

The following chart illustrates VCS's Year of Jubilee:

> "You are also to count off seven sabbaths of years for yourself, seven times seven years, so that you have the time of the seven sabbaths of years, namely, forty-nine years. You shall then . . . sound a horn all through your land. You shall thus consecrate the fiftieth year and proclaim a release through the land to all its inhabitants. It shall be a jubilee for you, and each of you shall return to his own property, and each of you shall return to his family." (Leviticus 25:8–10, NASB)

SCHOOL YEAR	YR #	SCHOOL YEAR	YR #	SCHOOL YEAR	YR #	SCHOOL YEAR	YR #
1960–1961	1	1967–1968	8	1974–1975	15	1981–1982	22
1961–1962	2	1968–1969	9	1975–1976	16	1982–1983	23
1962–1963	3	1969–1970	10	1976–1977	17	1983–1984	24
1963–1964	4	1970–1971	11	1977–1978	18	1984–1985	25
1964–1965	5	1971–1972	12	1978–1979	19	1985–1986	26
1965–1966	6	1972–1973	13	1979–1980	20	1986–1987	27
1966–1967	7	1973–1974	14	1980–1981	21	1987–1988	28
1988–1989	29	1995–1996	36	2002–2003	43	2009–2010	50
1989–1990	30	1996–1997	37	2003–2004	44	Year of Jubilee	
1990–1991	31	1997–1998	38	2004–2005	45		
1991–1992	32	1998–1999	39	2005–2006	46		
1992–1993	33	1999–2000	40	2006–2007	47		
1993–1994	34	2000–2001	41	2007–2008	48		
1994–1995	35	2001–2002	42	2008–2009	49	7th Sabbath of Years	

Construction began on the Conservatory of the Arts in June/July 2010, at the completion of the Year of Jubilee, fifty years since the founding of Valley Christian Schools.

One more thing: At the beginning of the 2006–07 school year, during my annual VCS keynote address, I had issued the challenge to our VCS community to raise funds for construction of Grace Public School in New Delhi on the land we had helped purchase. I shared the goal to complete the Indian school within the next four years, to coincide with the VCS Fifty-Year Golden Jubilee Anniversary by 2010. Building a school for the poor seemed like an appropriate way to dovetail with the command of the ancient jubilee to "proclaim liberty"[122] to captives and also symbolically repay the generous donors who had enabled us to build the VCS campus. Providentially, that same fall of 2006 VCS launched the conservatory program. Then by the end of our Jubilee Year, just as we accomplished our goal of building the school in New Delhi, God gave a bonus: Our own construction of the conservatory building began. Since music and the arts open the human soul, I even saw a parallel between the jubilee theme and the conservatory's mission of training young artists to bring God's message of freedom to spiritual captives.

Only God could orchestrate timing like this. What a confirmation of His hand of blessing on this endeavor! And we would witness another curious potential "message" from on high as framework for the new conservatory building rose.

CHAPTER 18

THE MYSTERIOUS LIGHT

WITH CONSTRUCTION finally underway, it seemed as if grading and foundation work would never end. As the project moved forward, I would occasionally take pictures to document the progress.

The first steel beams being lowered and attached to the
foundation of the conservatory building

On December 6, 2010, I was headed for lunch at 12:15 p.m. when a huge crane caught my attention. The crane's long arm was lowering a dangling steel beam toward the foundation. I ran to get my Nikon with the telephoto lens to take the shot. The beam danced in the sunlight as it found its way toward a waiting steelworker below. As my camera clicked, the steelworker with a bright red hardhat leaned toward the base of the beam to screw down the foundation bolts.

In no time a second beam was dancing in the air. Here was history in the making for Valley Christian Schools. The dream of a Conservatory of the Arts was coming into reality before my eyes.

Within seven minutes, the second beam found a new home to help support the wall for future generations of eager-to-learn conservatory students. Each day steelworkers arranged beams to form the shape and dimensions of the growing Conservatory of the Arts. Dedicated ironworkers assembled the building against the blue sky, and the distant rolling hills served as a canvas for construction of their work of art.

The giant crane

Angels from on High?

By Thursday, December 16, the backside of the building had taken shape. Workers had not yet begun construction of the Student Life Center portion of the building, where translucent aspiring canopies would eventually shelter beautiful transparent forty-foot-high panes of glass from floor to ceiling.

Around 3 p.m. that Thursday (the tenth day of erecting steel), I watched a brave helmeted welder climb to the top corner of towering steel nearest the Education Building to erect an American flag and a small Christmas tree, complete with electrical lights.

Erecting a flag and Christmas tree

Kenny Palmer served as foreman for the conservatory construction project. On Sunday evening, December 19, Kenny was working late—no doubt in preparation for the next day's work.

At 8:14 p.m., he took a photo of the building with his Olympus digital camera. When he printed the picture later that night, he was stunned. A bright round light, like a large star, appeared perfectly positioned on top of the evergreen tree.

The next day, on Monday, I visited the site to view progress. Almost immediately Kenny described what happened and showed me the picture with the mysterious image, which he had printed out on a black-and-white printer in his construction trailer. He showed it to his boss, Larry Patterson, and to several of his colleagues and friends, then to our VCS board building committee at the next meeting. I asked for a copy of the digital image file.

Later, as I was preparing to write this story, I remembered I still had Larry Patterson's cell number. I gave him a call to ask about the light. "Larry? Did anyone figure out a natural explanation for what caused the bright light to appear on the top of the Christmas tree and the flag?"

"We never did figure out what happened," he replied. "Kenny said he didn't see anything when he took the picture, but the light appeared when he printed it."

"I think it might have been an angelic message from God telling everyone He is really pleased and giving His blessings on the project and the conservatory."

Larry responded without hesitation. "I think just about everyone thought the same thing."

The mysterious light

Construction continued with very few hitches as we entered 2011, and the work proceeded swiftly throughout the spring and summer. Every day it seemed something new and interesting was happening in the building process, and we surged with excitement to see the Lord's plans becoming a reality. By August as we prepared for the 2011–12 school year, anticipation reached a fever-high pitch. I think all of us—parents, students, board, faculty, and administrative leadership—felt like Christmas 2011 was coming early to VCS!

CELEBRATING GOD'S CREATIVE WORKS

We set the conservatory's dedication and ribbon-cutting ceremony for Friday, September 30, 2011, our Homecoming Weekend. With the four-story building complete, the finished second and third floors comprised Phase 1 of the Conservatory of the Arts and Student Life Center. (NTS Construction, headed by 1988 VCS alumnus Brian Brager, built out the first floor—a lower level on the hill slope—over the coming year in time for fall 2012, and the fourth-floor interior by the fall of 2013, at a huge savings to VCS of $1.7 million.) The evening ceremony piggybacked on the theme chosen for the 2011–12 school year: "Building Lives to Reflect and Continue God's Creative Works."

After an overture by the Valley Christian Symphony Orchestra, opening remarks, and the invocation, Vera Shantz, VCS's board chair, rose to address the audience. "It is awe-inspiring to reflect on Valley Christian's Quest for Excellence and see how far we have come," she said. "Thanks be to God alone for His abundant blessings, grace, and provisions which have made all this possible. Up until January 2000, Valley Christian Schools did not have a permanent home and was leasing all its facilities. However, over the last ten years, thanks to God's provision through the generosity of donors and the support and funding of Bank of America, VCS has built and now owns over 321,000 square feet of state of the art facilities valued at well over $100 million."

Vera's words took me back to the days when VCS struggled seemingly from one crisis to another, yet saw God's miracles all along the way.

"Today Valley Christian Schools is considered to be one of the top private Christian college preparatory schools in the nation," she continued. "Valley Christian graduates are exceptionally well prepared to enter higher education and, even more, to become Christian professionals of influence to bring renewed credibility to the cause of Christ in the marketplace of ideas and help shape the spiritual and moral values of society through their personal Quests for Excellence. We hope and pray many generations of students will come through the conservatory to learn about the arts and that their love for the arts will grow. But most importantly, we pray their love for God will grow and flourish so they will go out into their communities and the world as leaders boldly reclaiming and transforming the arts with God's truth."

After a vocal performance, I stepped to the microphone. "As we look around this campus we can easily see how amazing things happen when determined people are united and motivated by the power of the Holy Spirit. Seemingly impossible things are accomplished when we allow our Creator to do His great works through His people. God is gracious to work through His people who are committed to give Him all glory and honor instead of seeking any credit for themselves."

I picked up on the school year's theme and told the audience my conviction about the key to our success. "The Quest for Excellence at Valley Christian Schools is so successful because we are determined to credit our Creator for all of His creative works. Our theme 'Building Lives to Reflect and Continue God's Creative Works'—through us and our students—helps emphasize this critical truth. We look forward to the many ways our conservatory students will bring goodness, peace, and joy and the light of Jesus to transform the dark places of our world."

Following another musical presentation, Robert Rubino, a member of the VCS board of directors, gave some history about our conservatory journey from vision to fulfillment. "Recognizing the importance of the arts to the individual, community, and society as a whole, we were determined to offer the best training possible with a mindset focused on our ultimate Creator and Lord God above, who has blessed each individual with the gifts they possess. You see, with the Quest for Excellence we understand excellence is found in the nature, character, and works of God. Whatever we do, we 'do it heartily as unto the Lord.' For we know it is by His grace each person is blessed with the abilities and talents they have, and God, in His infinite wisdom, has an unbelievable purpose for each individual, utilizing those talents they possess. Therefore, the purpose of this conservatory is to create leaders in the arts who will have a lasting influence to impact our schools, our community, and the nations in support of the Great Commission."

Later in the program, Troy Gunter, the vice president, director, and founder of the conservatory, spoke and revealed exciting news. "I am happy to share with you the conservatory's most recent joy and achievement: Our marching band has been accepted to perform with a high school from Beijing in Pasadena's Tournament of Roses January 2013! We will be traveling to Beijing to rehearse with the students this spring, and we will host them before our joint performance the following winter. We are seeing firsthand the boundary-defying power of the arts as we unite with other students across geographical, cultural, and linguistic barriers."

Troy's remarks turned philosophical. "It is evident, not only through these recent achievements but even in our own personal experiences, the arts are undeniably a powerful force. We all have experienced moments when the arts have deeply moved us. We find ourselves open, even vulnerable, in ways contrary to what society often dictates. It is God who has given us this wonderful gift of art, enabling us to connect with ourselves, our fellow man, and our Creator in a truly supernatural way. Plato was on to something some twenty-five hundred years ago when he proclaimed, 'Music is a more potent instrument than any other for education, because rhythm and harmony find their way into the inward places of the soul.'"

I got excited as I listened to his expansive vision for the wide potential influence of the conservatory and its students.

"Here at Valley Christian Schools," Troy said, "I believe we are charged with the task of developing Christian artists capable of using their gifts and talents to positively impact this world for the cause of Christ and to the glory of God. This goes much further than preparing artists for church ministry. We need Christian artists seated in our orchestras, acting on Broadway, composing film scores in L.A., singing and dancing on stages throughout the world. Moreover, our charge goes beyond creating professional artists. We need Christian scientists, athletes, ministers, doctors and nurses, engineers, teachers, and even politicians who possess a profound understanding and appreciation of the arts. That is what we are about at Valley Christian Schools, and it's what this building is about."

DREAM BIG

Wow! My heart soared through the final orchestral piece and benediction. The ribbon-cutting ceremony with our VCS founder, David Wallace, and other VCS leaders could not have done more to put icing on the cake.

Big dreams do come true. The dream to march in the prestigious Tournament of Roses Parade, as Troy Gunter announced during the conservatory dedication, was birthed way back in 1993, shortly after the inception of the VCS Quest for Excellence. Troy and I dared to imagine what seemed totally out of reach. It took twenty years of hard work and planning, but our big dream became reality. Valley Christian

Schools invited the band from Beijing Public School No. 57 to co-submit an application to march in the Rose Parade®, and we were accepted. The joint bands from Valley Christian High School and Beijing, China, marched together down the streets of Pasadena, California, on New Year's Day 2013 as the "East-West Fusion Band." We give thanks to God for all the talented efforts of our faculty and student musicians who dared to dream big with us.

Valley Christian High School band marching in the Tournament of Roses Parade
January 1, 2013, with the band from Beijing Public School No. 57, China

For the past seven chapters, I have led you on a journey through the process of how the Conservatory of the Arts and Student Life Center went from a mere dream to a shining reality. It's easy to say "the Lord made all this come about" while silently thinking we actually had more to do with the process than we care to admit. In the case of the conservatory, however, that is just not the case for me. I am fully convinced the series of dozens—if not hundreds—of key events leading to the building's completion could not have happened by chance or mere human effort and talent. The earthly odds of all the critical elements falling into place on their own are stacked against it! I am not a gambling man, but I imagine a person has better odds of picking the winner of the Super Bowl for the next twenty years than successfully planning how the conservatory events unfolded as they did.

The Conservatory of the Arts and Student Life Center serves as an example of how God works through the hands of talented and dedicated people to extend His goodness in our community and to the world. The building is more beautiful and much more amazing than I could have imagined. As of the 2014–15 school year, VCHS has more than 450 conservatory students with majors or minors enrolled. Thousands of gifted students are passing through this building to develop their talents and to commit their lives to bringing "goodness, peace, and joy" to those who need it. In doing so, they are serving as the hands of our Creator Himself.

And let us remember, lest we fail to acknowledge God as the provider of "every good and perfect gift,"[123] it is "not by might nor by power, but by My Spirit," says our Lord.[124]

No. There is no doubt: God has a passion for souls, and He brought about the conservatory to glorify Himself and equip artists to "go and make disciples of all the nations."[125]

We have another journey ahead of us—an unlikely one. Follow me on a road the Lord brought me down to learn a critical lesson: No school is too small. There is no school He can't use to do big things for His kingdom.

CHAPTER 19

SMALL BEGINNINGS

"Do not despise these small beginnings, for the
LORD rejoices to see the work begin."[126]

DURING THE LATTER PART of 2006, a letter
from Marilyn George, Associate Executive Director of the Western
Association of Schools and Colleges, arrived and received my immediate
attention. Valley Christian Schools had recently successfully completed
a midterm report as part of its six-year accreditation cycle. Three years
earlier, VCS had received the highest level of dual-accreditation from
the Western Association of Schools and Colleges (WASC) and the
Association of Christian Schools International (ACSI).

Marilyn George asked if I would serve as the chair of a school
accreditation visiting committee. As a beneficiary of accreditation
teams serving Valley Christian, I knew I had a duty to serve other
schools and had committed to serving on an accreditation team every
other year, but until then they had all been dual ACSI/WASC teams.
This was the first time WASC, a completely secular organization, had
asked me to chair one of its teams. *Quite an honor,* I thought, while

simultaneously wondering how I might fit another responsibility into my calendar.

I read more of the letter. *Great, it's a K–12 Christian school.* With relatively few such schools, I relished the opportunity to serve a comprehensive Christian school.

My gratification quickly eroded, however, as I read further: "Faith Christian Academy (FCA) in Coalinga. . . ." *The school is in Coalinga?* Coalinga is a small community a couple of hours south of San Jose. I continued reading. The school's total population was 149 students, including twenty in the preschool. *So much for being a comprehensive K–12 school!*

My conscience nudged me with the thought that my attitude might be a bit prideful or superior. But I am truly passionate about the Quest for Excellence in light of the generally poor quality of many Christian high schools. In my experience and awareness, small communities could often achieve a quality Christian educational experience for elementary school students, but with so many diverse programs needed for a quality high school, success at that level proved difficult and unlikely in a small community.

Years earlier I was asked to chair a visitation committee for a larger K–12 Christian school. After my first visit, the entire accreditation process was postponed because of so many educational and administrative problems at the school. I feared a repeat in Coalinga, and suspected a much smaller school would find it even more difficult—if not impossible—to develop a quality Christian high school. I dreaded becoming the bearer of bad news, disturbed by the thought of the embarrassment the FCA leadership might experience if it failed to meet accreditation standards. I suspected the school's limited resources, coupled with the small size of the community, would forever restrict the high school from achieving true quality—like a five-foot-tall man dreaming of playing forward in the NBA.

My executive assistant, Pam Watson, and I discussed the WASC request. Declining the invitation to serve as chair was unwise, we both agreed. So I accepted the role.

My first duty was to contact the school's administrator. Pam gathered information on Faith Christian Academy in preparation for my visit. As the recipient of calls from an accreditation chair every six years for VCS's own accreditation visit, I was acutely aware of the nervous anticipation the head of a school feels when receiving the first call from the chair of an accreditation visiting team. Even though VCS has always received a full six-year accreditation, I knew how the personality and disposition of the committee chair could make the visit positive and productive—or possibly just miserable. Horror stories abound about terribly led teams producing all manner of grief for schools seeking accreditation.

"School Size Matters"—True?

I determined to remain positive, helpful, and hopeful as I made my first telephone call to Mrs. Tara Davis, principal and founder of FCA. After my introduction as the chair of the school's accreditation team, we confirmed upcoming team visit dates for Sunday through Wednesday, February 25–28, 2007. We also arranged for my one-day pre-visit. Another challenge emerged from the conversation: FCA was not accredited, so this would be the school's first accreditation team visit.

Learning the vocabulary and process of accreditation can be exciting and at times scary. Tara Davis proved to be a creative, kind, enthusiastic, intelligent, hardworking, and determined leader. She confidently declared FCA a "great little school," but was willing to receive any insights she could gather in preparing for the accreditation visit. She loved the children and their families as her own, and it soon became obvious the community generously returned her affections and loyalty.

I hoped for Faith Christian Academy's successful accreditation, but the school community would be ultimately responsible for the outcome of the process. My doubts about the ability of a small school to provide a quality education for high school students unavoidably colored my perspective.

As part of the accreditation process, in June 2006 FCA had begun formally developing its Self-Study with the inclusion of representatives of the entire FCA community. After several revisions, FCA faculty, staff, parents, and students contributed to completion of their Self-Study Visiting Committee Report, portraying a vibrant and ambitious five-year plan for advancing the school.

As it happened, I had recently finished writing my book *Quest for Excellence,* which would hit print around the end of summer. At VCS, our determined steps were underway to launch the Quest Institute, with a mission, in part, to help struggling Christian high schools become large, comprehensive schools of excellence. At the time, I believed size was one criterion for comprehensive excellence in high schools. It seemed obvious to me that without an adequate number of subject-matter experts to offer a full range of vigorous college preparatory courses, a small high school would be handicapped in preparing students for college admissions. I couldn't imagine how a small school could offer all the excellent advantages of a larger one.

No doubt, my view raised conflicted emotions and serious questions as to the potential quality of such a small school in a small community with limited growth potential. An enrollment of even 100 students in high school would mean severe limitations for educational quality; I personally believed a quality, comprehensive high school required a minimum of 400 students. And regrettably, it appeared unlikely Faith Christian Academy could achieve a goal of 100 students in the foreseeable future given the community's modest population.

That same summer, as I began writing sections of *The Quest Continues,* one of my three big, central questions emerged: Is VCS's Quest for Excellence a model all schools can emulate? Is such success repeatable anywhere? Obviously, if being in the right place at the right time was VCS's great advantage, the answer is no. If, however, VCS was built and sustained by God through principles involving the Quest for Excellence, the VCS model for development might be repeatable in any school community—as long as there were enough people to populate a comprehensive high school. Sadly, I thought, *Coalinga just doesn't have enough people.*

GETTING ACQUAINTED

As I prepared for the visit to Faith Christian Academy, I desperately wanted to believe the Quest for Excellence was possible in any Christian school. I vaguely recalled a Coalinga road sign near Harris Ranch on Interstate 5, seemingly miles from nowhere. A little checking revealed Coalinga's location: ten miles west of Interstate 5, halfway between Los Angeles and San Francisco, and sixty miles southwest of Fresno, the closest sizable city.

The sky was still dark when I backed our gray Honda Odyssey out of our long driveway on the first day of the visit, February 25, 2007. By the time I hit Highway 5, the challenges of trying to help a very small high school achieve quality education troubled me afresh. Subconsciously I prayed, *How did I get into this, Lord?*

"Despise not the day of small beginnings" (a paraphrase of Zechariah 4:10) popped into my mind, and it struck my heart with unexplained emotion. A bit perplexed, I asked, "Is that You, Lord?" I filed the phrase into my mental notes, with the idea I should keep an open ear to what the Lord might be trying to say.

During one of my five trips to Coalinga, I stopped to take some pictures. The welcome sign seemed bigger than the town! I took a few pictures of the sign, but it looked lonely—so I waited for an approaching vehicle and then snapped a shot of the sign with the car in the background for effect.

Coalinga claimed 11,668 residents at the 2000 census; its green "Welcome to Coalinga" sign announced a population of 16,423. A recent population growth spurt resulted from the newly opened Pleasant Valley State Prison and Coalinga State Hospital, housing several thousand sexually violent predators. The prison's inmates were added to the city's population.

Our visiting team included Katie Nelson, from Capital Christian School in Sacramento, Carolyn Reed of Lafayette, California, and me. FCA Principal Tara Davis greeted us when our team arrived on Sunday, February 25, and our visit began with the usual facilities tour. Mrs. Davis directed the team first to her office, decorated with lots of wall-mounted pictures, news stories, and commendations telling the heartwarming story of Faith Christian Academy.

During the K–12 tour, Tara shared FCA's history and enthusiastically told her vision for new high school facilities. Faith Christian Academy began in 1994 as a kindergarten class with Sandra Chagoya and Tara Davis teaching their own children. Other families asked to enroll, and during that first year of kindergarten, the Lord led those parents to establish a private school where all parents could send their children to receive a godly education.

Mrs. Tara Davis, principal and founder of Faith Christian Academy

"We're located in Pleasant Valley, the heart of California's Coast Range Mountains," Tara said, as we strolled through the campus. "The city's population has recently grown and is approaching 17,000, including the new residents and employees of Pleasant Valley State Prison; the Claremont Custody Center, a minimum-security institution; and a state mental hospital, which opened in September 2005."

Coalinga's labor force, we learned, consisted of the oil industry (20 percent), agriculture (20 percent), state prison/mental health employees (30 percent), education (10 percent), and various service industries (20 percent). The prisons in the community aided Coalinga's economic recovery after a destructive earthquake in 1983 and the decline in the local oil industry.

The FCA Self-Study Visiting Committee Report had told us that although students left for various reasons, including financial issues and moving, the student population had steadily increased to reach an enrollment of 149, with about twenty preschool students and a high school program of eighteen students in March 2006.

For students above or below grade level, Faith Christian Academy made academic accommodations and learning modifications as needed. FCA aimed for all students to achieve at or above grade level. The school enrolled new students throughout the school year, including many students significantly below grade level. "Our faculty successfully helps improve their achievement so most of the newly enrolled, below-grade-level students can improve up to grade level or higher," Tara said.

CRITICAL MASS?

One high school program feature caught my attention. It was described in the school's Self-Study.

> One of the most important relationships FCA continues to foster is with the local community college. The West Hills Community College District has a campus in Coalinga. It provides counseling support to FCA students desiring to enhance their educational experience by taking college classes, for college credit, while earning credit concurrently at FCA. Students may take classes through West Hills College free of charge (up to 11 units) and students may take classes at the campus or online. This partnership with the community college has provided an expanded opportunity for students to achieve their educational goals. Seventy percent of Faith Christian High School students are concurrently enrolled in classes at West Hills College. Additionally, 100 percent of the high school students are enrolled in courses required for admission to the University of California or California State University system. (*Faith Christian Academy Self-Study*, p. 16)

Ironically, I had worked for years for VCHS to negotiate a concurrent credit arrangement with various colleges, but had had only marginal success. Valley Christian High School, with well over 1,100 students at that time, offered more than twenty Advanced Placement courses but only a couple of dual credit course opportunities. It had not entered my mind that a school with only eighteen high school students might offer a program opportunity not available at VCHS.

Still, my built-in bias colored my thinking as I pondered one of the questions I had asked God: Can I confidently tell everyone in any community that God is willing do for their schools the same kind of miraculous works He has done for VCS through the Quest for Excellence? Is such success repeatable anywhere?

If being located in a large community is a necessity for excellence, then VCS is not a Quest for Excellence model all schools can emulate. The answer to the "anywhere" question appeared to be a sad "no." A small, quality high school, I concluded, is an oxymoron.

To my dismay, the Quest for Excellence model seemed viable only in communities with enough people to build an excellent, comprehensive high school. I continued to associate the Quest for Excellence with high schools of at least 400 students—the minimum number I believed necessary to achieve critical mass and comprehensive quality programs.

In my own notes, I personally concluded: The concurrent high school and community college credit program at FCA is amazing, but the implementation wouldn't work for many more mature high schools in larger communities. FCA's students are taught off campus or online by college instructors, and West Hills Community College is nearby in their small town. Such a program is not scalable for schools like Valley Christian High School, I reasoned. Having students leave campus for junior college courses simply wouldn't meet the expectations of VCHS's students and parents. And parents paying thousands of dollars in tuition each year for their students would not perceive an online course with a distant professor as a good value proposition. At VCS, parents and students want a personal relationship with a really amazing teacher who serves as a role model and guide.

A Sense of Jeopardy

At the conclusion of the visit, our WASC accreditation committee was pleased to validate Faith Christian Academy's mission, programs, expected learning results, and Action Plan to improve the high school facilities and program offerings. The committee recommended a six-year accreditation term, with a midterm return visit to verify progress on the Action Plan.

The FCA teachers were lovingly instructing their students and the students were happily learning. But by the conclusion of our visit, the magnitude of FCA's self-imposed first of seven school-wide three-year Action Plan initiatives appeared more daunting than ever.

The first Action Plan initiative aimed to develop a new high school and an athletic complex on their recently acquired 16.8 acres. The complex would include a gymnasium, baseball field, tennis courts, football field, classrooms, offices, restrooms facilities, and a snack bar. Before our visit, I had counseled Tara Davis to set high but reasonable goals in their Action Plan and ensure they were sufficiently on track by the school's midterm visit in the spring of 2010. If the accreditation committee's three-year midterm report indicated achievement of the Action Plan was unlikely by the end of a six-year accreditation term, the school's WASC accreditation would be in jeopardy.

The faith of Tara Davis seemed far greater than could be justified by the school's total high school enrollment of fewer than twenty high school students. Given her enthusiasm, I was not about to show any signs of disbelief. The visiting team's role must absolutely avoid being prescriptive. But I secretly worried about the midterm visit, and what the midterm visiting team would be required to report about whether the school's Action Plan initiatives could be accomplished by year six of the accreditation term.

My own experience with school construction told me even a large, well-funded school would have difficulty achieving such monumental construction goals within a six-year horizon. The three-year midterm visit's requirement of significant progress made matters even more challenging.

Honestly, as chair of the visiting committee, I immediately began to dread the midterm visit I was expected to make in 2010. The school's success in meeting its school-wide Action Plan would determine whether Faith Christian Academy kept its accreditation—and success looked dicey at best.

CHAPTER 20

THE DREADED VISIT

IN SEPTEMBER 2009, I responded to an email request from Principal Tara Davis for guidance and clarification on how she should proceed with Faith Christian Academy's midterm report as part of the six-year accreditation term. In my response, I told her I was looking forward to returning to FCA to see her and her team and their wonderful school. I clarified the purpose of the midterm visit: to review FCA's progress in implementing their school-wide Action Plan, as laid out in Tara's "Focus on Learning" report presented to our visiting WASC team in March 2007 after our first visit. After reviewing the seven school-wide Action Plan initiatives, I described the process FCA could follow to respond to each one, and encouraged her to contact me if she had any questions.

Soon her reply popped up in my email in-box. She thanked me for the additional details, but also requested to push back my next visit so she could have adequate time to prepare her midterm report. "I look forward to seeing you again," she said. "We have made a lot of changes since you were here last, and I am excited for you to see them."

Though the tone of her email sounded hopeful and positive, it contained no indication of progress underway on new campus construction. When I reread FCA's Self-Study and Action Plan, their first of seven school-wide Action Plan initiatives still seemed extremely daunting, with its bold goal to build a new high school campus. The initiative stated FCA's intent "to develop an athletic complex to assist in promoting healthy individuals." It included a five-year timeline to complete three phases, including a parking lot, gymnasium, six class-rooms, and three multi-purpose rooms. The proposed buildings totaled more than 28,000 square feet with a multi-million-dollar price tag.

FACILITIES CONSTRUCTION TIMELINE

PHASE	TIMELINE	PROJECTS	COST
Phase I Land preparation Ball fields Parking lot	2 years	Water well Drainage and land engineering Sprinklers Parking lot with crushed rock Basketball and tennis courts	$ 75,000 $ 200,000 $ 20,000 $ 50,000 $ 200,000
Phase II Gymnasium	18 months	Gymnasium: 16,800 square feet	$ 1,200,000
Phase III Classrooms	18 months	6 Classrooms: 6,000 square feet 3 Multi-purpose rooms: 6,000 square feet	$ 450,000 $ 450,000

The remaining six Action Plan initiatives included more normal and feasible plans: improving student achievement, developing the spiritual life of the students through an added community service pro-gram, improving the college admissions success of students, increasing enrollment, improving teacher compensation to promote retention of qualified teachers, and completing the curriculum guideline binder to ensure all materials being taught align with California standards.

The two other members of the February 2007 accreditation visiting team were unable to return for the midterm visit, so WASC arranged for Shirley White from Center High School in Antelope,

California, to join me. When we received Faith Christian Academy's midterm report in advance of the one-day visit, I quickly reviewed the school's progress on the seven initiatives in the school-wide Action Plan. A telephone discussion with Tara Davis confirmed progress on acquiring the high school campus. The information was encouraging, but I was still cautiously skeptical. Building is one thing, but building a quality high school is another.

THE CAMPUS TOUR

Shirley White and I met Tara Davis at Faith Christian Academy on the morning of Thursday, March 11, 2010. The office staff warmly greeted us and gave us a leisurely tour of the campus, beginning at the preschool. Immediately, I sensed warmth and happiness among the students and faculty. Children played in an especially well-appointed and loving learning environment. Well-trained teachers engaged and connected with students in positive ways. The interaction was natural and unforced—evidence of an ongoing and meaningful relationship between teachers and students, which couldn't be staged for an accreditation visit.

Cheerful teachers and happy children at Faith Christian Academy

Tara Davis reminded me that I had given her a copy of my first book, *Quest for Excellence,* at the end of the February 2007 accreditation visit. "I read it eagerly," she told me. "I realized you at VCS have had many of the same struggles and challenges to overcome as we have. And we share similar values and goals—FCA also emphasizes excellence in our educational plan. Your book has helped us define teaching excellence in a small school setting, and it gave me confirmation that Faith Christian Academy is on the right track."

Her words greatly encouraged me. Shirley White and I learned that after the initial accreditation visit, FCA had purchased one of the finest buildings in town as the new home for Faith Christian High School. Improvements to the building were made through the summer of 2007, and the school opened that fall.

The Great Recession, however, hit Coalinga and FCA hard. Yet even in the face of such difficulty, the high school grew from eighteen students in March 2006 to thirty-four students in 2010.

The quick history lesson and elementary campus tour concluded. Mrs. Davis was then eager to drive us to the new high school campus a few blocks away. Halfway between North Coalinga Street and North Monterey Avenue, Faith Christian High School came into view, located on the north side of Monroe Street directly across from beautiful Keck Park.

Faith Christian High School, Coalinga, California

After a tour of the campus, we walked out to the front of the building where we admired two huge marble plaques of the Ten Commandments, mounted on the front wall of the school—each about eight feet tall, mounted three feet off the walkway so they reached eleven feet toward the ceiling.

How could a school of this size manage such a costly project? I wondered. Memories returned of my own efforts to install two five-by-five-foot granite plaques at the entrance to Valley Christian Schools' Skyway campus mall, with inscriptions from Genesis 1:1 and Revelation 22. We were inspired to have the first verse of the Bible alongside verses from the last chapter of the Bible inscribed on the stones to greet all who enter the campus. We secured two donations of $10,000 to pay for the stones, lettering, and installation.

Ten Commandments plaques on Faith Christian High School front wall

Pondering, I realized, *If our relatively small five-by-five-foot plaques cost $10,000 each, these more beautiful four-by-eight-foot plaques might have cost much more.*

Then Tara Davis told the story of a generous marble craftsman. He was inspired by the good work of Faith Christian High School and donated the Ten Commandments plaques.

Bang! The thought hit me between the eyes: *That's the second time tiny Faith Christian High School has beaten Valley Christian High School on quality, and we are the largest Christian high school in the United States!* The first upstaging was their concurrent college credit program, and the second was the miracle of the Ten Commandments plaques. *Hmm.* This picture wasn't fitting neatly into my Quest for Excellence paradigm—the one requiring a minimum enrollment of 400 students to achieve critical mass and provide high school students with a high-quality experience.

No Limits for God

Realization was dawning on me that the Quest for Excellence could indeed be achieved in a small community. Earlier I had concluded, "A small, quality high school is an oxymoron." Now I pondered another question: *Perhaps my oxymoron is God's profundity?*

Miss Rebecca Davis lovingly interacts with her third- and fourth-grade students.
She graduated from college with a teaching credential in only two years after
completing two years of concurrent college credit while attending Faith
Christian High School. Her married name is now Mrs. Rebecca Buckner.

My concerns for a quality comprehensive high school of fewer than 400 students began to evaporate as I learned more about Faith

Christian's comprehensive concurrent community college partnership allowing students to earn college credits. The dual credit program brought legitimacy to Faith Christian High School's college-prep program. And the school's student access to West Hills Community College settled the question of comprehensive offerings in a big way.

Tara Davis continued her show-and-tell tour. She pointed out campus development achievements since the initial February 2007 visit of the WASC team to process FCA's accreditation application.

Then we took a short drive to the 16.8 acres donated to the school in 2006. Climbing out of the car, we were greeted by a sign announcing the "West Hills College Heavy Equipment Class Project." On the large dirt lot we saw skip loaders and other equipment working the ground for construction of the Faith Christian High School baseball field. I took a photo as members of the college's Heavy Equipment Class erected the field's backstop. Adjoining athletic grounds would accommodate a practice field for the Faith Christian Eagles football team.

Principal Tara Davis at the high school's future baseball field

While she stood in front of the baseball field construction project, Tara Davis explained how God had provided. "Dr. Daugherty often talks about the Quest for Excellence, and at Faith Christian High School funds are always limited, so we have to give it to God through prayer. We received the gift of this land almost four years ago and didn't have funds to build. But we just kept praying and said to God, 'This is Your project. We know we need ball fields and other activities for students in order to be an excellent school.' God is answering our prayers. He brought us West Hills College Heavy Equipment Class to do this project. Their students are learning and getting college credit for it while we are getting a beautiful ball field—and it is all from the Lord."

Once again, I could only marvel at how the Lord was exploding all the constraints of my logical paradigm. Truly, nothing is impossible with Him.

He had yet more to say, and I had much more to learn.

CHAPTER 21

THE POWER OF ONE:
BIG THINGS IN SMALL PLACES

*"I have come that they may have life, and that
they may have it more abundantly."* [127]

AS I SPENT TIME with the Faith Christian Academy
team during the midterm accreditation visit on March 11, 2010, I was
awestruck by a powerful sense of God's goodness, peace, and joy. The
power and force of the school's "happiness" culture was very evident. I
could see God's loving presence visible in the twinkling of the students'
eyes, the smiles on the faces of parents, and the exuberant love of the
teachers for their children.

The impact of this experience left me with the same magnitude
of awe I so often sense at Valley Christian Schools. I never expected
such a powerful learning environment in a small school.

How could this be? I reflected on what I have come to call the Awe
Quotient: The Awe Quotient (AQ) of any school can be described as the
perceived value of each student multiplied by the number of children

in the school, or (AQ=N*PV). In this formula, the number of students is N, and PV is the perceived value of one student.

It made sense to me: The greater numbers of highly valued students enrolled in a school, the greater sense of awe the school can project to campus guests and the community.

However, if I applied the formula to Faith Christian Academy and Valley Christian Schools, with their highly valued students, FCA would have an AQ of 110 and VCS's AQ would be 2,250, since FCA enrolled 110 students and VCS's enrollment was 2,250.

It was a bit disturbing, actually. How could little Faith Christian Academy inspire the same kind of wonderful awe I sensed at VCS, when VCS had more than twenty times the number of students and probably more than a hundred times the capital investment? *Where is the logic in this?*

During this one-sided conversation with God, I noticed some children playing happily on the FCA playground during recess. They looked like second-, third-, and fourth-graders, boys and girls playing jump rope, kicking the ball, laughing and talking.

Another question interrupted my thoughts. But this question wasn't from me to God. It was a question from God to me: *How much do you think one of these children at Faith Christian Academy is worth?*

My mind raced. I've read articles about what parents pay to rear a child. With private schooling and college, the cost can easily approach $500,000 to $1 million over a twenty-plus-year period. The price tag for a child under a bare-bones budget with no college costs after public schooling to age eighteen exceeds $200,000. I dismissed the idea in favor of another.

The real value of anything is dependent upon how much someone is willing to pay, I replied to the Lord's question. Explaining further, I told Him in my thoughts, *Housing appraisers determine the value of a house by checking on what the most recent buyers paid for comparable home purchases.*

God nudged me. *Yes, and what was the most recent purchase price paid for one of these children?*

The oft-quoted verse came to mind: "For God so loved the world that He gave His only begotten Son, that whoever believes in Him should not perish but have everlasting life."[128] The Grand Assessor of the heavens and the earth paid the most recent price.

I exclaimed to God, *You set the value of every child by redeeming each and paying the ultimate price tag when you gave Your son Jesus to die on the cross for each and every person.* The realization hit me: This means each one of these children is worth what Jesus is worth, since He gave Himself in exchange for every child.

And how much do you think Jesus is worth? God asked.

I recalled scripture identifying Jesus as God who came to earth to pay the price of redemption for every single person, including the children who were playing at recess. Genesis 1:1 says, "In the beginning God created the heavens and the earth," and the Apostle John wrote about Jesus in his Gospel, ". . . the Word was God. He was in the beginning with God. All things were made through Him, and without Him nothing was made that was made."[129]

Jesus Himself said, "He who has seen Me has seen the Father"[130] and "I and My Father are one."[131] The answer to God's question is as profound as it is obvious to those who believe the Bible: There is no doubt Jesus is of infinite value because He is God come in the flesh, and God is of infinite value since He is eternal, omnipotent, omnipresent, and omniscient.

I was humbled by the Lord's next response: *Since I, Lord God Almighty, am of infinite value and I gave Myself to pay for one of these children, how much is each of these children valued by the Grand Assessor of the heavens and the earth?*

Given that the value of anything is what someone is willing to pay, I knew the answer. *Each child is of infinite value to You, Lord. That is why You died on the cross to redeem them, because nothing and no one else could afford to buy even one of these children.*

The Grand Assessor set the price tag for every person as being equal to Himself when He gave Himself to redeem each and every one.

I wondered where the discussion was headed.

So, your formula is correct, God explained, *but PV, your perceived value, must represent the real value I paid for every person, and I gave Myself on the cross in payment to redeem every person. If the fair market value of every person is based on the most recent purchase price, even one small child is of infinite and equal value to Me, since I am of infinite value.*

God went on: *So look what happens to your formula when (FCA's AQ=N*PV→∞) and (VCS's AQ=N*PV→∞)! The Awe Quotient of even one homeschooled child equals the Awe Quotient of all the students, programs, and capital investments at Valley Christian Schools. The number of children is irrelevant.*

"Wow!" my soul screamed. It's true: All people are created equal and endowed by their Creator, just as the Declaration of Independence says. Each one is equally infinitely valued by our Creator. The power of the Creator is present with infinite potential wherever students are discovering their God-given worth and developing their God-given talents to achieve their God-intended purposes. God is just as big in small places as He is in big places. *This means,* I realized, *I can tell everyone the Quest for Excellence principles can be as powerful and successful for schools in small communities as for those in large communities.* When God is at work in any school community—where Light, Life, and Learning are flourishing, bringing goodness, peace, and joy—the Awe Quotients are equally infinite.

God was teaching me about what I have come to call "the Power of One."

The March Winds

The late winter winds seemed to blow away my concerns that such a small high school might not be capable of offering quality comprehensive programs. I drove home from the midterm accreditation visit to Faith Christian Academy wrapping my thoughts around a major paradigm shift.

After our day listening to Principal Tara Davis describe the school's extraordinary accomplishments since our 2007 visit, Shirley White and I put together our Midterm Visiting Committee Report. We wrote:

> FCA serves students with a wide range of ability. Many of the students are admitted with achievement significantly below grade level. Significant attention is given to student support and improved learning. The committee observed that the school provides a nurturing and caring environment that is combined with a commitment to remedial academic growth for students performing below grade level. Concurrently, and in the same educational environment, students who are at grade level and above are adequately challenged. A close association and cooperation with West Hills Community College provides opportunities for advanced college prep classes for more capable students.

Significant Improvements[132]

- The purchase of a new high school campus has allowed the opportunity to provide a well-rounded educational experience.

- Construction of the baseball field is underway.

- New athletic programs have been added at the elementary and high school levels.

- All teachers hold a bachelor's degree; teaching credential; certification in CPR, first aid, and blood-borne pathogens; and have obtained fingerprint clearance.

- A Campus Management System was implemented.

- A high school computer lab was added to the new facility and is a significant component of the educational program.

- The high school curriculum guideline binder has been completed.

- Additional sports programs have been added at the elementary and high school level.

- A new foreign language program has been implemented at the high school level.

- The high school grew from eighteen students to thirty-four students.

- The concurrent credit program with West Hills Community College expanded.

The report affirmed the school's commitment to ensuring "all students are learning" and commended FCA for an "appropriate instructional program for the wide range of student ability levels."

In the Justification Statement concluding the Midterm Visiting Committee Report, we wrote, "The school leadership team, faculty, and staff diligently pursued the implementation of visiting team recommendations. . . . Therefore, we recommend that Faith Christian Academy not be subject to any additional visits during the remaining three years of their accreditation period and that no new conditions be imposed."

A RETURN VISIT

By April 2010, I had accepted an invitation from Jerry Haddock, director for the Southern California Region of the Association of Christian Schools International (ACSI), to speak at the 2011 ACSI Administrators Conference the next February at the beautiful Hyatt Champions Resort in Indian Wells, California. Four hundred Christian school administrators, board members, and spouses were expected to be in attendance.

The Faith Christian Academy midterm visit of the previous month remained as a huge paradigm shift for me. The revelation of how the Quest for Excellence can have a big influence in small places was still sinking in to my mind and spirit. I decided to center my keynote on three big questions, which evolved into the three big questions discussed in this book:

1. Can I confidently say God is willing and able to do the same miraculous works to build schools like VCS in any community where people are praying and working to bring His goodness, peace, and joy to the children in their schools?

2. Are there really enough resources to build great schools in every community, even during difficult economic times?

3. If the answers to the first two questions are yes, what can I say to help people find enough resources to build great schools like VCS? In other words, how can ordinary people with ordinary means get "Access to the Omnis" (omnipotence, omnipresence, and omniscience) to accomplish the Quest for Excellence in their schools, their businesses, or their professional lives?

No doubt, since my experience at FCA, God had blown up my original paradigm about critical mass. I no longer believed high schools must have at least 400 students in order to achieve a quality comprehensive program. I was now fully convinced God does big things in small places through His people—even one person—when they access the nature, character, and works of God to achieve His purposes and desires, as transplanted into our hearts.

The Faith Christian High School story, I concluded, would provide the best way to illustrate and answer these questions. In an email to Principal Tara Davis about the invitation to speak at the ACSI conference, I told her, "The theme is to be about 'hope' for Christian school administrators during the Great Recession. God is doing so many wonderful things in your school. Would it be okay with you if I visit again, take some pictures and video, and use you and FCA as an example for my talk of what BIG THINGS God is doing in such a small community?"

Tara promptly replied, saying she would be both humbled and proud for FCA to serve as an example for my conference keynote. "Please come back anytime to take pictures and videos of the work the Lord is doing in our fine city."

VCS Faculty/Staff Chaplain Werner Vavken joined me on Monday, May 10, 2010, when we returned to Coalinga. The video he created from this visit—four and a half minutes, with soundtrack—was well received at the Administrators Conference. It is now posted online for all the world to see.[133] What a testimony of God's power and provision!

Surprise Benefit: Dual Credit

My connection with Faith Christian Academy also led to a major benefit for Valley Christian High School students. The FCA program allowing its high school students to earn concurrent college credit opened my eyes to the possibilities for VCHS. During the midterm accreditation visit at FCA, I met with Dr. Willard Lewallen, then president of West Hills Community College, the local campus in Coalinga where Faith's high school students take college classes. I wanted to see if Valley might develop an arrangement with the West Hills Community College District for VCHS students to get dual college credit while attending high school courses on our Skyway campus in San Jose. He agreed.

Dr. Lewallen and his executive team visited Valley Christian Schools, and over the coming months we worked together with legal counsel to draft and complete a contract outlining the agreement. West Hills Community College District would hire VCS faculty who met WHCCD qualifications as adjunct college professors for additional salary to teach VCHS students dual credit college courses.

The program began in the fall of 2011, with great success. Now Valley Christian High School offers dozens of dual credit courses in partnership with various colleges and universities, giving our students access to more than 100 units of college credit. In most cases these credits on college transcripts transfer smoothly to four-year colleges and universities. Courses are reviewed to ensure they have the same content and rigor as those taught at the partner college or university, which is possible because most courses taught in one semester at the college are spread over the entire year in high school. Starting in ninth grade, VCHS students can acquire up to two years of college credit during their regular school day without leaving our Skyway campus. By fulfilling general education requirements, this innovative program allows these VCHS students to enter a four-year college or university program as juniors after high school graduation.[134]

I could never have dreamed all this would grow out of chairing the accreditation visiting team for Faith Christian Academy. When the invitation letter arrived, I was tempted to think, "Can anything good come out of Coalinga?"[135] Then, through this small school I thought I was helping, God brought an amazing dual college credit program to VCHS. It is for certain: God can make the Quest for Excellence a reality in every community!

CHAPTER 22

THE SKY IS NOT
THE LIMIT!

MY EXPERIENCE WITH the Faith Christian Academy accreditation process caught me completely by surprise. Going in, I was skeptical a small school could achieve such big dreams. God taught me vivid, powerful lessons about "the Power of One" and the priceless value of every single student. What I learned in Coalinga opened up my own faith and made me see that God wanted to do more at VCS, too—more than I could ever hope and imagine.

After the successful launch of the Conservatory of the Arts, a passion grew in my soul to further enhance the academic portion of VCS's A³ vision encompassing Academic Achievement, Artistic Beauty, and Athletic Distinction. *What better place than VCS in Silicon Valley to develop an Applied Math, Science, and Engineering (AMSE) Institute?* I thought prayerfully.

Embracing a vision for AMSE represented a turnaround for me. The idea was birthed in our intercessory prayer group years before, when Werner Vavken shared his burden for VCS to offer practical, hands-on electrical and mechanical opportunities. At the time, I debated the idea with him, claiming a rigorous college preparatory curriculum didn't have the bandwidth to fill student schedules with occupational, pseudo-academic courses.

We both agreed to put the matter to prayer. I had no idea what God had in mind. But wow! It was big! Little did I know how our new AMSE vision would transport our student achievements to the most infinitesimal corners of *inner* space and the limitless wonders of *outer* space. Over the course of the next few years, we were again humbled and amazed not only to lay out two BHAGs (Big Hairy Audacious Goals)[136] but to see God make them a reality.

In August 2009, Valley Christian High School Principal Mark Lodewyk and I announced the launch of the Applied Math, Science, and Engineering Institute. Our plans took shape over the coming school year.

AMSE is the school's STEM (science, technology, engineering, and math) focus on steroids. The AMSE Institute pairs in-depth instruction with hands-on clubs and programs, with mentoring provided by amazing scientists and engineers from Silicon Valley. These professionals offer their time and expertise to coach students as they develop their remarkable science projects. AMSE and the Conservatory of the Arts are excellent expressions of Academic Achievement and Artistic Beauty, respectively.

As with the conservatory, students were challenged to enroll in an AMSE major or minor. Ninety-nine students enrolled during the launch year, and the numbers encouraged us. In comparison, by 2009 the three-year-old conservatory had about 100 students enrolled in majors and minors, after starting with twenty-six students in 2006. To enroll ninety-nine students in AMSE in the first couple of months showed great promise for the institute.

THE FIRST BIG HAIRY AUDACIOUS GOAL:
VCS's NANOTECHNOLOGY LAB

Scott Vander Veen, high school science chair, and I attended Azusa Pacific University's Segerstrom Science Symposium on October 23, 2009. While there, we took the opportunity to tour the university's newly dedicated $54 million, 71,000-square-foot LEED-certified science center. During our tour, we watched a demonstration of a Scanning Electron Microscope (SEM).

"Why doesn't VCHS's science department have one of these?" I asked Scott.

Scott responded with a "Yeah, right—you're dreaming!" smile.

The power, compact size, and seeming ease of use of the SEM at Azusa Pacific impressed us. An SEM is capable of creating detailed sample images at very high magnification—on the scale of nanometers. A nanometer (nm) is a unit of measure equal to one billionth of a meter. The tip of a pin is almost 1 million nm across, and the width of a human hair is about 60,000 nm. A single strand of DNA molecule is about 2–6 nm wide.

It became my personal mission to secure an SEM for VCHS. Acquiring and using an SEM became the first of two Big Hairy Audacious Goals to give a sense of "Yeah, this is for real" to the high school AMSE initiative.

My pursuit inspired a lunch with Dr. Bruce and Michelle Roth at the Mandarin Gourmet, my favorite Chinese restaurant. Bruce is the inventor of Lipitor, the best selling drug in the history of pharmaceuticals. He and Michelle enrolled their children, Rebecca and Aaron, at VCS when Bruce accepted the vice president position for Genentech's Discovery Chemistry Lab. Michelle joined VCHS's science department faculty during the 2007–08 school year.

After enjoying the conversation, lettuce wraps, and sizzling rice soup, I asked a seemingly absurd but serious question. "Bruce," I began, "I put a hold on all capital expenditures during this economic downturn except for investments 'strategically necessary' to sustain and advance VCS's mission. Do you think it 'strategically necessary' for VCS to spend about $250,000 to purchase Scanning Electron Microscopes? VCHS would be the first high school in America to develop such a high-powered microscopy lab."

Without hesitation, Bruce looked me square in the eyes and replied firmly and with conviction, "Absolutely!" In that moment Valley Christian High School's AMSE program took on an entirely new reality for me. Bruce agreed to accept a seat on the newly forming Applied Math, Science, and Engineering Advisory Board, and to champion the Scanning Electron Microscopes initiative.

Bruce did not hesitate. He requested assistance from the microscopy department at Genentech, and before long, Bob Monteverde, marketing manager at Nanounity, a company distributing and servicing microscopes and microscopy needs, was making a presentation in my office.

While Nanounity did distribute Scanning Electron Microscopes, Bob Monteverde pointed out that a different kind of instrument—an Atomic Force Microscope (AFM)—would better support VCS's goals and budget. With Bob's guidance, VCS purchased two AFMs—capable of nano-scale resolution and significantly less expensive to maintain and operate than electron microscopes. The AFMs were ordered in the spring of 2010 and installed by the start of school that fall.

At the end of our first meeting, Bob Monteverde asked, "You know I'm a Valley Christian parent, right?"

I hadn't made the connection.

"Our daughter Caitlin is a vocalist. We chose Valley Christian because of the conservatory," Bob explained.

My face registered surprise. "I imagined your children might have a passion for science."

"Well, of course my entire professional life involves science, but we are thankful for the conservatory because Caitlin loves to sing and she's definitely gifted as a vocal artist."

Wow! I thought. *That's just more confirmation of how important a comprehensive program is to help parents discover and develop the God-given talents of their children so they can achieve all God intends for their lives.*

That discussion gave me additional assurance we were on the right track with our A³ comprehensive programs.[137]

THE AMSE ADVISORY BOARD

While attending the Segerstrom Science Symposium at Azusa Pacific University in October 2009, I had met Jon Prange, who served as the venture business manager at the San Diego Zoo. Jon expressed excitement about Valley Christian's AMSE initiative and was the first to agree to serve as an AMSE Advisory Board member. When Dr. Bruce Roth accepted my invitation, he became the second of several more amazing science and engineering professionals who joined the board during this organizational timeframe.[138]

Without hesitation, I asked my dear friend and longtime VCS prayer intercessor, Werner Vavken, a retired engineering genius and VCS administrator, to chair the Advisory Board. Then while golfing with Dan Saldana, a retired NASA engineering manager and VCS alumni parent, Werner asked Dan to serve on the AMSE Advisory Board, and Dan agreed. During a pancake breakfast, I struck up a conversation with VCS parent Dr. Eric Phelps, an extraordinary Christian orthodontist, and he too agreed to serve on the board. Werner also had a great contact with Stephen Ferrero, then an Apple iPhone engineering project manager, and he accepted the invitation to serve.

Our first AMSE Advisory Board meeting was held on Wednesday, January 20, 2010. We gathered for a dinner meeting in the VCS high school library, overlooking the beautiful lights of Silicon Valley. Every person on the newly formed AMSE Advisory Board was present, including (in addition to those just named) Brian Cronquist, Jean Fairweather, Larry Fennern, Yoon Berm Kim, and Bob Monteverde.

Werner Vavken, newly appointed director of VCS's AMSE initiative, opened the meeting with prayer. I welcomed everyone to VCS, and the two of us described our vision for AMSE. Werner made a brief illustrated presentation on how the United States had fallen to twentieth place in the world for math and science achievement scores. He emphasized the important role of the Advisory Board members to assist and advise students with their science projects, and to help innovate and develop significant projects and programs for AMSE students.

In my comments, I described why Valley Christian Schools is so passionate about applied math, science, and engineering. As Christians, I emphasized, we believe in the Creator and are naturally and intensely focused on God's creation. Christian educators and scientists should be the most passionate about good science and the effective application of scientific insights to sustain and improve the world. We, of all people, must care the deepest about the lives of people and animals, because we should understand that good people are good stewards of God's good creation.

High school principal Mark Lodewyk expressed appreciation to Advisory Board members for their help launching the AMSE Institute. Junior high principal Lisa Arnett then described the unparalleled excitement for Project Lead the Way, the junior high school's STEM (science, technology, engineering, and math) initiative.

Every Advisory Board member participated in a brainstorming session to propose ideas for projects and program initiatives for AMSE students. Bruce Roth brought everyone up to date on the strategic initiative for the procurement of an Atomic Force Microscope lab to support AMSE student science research projects. I pledged to budget the needed capital funds. The energy in the room was electrifying as Bruce led the discussion.

Then Eric Phelps recommended a monthly AMSE Lecture Series, with a purpose to enable students to imagine and discover their potential future careers in science, technology, engineering, and medicine by learning from practicing professionals. "The speakers will share insights and stories about what it's like to work in their field of endeavor and how to prepare for their varied careers," Eric explained. "Each professional will inspire our AMSE students to embrace their life's dreams—to dream big about their educational goals and career paths."

As it turned out, Eric Phelps helped implement his idea almost immediately. The AMSE Lecture Series has become one of the most influential programs of the AMSE Institute. Every month on a Sunday evening throughout the school year, the series sponsors a speaker who gives an informative and inspirational presentation. All AMSE students participate in at least five or eight of the lectures, depending on whether they are a minor or major AMSE student, and many of their parents attend with them. Eric and his wife, Suzanne, sponsor an annual lecture in memory of their son Dane Christian Phelps, who was three and a half years old in 2008 when he succumbed to the effects of a rare form of ichthyosis, a congenital skin disease most known for extreme scaling and sloughing of the epidermis. Dane's life and memory continue inspiring our AMSE students toward careers of significance where they can make a difference solving real world problems, such as helping to find a cure for ichthyosis.[139]

AMSE's Second Big Hairy Audacious Goal: The VCS Space Program

Back at the initial AMSE Advisory Board meeting, the brainstorming continued, and Dan Saldana put forth his idea. I'll never forget his first sentence: "I'll help the students put a satellite in space." With that, he looked around the room to gauge interest in his idea. Everyone in the room seemed to have pushed "pause."

I instantly felt a sense of warped reality. Enveloped in cognitive dissonance, my logical mind wanted to say, "This is a high school program, not NASA!"

President Obama's recent decision to defund many of America's space initiatives, including the space shuttle program, crossed my mind. I imagined trying to answer questions from VCS board of directors as to why we would pursue a satellite program when the president had the sense to back off from what he considered excessive spending.

All I could pull myself together to say was, "Are you serious? How could VCS afford to put a satellite in space?"

Dan backed up and began describing his background.

"During my career working with NASA at Lockheed, I headed eighty-nine satellite projects. Most of them were 'secret' projects for the Defense Department. When I retired, I wanted to give back to students, so I offered to help bring science and math into our public schools but was told I needed a teaching credential.

"As I looked into the fastest route to get a teaching credential, I received a call from Bob Twiggs, a professor at Stanford University. He asked if I would work with him at Stanford to help students develop satellites." Dan told us Bob had co-invented the CubeSat, a miniaturized satellite for space research, which usually has a volume of exactly one liter (ten centimeters cubed) and a mass of no more than 1.33 kilograms. The CubeSat typically uses commercial off-the-shelf components for its electronics.

Dan agreed to work with Professor Twiggs on the project to help Stanford students develop and fly space payload modules of similar design called CubeLabs. Dan was pleased with the arrangement—especially since Stanford didn't think he needed a teaching credential!

Then in 2009, Dan explained, Bob Twiggs was recruited by Kentucky Space, a non-profit consortium of private and public universities, companies, and other organizations, to help them design and lead innovative space missions within realistic budgets and objectives. Kentucky Space, Space Tango, and related companies are built around the goal of creating space-related technologies and products with modest costs but high value. Such companies pioneer opportunities with "the apps side of space" for businesses in micro-technology, biomedical, and bioengineering product areas, using NASA's payload capabilities.

I learned that Bob is now a Stanford professor emeritus and concurrently serves as professor of astronautical engineering at Morehead State University and the University of Idaho. (Later in 2010, *SpaceNews* would name Professor Twiggs, along with Elon Musk, CEO of SpaceX and Tesla Motors, and others, as one of the year's ten most influential space professionals who have made a difference in space.[140])

"It's been a great experience to work with students at Stanford," Dan said. "As I've been sitting here thinking about what I could offer AMSE students, I realized there is no reason why we can't put together a team of really bright and motivated students at Valley Christian to put a satellite into space."

It's a rare occasion, I must admit, but I was speechless for a moment. I love it when people "out-vision" me! After gathering my thoughts, I told Dan, "If Stanford doesn't think you need a teaching credential, I think you will be qualified to teach at Valley Christian."

Eventually I mustered the courage to ask the money question. "How much will it cost to launch a satellite?"

"Getting aboard a scheduled launch is the key. At Stanford we brought the cost down to $100,000 and I think we can lower the costs even more."

I had an absurd thought: *The good ship VCS is headed for space!*

BLAST OFF!

When Dan Saldana promised to recruit Professor Twiggs to help launch Valley Christian High School's AMSE program, I was excited, amazed, and apprehensive. Dan is a man of few words and lots of action. Less than three months after Dan made his offer at the January 20th AMSE Advisory Board meeting, none other than Professor Bob Twiggs himself came to my office with options for how VCHS could become the first high school in the world to put student-designed and -developed CubeLab science experiments on the International Space Station (ISS). As a second phase of the program, he said Valley Christian AMSE students could put the first high school CubeSat satellite in space orbit around the earth.

L to R: Professor Bob Twiggs presenting options for the VCS space program, executive assistant Pam Watson, and Dr. Clifford Daugherty

Five options were presented, and we undertook a comprehensive discussion of the pros and cons of each option. We finally agreed on the International Space Station CubeLab option. Within twenty hours, Jeffery Manber, managing director of NanoRacks, presented a contract for launching the world's first high school CubeLab science experiment on the ISS.

NanoRacks would provide the interface with NASA and the ride to the ISS. Our students had to design, fabricate, and build the CubeLab from scratch. This was key. We stipulated that the project needed to be a student-conceived and -developed science experiment in order to go aboard the ISS. Our students chose a plant growth experiment, researching which plants would work best in the microgravity environment. They installed an internal camera to document stages of growth during the experiment. Astronauts on the ISS would "plug in" the CubeLab's USB outputs to their laptops to download the data to students at VCHS.

Valley Christian's AMSE Institute kicked off the 2010 school year with a bang, or more accurately, a blast—a blast into space. Students met their biggest challenge through their successful design, fabrication, building, testing, and launch of the nation's first high school CubeLab science experiment. The project literally launched into space in late January 2011 on the HTV-2 Japanese cargo spacecraft, boarded the International Space Station, and hitched a ride back to Earth in mid-March aboard the Russian Soyuz vehicle on an astronaut's lap.

THE HIGH SCHOOL RACE TO SPACE

The final page in this story recounts possibly its most exciting angle.

Dr. Yvonne Cagle, a NASA astronaut and medical doctor who joined the AMSE Advisory Board, and I had approached several large school districts to invite them to participate in the AMSE Institute's International Space Station project, but all declined. When large high schools couldn't think big enough to provide their students the opportunity to put an experiment on the ISS, Dr. Cagle and I made a full-day trip to isolated Coalinga to ask Tara Davis if tiny Faith Christian High School would consider the challenge. She didn't hesitate, once again confirming how God does big things in small places and the Quest for Excellence can happen in any school, small or large.

International Space Station

Feature

Text Size ☐ ☐   Tweet 25   Like 125   +1 3   Pinit   ★★★★☆ ?

Students Blaze a Trail Using NanoRacks-CubeLabs for Space Station Research   12.22.10

A good education is the launch pad that enables students to shoot for the stars with their future goals. They work their way up by preparing in grade school for college, which leads to their subsequent career of choice. Students at Valley Christian High School in San Jose, California, however, are not waiting for the university setting for ignition on their dreams. Instead they are seizing the opportunity to embrace math and science education via the school's Applied Math Science and Engineering Institute, AMSE for short.

Students participating in AMSE conceptualized, designed, built, tested, and are now flying an experiment on the International Space Station as part of Expedition 25/26. The AMSE advisory board collaborated with NanoRacks, a private company that provides research opportunities on the space station through the International Space Station National Laboratory. Together they enabled Valley Christian High School students to be the first high school to take part in space station research using NanoRacks-CubeLabs.

Students at Valley Christian High School (left to right: Taehyun Park, Veronica Lane, and Michael Lee) work with mentor George Sousa to construct their NanoRacks-CubeLabs hardware. (Credit: Valley Christian High School)

Valley Christian students underwent a rigorous application process to qualify to participate in this exciting chance for hands-on microgravity science and engineering. The final project team includes 24 students guided by Dan Saldana, a retired satellite design engineer. The team chose a plant growth experiment for their focus. This experiment uses a student-designed, self-contained plant-seed growth chamber that plugs into the NanoRacks-CubeLabs platform onboard the station. An internal camera provides snapshots of the stages of growth during the experiment, which crewmembers then downlink to the school as data for analysis.

Students gained real world experience by planning, working, and seeing a project like this through to launch. They designed hardware and worked within specific parameters for safety, weight, etc. This included researching which plants would likely work best in the microgravity environment, given the 4 by 4 by 8-inch size of the NanoRack-CubeLabs unit. The plants had to be small enough to avoid outgrowing the growth chamber, while sturdy enough to survive limited irrigation and flight duration. William Kohlmoos, CubeLab Design Engineering Manager and student, recalls the selection process, "The payload group chose three plants: basil, marigold, and Wisconsin fast plant. The reason we picked these was because they were an appropriate decision based on the time we were allotted, which was 30 to 60 days."

The students plan to make a video documentary of their efforts, as well as maintain a Web site and blog. The AMSE Institute also hopes to hold a CubeLab Education Conference in 2011 to raise awareness of such opportunities for other schools. Veronica Lane, CubeLab Program Manager and Project Manager of Robotics and Senior at Valley Christian, comments on the range of influence hoped for in this project, "The mission of [this study] is to research, design and fabricate a plant growth experiment that will grow aboard the international space station. We also want to help other schools do a similar experiment and grow our own Applied Math Science and Engineering Institute."

The goal of this project is for students to learn to balance school commitments, along with a successful space station project. Benefits include engineering experience, project management skills, science education growth, applied research, and technology studies. The inspirational act of conducting a hands-on space station experiment is the fuel that will ultimately fire these students imaginations and lead them on an already bright trajectory towards careers in math and science.

by Jessica Nimon
NASA's Johnson Space Center
International Space Station Program Science Office

And yes, it happened! This little school partnered with VCS to do something unprecedented and normally unthinkable. FCHS students put a science experiment on the International Space Station! Their amazing accomplishment proved small schools can achieve big dreams. They even received a letter of commendation from President Obama.

The Faith Christian students realized that as humans begin to explore and inhabit space, a time will come when buildings will be built. FCHS students studied the effects of mixing concrete in space two ways: 1) by stirring the concrete mixture, and (2) by vibrating the concrete mixture. They analyzed the structural integrity of both kinds of space-mixed concrete and earth-mixed concrete with Valley Christian's Atomic Force Microscope at the molecular level.

Two schools. Two hugely different-sized student bodies—one small and one large. But one thing very much in common: one limitless God, challenging His children to see, indeed, the sky is not the limit!

Tara Davis, Faith Christian High School principal, the students
on the ISS team, and their mentors
Photo courtesy of Faith Christian High School

CHAPTER 23

THE DECLARATION

"CAN I CONFIDENTLY SAY God is willing and able to do the same miraculous works to build schools like VCS in any community where people are praying and working to bring His goodness, peace, and joy to the children in their schools?" This was my first big question.

Yes, I'll admit it. When I first asked the question, I had a spiritual blind spot when it came to believing the answer to my question could be "yes" for small high schools in small communities with growth potential of fewer than 400 students. But because of my lessons learned about "the Power of One," I became a believer. While that was an amazing paradigm shift for me, I had an even bigger blind spot.

When Valley Christian Schools founded the Quest Institute, now known as the Quest Institute for Quality Education, it was named the Quest Institute for Christian Education because my vision was limited to serving and developing Christian schools. I prayed for God's good works to happen in public schools, but I thought the U.S. Supreme Court had put the public schools off-limits to Christians. So when I asked God my big question—whether I could say that the excellent works He has done at VCS He could do in any community where people are praying and working to bring His goodness, peace, and joy to the children—I wasn't thinking of public schools.

Through the transformation I described in Part I, with the development of Junior University and the Lighthouse Initiative, my vision dramatically expanded to incorporate all schools, including public schools! This was a huge leap of faith, fueled by God's passion and love for all children.

The budget crisis in the local Franklin–McKinley School District had set the stage for this change. Due to budget cutbacks, all arts and athletic programs in the Seven Trees public schools got the ax many years ago. The district simply did not have the resources to provide all of the academic support students needed, let alone to offer art, music, or athletic opportunities. For more than a decade, students had no options for choir, dance, music lessons, instrumental instruction, or other similar programs.

The desperate need to restore Academic Achievement, Artistic Beauty, and Athletic Distinction to our local public schools—and our growing awareness and compassion—opened the door for VCS's high school and junior high students to learn how to make a huge difference in our neighborhood schools. Our students learned how they can connect with and mentor precious elementary children. Children learn amazingly well if they simply have the opportunities they deserve.

And elementary schools were not the only ones being transformed.

LIGHTING UP THE PUBLIC HIGH SCHOOL

In March 2014, Joshua Greene, an educator and the Junior University/Community Service Coordinator at Andrew Hill High School (AHHS),[141] asked to meet with VCHS Community Service Director Cindy Nardi and me. The administration of Andrew Hill initiated this contact, and Vice Principal Bjorn Berg hosted our meeting in Principal Bettina

Lopez's conference room. When we arrived, Israel Lara and Cisco Regalado from the Firehouse Community Development Program in San Jose joined the meeting. The mission of the Firehouse, according to its website, is "to empower youth and their families to break the cycle of poverty...."[142]

The Andrew Hill educators had a specific request for us: Could Cindy train and certify Joshua Greene and Firehouse staff members to teach the Light Up Your World (LUYW) curriculum to AHHS students?

Andrew P. Hill High School serves 2,173 students (9–12th grade) with a wide range of performance levels. High achievers can choose from twenty AP (Advanced Placement) courses, while lower-performing students often suffer the consequences of unhealthy peer pressure. For the 2012–13 school year, 48 percent of all AHHS students scored at a proficient or advanced level in English Language Arts, and 53 percent of all students achieved a proficient or advanced level in Mathematics.[143]

As requested, Cindy Nardi trained and certified Joshua Green and members of the Firehouse staff over the next couple of weeks to teach the LUYW curriculum. Then Joshua Greene and the Firehouse staff launched a pilot LUYW program during April 2014 for 160 Andrew Hill High School students in an effort to further improve self-perceptions, intrinsic motivation, achievement, and the school culture. The pilot encompassed a wide range of demographics, including low to high academic and behavioral measures as well as diverse ethnic and national origin groups. The administration wanted to discover if the LUYW curriculum would be well received by virtually all high school students, and whether the curriculum would empower these students "to discern how to make choices..."[144] to positively affect their lives, their school culture, and the world around them.

When the pilot ended, Joshua Greene reported the LUYW results as "eyebrow-raising, jaw-dropping amazing for all of the students."

The students wrote scores of lengthy thank-you notes to their LUYW instructors to express their appreciation for the training.

With such remarkable results in hand, the board of the Quest Institute for Quality Education awarded a grant requested by the Andrew Hill educators to fund a summer school program for incoming AHHS ninth-graders who had four or more Fs in eighth grade upon graduation in May 2014. The LUYW training, in addition to other academic courses, was considered a requirement for these "at-risk" students for promotion to ninth grade. As it turned out, the Andrew Hill LUYW summer program taught 166 students, about three-quarters of them incoming ninth-graders, with about half the participants considered at high risk with four or more Fs during the previous semester.

The Quest Institute also commissioned a study to track the anticipated positive results of the LUYW training led by the Firehouse staff and Joshua Greene. Dr. Peter Ellis, founding partner of CCPA—The Resiliency Group, agreed to conduct the study in two phases including pre-program and post-program LUYW participant assessments during summer school. At the conclusion of the summer school program, students reported high satisfaction with the program services and good scores on service productivity (defined as positive change due to the services).[145]

This program filled me with great satisfaction. Looking back, I could see how far we had come—the VCS community, the local public schools, and my own paradigm shift. This transformation finally became absolutely real to me at a milestone event that somehow seemed to encapsulate our journey over the past decade.

FLASHBACK AT THE FESTIVAL

Dr. John Porter, superintendent of the Franklin–McKinley School District, stood with me at the Festival of the Arts concert on May 16, 2014, watching as more than 500 students and parents from the schools of the Seven Trees community streamed into Valley Christian's large gymnasium. This Friday evening was special. The concert represented the culmination of more than a year of a partnership between four public schools and Valley Christian Schools.

How this all came about still amazes me. Public school principals, Valley Christian principals from both the high school and the middle school, and I had worked together to develop our strategy to bring new program opportunities to the public school students, reinforcing Light, Life, and Learning as well as a culture of goodness, peace, and joy. We implemented the Light Up Your World curriculum with amazing success, and we successfully expanded the Hellyer Junior University and Lighthouse Initiative to three more public schools. Andrew Hill High School students partnered with VCHS students to mentor elementary students, and we hoped Sylvandale Middle School students would soon join our VCS middle school students as mentors to the younger children.

Principal Dan Fowler of Sylvandale had attended several Junior University meetings and expected to join the initiative during the coming 2014–15 school year. He commented about the high quality of students Sylvandale was receiving from Hellyer and wanted to help. Because his students had benefited from their experience with Junior University and the Lighthouse Initiative while in elementary school, Dan said he believed they would make great mentors to elementary students because they wanted to give back.

In all, five public schools in two school districts were now committed to the Junior University and Lighthouse Initiative along with Valley Christian High and Middle Schools, totaling seven schools with an enrollment of more than 6,800 students.

The 2013–14 school year, coming to a climax around the Festival of the Arts concert, had brought great strides in our understanding and implementation of how a culture of goodness, peace, and joy could take root in the public schools. We had discussed the plight of the *Bismarck's* lost rudder and the parallels in that story for American education. We became determined to repair the rudder of our educational system and to restore the moral compass in our schools by calling upon the legacy of our Founding Fathers. We developed and discussed the illustrations of the red public schoolhouse and the flowing faucet, presented in Chapter 7. We agreed to reconnect the hinges of Common Virtues to the door of educational opportunity, based on the values of our Founding Fathers as found in the Declaration of Independence. Among other strategies, we purposely opened the valve of community resources by teaching students the "Declaration" song, which includes the exact language of the Declaration of Independence. We were convinced the same self-evident truths that gave birth to our nation could produce a rebirth of Light, Life, and Learning and a culture of goodness, peace, and joy in our public schools.

Founding Fathers

A RARE PARTNERSHIP

Valley Christian Schools has held its Festival of the Arts, an annual family event, for many years. It takes place on a full Saturday in May and features children from all grades, K–12. The atmosphere is always filled with thousands of happy guests, jump houses, scents of tasty foods, face painting, an art show, a photography show, a ceramics show, dance shows, multiple jazz band performances, theater shows, band performances, and a concert by the full VCHS Symphony at the end of the evening. Our idea was to add a Friday evening concert on May 16, 2014, to launch the Festival of the Arts, with the Junior University and Lighthouse Initiative public school mentees performing for their families. Valley Christian High School and Andrew Hill High School mentors would help showcase their mentees' accomplishments in a program we planned as a new annual event. We invited all public school parents and friends to attend and help celebrate the new opportunities these initiatives had opened up for Academic Achievement, Artistic Beauty, and Athletic Distinction for their children.

The Valley Christian High School students had created a short video to open the concert with highlights of the year from Junior University and the Lighthouse Initiative. The Quest Institute later incorporated it in a video of the evening's program as a gift from the children to their parents.[146] The Quest Institute agreed to sponsor a catered Italian meal after the concert for the public school children and their families for only $1 per person. We set a nominal charge to get the count right for the number of meals. Buses transported families from their schools to the VCS Skyway campus and back, ensuring that families without transportation could come. We had the Festival of the Arts program printed in English, Spanish, and Vietnamese.

That evening, as president of Valley Christian Schools, I welcomed everyone to our Skyway campus and recognized Dr. John Porter, superintendent of the Franklin–McKinley School District.

"Dr. John Porter is a forward-thinking visionary," I said. "It is this kind of opportunity that comes from a man who thinks out of the box, makes things happen, and supports his principals and their ideas. It is such a privilege to have this partnership, Dr. Porter. Thank you so much for joining us this evening."

We shook hands, and Dr. Porter took the microphone. "It's my pleasure to share with Dr. Daugherty this wonderful partnership with Valley Christian High School, Middle School, and several of our schools." He introduced his principals from the public schools before continuing. "I would like to give the high school students of Valley Christian a personal thanks from the Board of Trustees and myself for being the wonderful role models you are for our students, and for your devotion and dedication to the work you do with us. Tonight is a tribute to our partnership—a rare one that I have never seen across this country. I've never seen a partnership like this between a parochial school and an elementary school district. This is a unique opportunity for us, and I think we are all grateful."

The program began with the high school student mentors, who taught weekly instrumental music lessons for about twenty-five elementary mentees, playing jazz alongside their mentees in their mentees' first concert, under the leadership of Dr. Marcus Wolf, Valley Christian High School Conservatory jazz instructor. I listened as twenty-two Franklin–McKinley elementary mentees played their hearts out, their cheeks puffing on their woodwind and brass instruments, bows passing across strings, or fingers bouncing off keyboards. Dr. Porter leaned toward me and said, "They sound like a real band!"

I agreed, but didn't want to admit I had purposely planned for our VCS jazz band to drown out what I expected to be the fumbling efforts of the younger musicians. The elementary students, I hoped, would be encouraged and inspired simply playing alongside the very talented high school musicians. I didn't expect they could really learn to play only months after their lessons began. But play they did! The high school members toned down their volume to highlight the new talent and skill of twenty-two young musicians who would likely never have enjoyed a music lesson without the dedication and commitment of their teenage mentors.[147]

Brandon Peters (second from left) playing cello alongside his mentee, Carlos

FULFILLMENT OF A VISION

As the program continued, the elementary robotic mentee students showed the robots they built, dancers danced, and singers sang in a large combined choir from three elementary schools. The songs included "This Land Is Your Land" by Woodie Guthrie, "Come In My People" by Los Arboles Principal Ricardo Balderas, and "Declaration," one of the highlights of the evening for me. This last piece (with music by Plank Road Publishing, adapted by Teresa Jennings) contains the exact words penned by Thomas Jefferson in the Declaration of Independence: "We hold these truths to be self-evident, that all men are created equal, that they are endowed by their Creator with certain unalienable Rights, that among these are Life, Liberty, and the pursuit of Happiness."

Matt DeMeritt, Valley Christian Schools Theater Director, had produced an outstanding video of the "Declaration" song using one Valley Christian elementary student and three Franklin–McKinley elementary actors to "star" in the video. Fantastic public school teachers and high school mentors used this video to teach their public school children the "Declaration" song for the concert by simply playing the video in class as students did their work. Even kindergartners and first-grade students easily learned to sing the fairly complicated words. As they practiced, we dreamed that perhaps teachers in any school anywhere in America might use the Declaration video to teach the "Declaration" song to their students.[148] Our local students had held their first combined rehearsal that Friday morning under the leadership of Dr. Mark Hulse, Valley Christian Conservatory vocal instructor.

Mentees from three elementary neighborhood public schools sing the "Declaration" song, as taught by their hard-working Junior University and Lighthouse high school mentors.

During the evening, just before the award presentations to mentors and mentees, Carla Haakma added some very kind and insightful comments.

> Last year when I was principal at Los Arboles, Dr. Daugherty asked Jerry Merza, the principal at Hellyer, to reach out to us at Los Arboles to become part of this partnership, and I was so honored. I said, "We have a sister school, Lairon Elementary, and we work side by side, so it would be really great if we can also include them."
>
> Dr. Daugherty agreed, and so pretty soon we had three elementary schools coming up the hill to Valley Christian for meetings to plan these opportunities for our students together. It became like, "Oh my gosh, how are the Valley Christian High School students going to provide all of the mentorship needed for three elementary schools?" So Dr. Daugherty had another vision of bringing Andrew Hill High School students into the fold as mentors so they too could give back to the elementary schools in the district.
>
> So here we are today after our first year of a successful partnership with Valley Christian and Andrew Hill High School students serving as mentors for our elementary students at Hellyer, Lairon, and Los Arboles elementary schools. I'm so proud of all the effort and the relationships we have built this year through this program. Valley Christian has been very generous by providing bus transportation to round up the high school students after school and bring them to the elementary schools, and helping to keep this program organized.
>
> The Junior University and Lighthouse Initiative has been such a great opportunity, and we see nothing but growth in

the future. We are planning to add Sylvandale Middle School into the partnership next year. As our elementary kids grow up and they get into middle school and high school, we hope they will want to give back and become mentors and work with the younger students.

I just wanted to give a little background on the program, and I'm just so very proud of it. We are just at the beginning stages, but we've had a great year and I only see bigger and better things to come.

Listening to Dr. John Porter and Carla Haakma speak with such encouraging words, I couldn't help but recall how I had suddenly received what I believed was a divine strategy to bring Light, Life, and Learning and God's goodness, peace, and joy to our neighborhood public schools. Tonight I was certainly experiencing the fulfillment of the vision God gave me in October 2012 for expanding the Junior University and Lighthouse programs.

My heart stirred. *Yes*, I thought. *The best definition of vision I can think of is "getting a glimpse of what God wants to do."* As we align ourselves with His will, He allows us to tap into His Omnis, and He does His great works through His people.

As I sat in the large gym at Valley Christian High School during that momentous Festival of the Arts evening, I looked across on the gym wall and again saw our motto, "Quest for Excellence." The best definition of true excellence really is "the nature, character, and works of God," as I wrote in Chapters 8–9. And it is truly nothing but joy to see His vision and great works coming to pass through our lives. I'm so thankful God is doing His great works, because I could never even begin to do them myself. As Thomas Jefferson wrote in the last paragraph of the Declaration of Independence, he and his fellow Founding

Fathers could take their bold stand in support of liberty only "with a firm reliance on . . . divine Providence."

Focusing again on the evening's program, I watched the award presentations and then listened as a young girl from Hellyer Elementary School closed the concert with a vocal solo of the first verse of "Amazing Grace."

A sense of awe filled my heart as I reflected on all I saw and heard—a snapshot of all God Himself had achieved through our public school partnership. This Festival of the Arts event with our VCS and public school students seemed to stand as a proof of concept, like a flag planted on a hill and waving with the message to all: "Any school, church, or people of good will can do this!"

PROMINENT PROCLAMATION

In the fall of 2014 I got exciting news about another Quest Institute public school initiative to help restore the foundation of America's godly heritage. Jerry Merza, principal of Hellyer Elementary School, had an inspiration about how to use the money his school received from VCS high school students who had organized a 5K charity run and raised thousands of dollars to improve education for disadvantaged children.

With his donated funds, Principal Merza hired local artist and muralist Paul J. Gonzalez to design and paint, on the most prominent exterior wall at Hellyer, a fifty-foot mural featuring the Declaration of Independence and iconic images from our nation's history. Jerry Merza is determined to restore and sustain the educational rudder and moral compass at his school—legally—by supporting the Common Virtues of our Founding Fathers. The mural, strategically located at the school's entry where everyone who comes to campus easily sees the words of the Declaration, should be finished in the spring of 2015 after the weather warms.

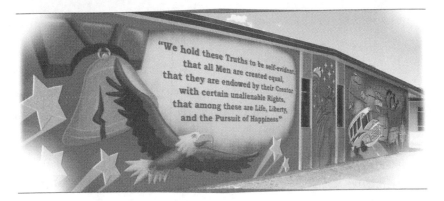

Wall at Hellyer Elementary School with the Declaration mural

Later, at a Junior University and Lighthouse Initiative meeting, I distributed a draft copy of *The Quest Continues* with endorsements from the public school principals and others. I was proud to show Peter Gloege's LOOK Design Studio cover with the beautiful lighthouse. Ricardo Balderas, principal of Los Arboles elementary school, pointed to the cover and announced, "That lighthouse will go on our wall mural at Los Arboles with the Declaration of Independence words, 'We hold these truths. . . .'" Within a month, Ricardo was pleased to get a matching grant and the support of excited parents to fund the project.

What if every school in the country commissioned such a mural, each uniquely portraying our national heritage as found in the Declaration of Independence?

WHAT HAVE I LEARNED?

To conclude Part II, I'd like to summarize what I have learned on my journey to find answers to some of the questions posed at the beginning of this book.

What makes the Quest for Excellence so powerful? When we get a glimpse of what God wants to do, His vision is never lacking His provision. For me, as a Christian, the ultimate definition of excellence is the nature, character, and works of God. As I seek His wisdom and understanding, I better get to know Jesus and His good character. As I learn of Jesus, He helps me to become more and more like Him, experiencing His faith, hope, and love along with His goodness, peace, and joy.[149] Then by His kind mercy, He elects to do His great works in and through my life. He will do the same for anyone who truly seeks His wisdom and understanding and accepts Jesus' offer to "learn of Me."[150] That is the power of the Quest for Excellence!

No, Valley Christian Schools' Quest for Excellence success cannot be explained simply by being at the right place at the right time. We've discovered that any place is the right place, and any time is the right time, when we submit our lives to the mighty power of God's purposes and His leading. "But without faith it is impossible to please Him, for he who comes to God must believe that He is, and that He is a rewarder of those who diligently seek Him."[151]

So can I confidently say God is willing and able to do the same miraculous works to build excellent schools like VCS in any community where people are praying and working to bring His goodness, peace, and joy to the children in their schools? The answer is a resounding "YES." God is just as big in small places as He is in big places. His resources are infinite and available to ordinary people who have learned how to get "Access to the Omnis." He does big things in small schools, and He will make every school among the finest in its community when His people pray and strive toward a culture of true excellence.

Excellence differs in size and shape from place to place, just as communities differ. Aiming to produce clones of Valley Christian Schools everywhere would be a fool's errand. But all excellence ultimately reflects the nature, character, and works of God. And God is very creative. The same excellence displayed at Valley Christian Schools can manifest in innumerable ways wherever any community is committed to cultivating goodness, peace, and joy, as well as Light, Life, and Learning, through their own Quest for Excellence.

The public schools are not off-limits to the Christian community. For all of our children, we can call on the legacy of our Founding Fathers' values, including Common Virtues. These Common Virtues shaped the lives of the brave men and women who formed our nation, and as we uphold these ideals they can now transform all of our schools, including our public schools. By working together we can repair the rudder and restore the moral compass to American education. When properly deployed, our nation's Common Virtues will bring Light, Life, and Learning, as well as goodness, peace, and joy and A[3] (Academic Achievement, Artistic Beauty, and Athletic Distinction), to students anywhere! And no—"The sky is not the limit!"

CONCLUSION

ALL THINGS ARE POSSIBLE

IN OCTOBER 2013 I came across an article on *MailOnline,* the world's most-visited newspaper website.[152] The interview featured Lieutenant Commander John Moffat, the British Swordfish pilot who is credited with launching the torpedo that disabled the rudder of Nazi Germany's greatest warship, the *Bismarck.* At this writing, Mr. Moffat, born June 17, 1919, is age 95 and still living in Scotland.

"What nobody talks about were the conditions—they were unbelievable," recalled Moffat, speaking in the spring of 2009. Then age 89, he had recently written a book, *I Sank the Bismarck,* about his experiences.

Moffat was one of fifteen Swordfish pilots who took off May 26, 1941, from the aircraft carrier *Ark Royal* on their attack mission.

"The ship was pitching sixty feet, water was running over the decks, and the wind was blowing at 70 or 80 miles per hour.

"And nobody mentions the deck hands who had to bring the planes up from the hangars—they did something special. After they brought them up they had to open the wings, which took ten men for each wing. And then they had to wind a handle to get the starters working. . . . After take-off we climbed to 6,000 feet to get above the really thick clouds, and we knew when we were near because all hell broke loose with *Bismarck's* fire. We got the order to attack and I went down and saw the enormous bloody ship. I thought the *Ark Royal* was big, but this one, blimey.

British Swordfish pilot John Moffat, whose torpedo sank the *Bismarck*

"I must have been under 2,000 yards when I was about to launch the torpedo at the bow, but as I was about to press the button I heard in my ear 'not now, not now.'

"I turned round and saw the navigator leaning right out of the plane with his backside in the air. Then I realized what he was doing—

he was looking at the sea because if I had let the torpedo go and it had hit a wave, it could have gone anywhere. I had to put it in a trough.

"Then I heard him say 'let it go,' and I pressed the button. Then I heard him say 'we've got a runner'—and I got out of there."

The term "runner" means a torpedo that would run clear to its target without bouncing off a wave. Moffat pulled up before the torpedo hit and didn't see it strike.

The next morning, he flew back to the *Bismarck* with a second torpedo. But no further attack was necessary. He watched as the huge warship, fatally crippled and under barrage by the Royal Navy, rolled over. Hundreds of German sailors leaped overboard as the vessel started to sink.

"I didn't dare look any further. I just got back to the *Ark Royal* and I thought: 'There but for the grace of God go I.'"

Not until 2000, when the Fleet Air Arm (the British navy's air force) wrote to him, did he learn it was his torpedo that had disabled the *Bismarck's* rudder. He said, "It gave me a sort of satisfaction."[153]

DEFENDING OUR VALUES

As I read this article about British naval hero John Moffat, I thought of the life-changing lesson I had learned about every child's value. What I shared in Chapters 19–21 about my Faith Christian Academy accreditation experience bears repeating: The Grand Assessor set the price tag for every person as being equal to Himself when He gave Himself to redeem each and every one. If the fair market value of every person is based on the most recent purchase price, even one small child is of infinite and equal value to God, since He is of infinite value. The Awe Quotient of even one homeschooled child equals the Awe Quotient of all the students, programs, and capital investments at Valley Christian Schools.

John Moffat exemplifies "the Power of One" principle—and the Awe Quotient—in action. Think of that tiny, obsolete-looking Swordfish biplane, armed with a single torpedo, one courageous pilot, and his navigator. These were men who would rather have died for the cause of freedom than surrender to tyranny! Pilot John Moffat and his navigator, John "Dusty" Miller, turned the tide of battle from the likely escape of the formidable *Bismarck* to a crucial victory, a milestone in winning the war.

Those who stand to affirm the legacy of our Founding Fathers in our nation's schools might appear to be a minority, and our voice may seem feeble, but let us not grow faint.

Standing with truth and justice makes the weakest mortal a triumphant warrior, for "if God is for us, who can be against us?"[154]

Significantly, John Moffat did not learn about his successful torpedo attack on the *Bismarck* until the year 2000—fifty-nine years later! What an example! How selfless we should all be in our commitment to serve the children of our nation, regardless of whether we have any assurance of recognition for faithful service or even living long enough to see the fruit of our labors. We should have confidence that the Supreme Judge of the Heavens and the Earth will reward the faithfulness of all who help restore Common Virtues and goodness, peace, and joy to our families, schools, communities, and beyond with pure motives.

The rudder of our Founding Fathers' values, embedded in the Declaration of Independence, must be safely reconnected to our nation's schools. We, like our Founding Fathers, must firmly "hold" and teach the same unchanging, "self-evident" truths to all children in American schools.

The values that gave birth to our nation are strong enough to withstand outside attacks from competing ideologies. Our liberties and freedoms will sink to destruction only if America loses its rudder—its sense of direction of who we are and what makes us great. We have reason for concern. Sadly, many school children today remain ignorant of the legacy given to us by our Founders and of the universal values they fought for and won. This vacuum of truth stemming from rudderless schools makes many of our precious children vulnerable to horrific competing ideologies we hear about on our daily news. It is time for action to call upon the legacy of our Founding Fathers.

The American ship of state was forged in hardship, christened by men and women who understood how critical it was to embrace an unchanging set of sacred founding values. Those values have guided our ship through adverse seas of revolution, civil war, multiple world wars, economic recessions, depressions, and the attacks of religious radicals on 9/11. Those values endure in the very document upon which our nation was forged: The Declaration of Independence.

WINNING THE AIR WAR: A MESSAGE TO CHRISTIANS

The battle for the hearts and minds of our children is ongoing and fierce. In the case of the *Bismarck,* the nation ruling the air ultimately determined the outcome of the battle. Indeed, the ability of a tiny, slow-moving, lightly armed biplane to render ineffective Europe's mightiest battleship is astounding. Moreover, the sinking of the *Bismarck* convinced Hitler his own surface fleet could not stand up to the Royal Navy, so thereafter the dictator deployed his ships cautiously, under plenty of protection. And it all started with a little Swordfish armed with only one torpedo![155]

In reading the story of the *Bismarck,* I was reminded that the Bible identifies Satan as the enemy of our children and all that is good. He is called "the prince of the power of the air."[156] Nevertheless, the enemy's power, most Christians concur, cannot stand up against those who prayerfully call upon "the exceeding greatness of [God's] power toward us who believe, according to the working of His mighty power which

He worked in Christ when He raised Him from the dead and seated Him at His right hand in the heavenly places, far above all principality and power and might and dominion, and every name that is named, not only in this age but also in that which is to come."[157]

To achieve his calling in the face of seemingly insurmountable persecution, Paul bowed on his knees in prayer to summon heaven's air force to overpower the "prince of the power of the air." Paul's prayer in the book of Ephesians reads:

> For this reason I bow my knees to the Father of our Lord Jesus Christ, from whom the whole family in heaven and earth is named, that He would grant you, according to the riches of His glory, to be strengthened with might through His Spirit in the inner man, that Christ may dwell in your hearts through faith; that you, being rooted and grounded in love, may be able to comprehend with all the saints what is the width and length and depth and height—to know the love of Christ which passes knowledge; that you may be filled with all the fullness of God.
>
> Now to Him who is able to do exceedingly abundantly above all that we ask or think, according to the power that works in us, to Him be glory in the church by Christ Jesus to all generations, forever and ever. Amen.[158]

Imagine the Apostle Paul, a scarred man, stooped and hobbled by his many persecutions, beatings, imprisonments, and shipwrecks, falling in weakness on his knees to pray with confidence to the Supreme Commander of the universe. Paul had faith the High Commander would release His heavenly host and dispatch a mighty armada of airborne angels to answer his prayers. The "prince of the power of the air" is no match for God's angelic host. When Paul prayed, angels cleared the heavens of diabolical airborne powers and principalities who controlled the skies. And today God will do the same for anyone who is "strengthened with might through His Spirit."

Like John Moffat flying into the teeth of seventy-five-mile-per-hour winds on that stormy day in 1941, the outcome of Paul's prayers might have appeared dubious to others—perhaps, at times, even to himself. After all, Paul lived in a dangerous world. Scholars believe his epistle to the Ephesians was written around AD 60–63, at the onslaught of the first Roman persecution of Christians by Emperor Nero.[159]

Earlier, Paul wrote to the Corinthians, "a great and effective door has opened to me, and there are many adversaries."[160] The odds of Paul's success as a missionary must have seemed dismal to him as he sat beaten and broken in prison. Similarly, the prospects for American education appear grim today, with discouraging student achievement scores and a ranking of only seventeenth in the developed world for strength of its education system.[161] But now as then, "the god of this world"[162]—"the prince of the power of the air"—is no match for those who boldly pray and courageously act to promote truth and justice.

On his knees, Paul called in the air force of the heavenly host to push back the darkness. In response to Paul's prayers, God's heavenly angelic host opened a great door in the heavens. Paul's writings now comprise at least one third of the New Testament, including about half of its twenty-seven books. A "great and effective door" indeed! It's a door millions of Christians have walked through since Paul's martyrdom around AD 67. As with the lone Swordfish biplane in 1941, the impossible became possible when the power and love of God flowed through the words and pen of one man to fill generations of hungry hearts.

ALL THINGS ARE POSSIBLE

My goal is to encourage you to launch your personal Quest for Excellence, because no matter how large or small you—or your school, business, or profession—might be, God as the Grand Assessor of the Heavens and the Earth has assessed your value as infinite. He has a passion for you and every child, teenager, and adult who enters the gates of your home, school, and community. He will give you, and all who are committed to the Quest for Excellence, access to His Omnis—omnipotence, omnipresence, and omniscience—as He works to accomplish His purposes through you.

It has been a joy for me to share with you what God has done and is doing through our Quest Institute schools, beginning with Valley Christian and stretching to the opposite side of the world. I am especially gratified to build a collegial relationship with our amazing neighborhood Quest Institute public schools. We are working with remarkable teachers and administrators who serve selflessly in our local neighborhood schools every day!

But ours is only one story among many. Everyone in every sphere of influence has a personal story, a personal Quest for Excellence to fulfill. Although we all face human limitations, God perceives the value of each one of us as infinite, and with God all things are possible. God's excellent works are as broad and varied as there are people, and His power is limitless.

This is my story and our journey. What is yours?

The Quest continues. . . .

THE TWENTY
INDISPENSABLE PRINCIPLES

THROUGHOUT OUR FAITH journey, we at Valley Christian Schools have learned many humbling and rich faith lessons about living a supernatural life naturally. God has accomplished His wonderful works through us even when situations seemed impossible. I have encapsulated and summarized many of our faith lessons into twenty principles, which hold timeless truths for anyone with faith to love God and the discipline to pray persistently. You, too, can witness His amazing supernatural leading in your everyday life.

The power of God is available to anyone who will seek Him on His terms. We can never put a leash on God to lead Him where we want Him to go. On the contrary, the key to experiencing His power is to surrender ourselves to the Lord for His purposes, dying to selfish aspirations and inviting the excellence of Christ to live through us—supernaturally.

1. Get to Know "The Boss"

Devote yourself to knowing God at increasingly deeper levels. The more you get to know His nature, character, and works, the more He will accomplish His supernatural work through you—naturally.

2. Stay in the Book

Feed your soul on God's written Word. Maintain high regard for God's ability to guide and direct through the eternal principles of scripture. Memorize passages so God can use them to speak to you at any time. I have committed to reading God's Word for at least five minutes every day. Five minutes often leads to much more time. When I read, I am praying for God to direct me personally through His Holy Spirit. The Word of God is alive, and He will personalize parts of scripture that seem to joyfully scream at you as though God is speaking to you alone. God will use His words in the Bible to guide you through an adventurous journey as you follow Jesus and the leading of His Holy Spirit.

3. Stay Tuned and Keep Talking

Pray regularly as a spiritual discipline. Give God your full attention so He has an opportunity to speak to you about anything, including matters not already on your mind. As you develop a God-consciousness in all you do, you will find it easier to keep your ear tuned to God's Spirit and maintain a dialog with Him throughout the day. Listen for God to speak into your thoughts in every situation. Even if the answer seems obvious, He most likely has something to say, if only to confirm your thoughts. He may surprise you. These adventures with the Lord will become amazing testimonies of God's miraculous works. Be sure to disclose those supernatural works to inspire others to follow Jesus.

4. Get a Heart Transplant

Allow God to transplant His thoughts, desires, and purposes into your heart. Be willing to let go of previous assumptions and practices, even those long held. In particular, do not confuse personal or cultural preferences with timeless Christian principles.

> "And I will give you a new heart with new and right desires, and I will put a new spirit in you. I will take out your stony heart of sin and give you a new, obedient heart. And I will put my Spirit in you so you will obey my laws and do whatever I command."[163]

5. Walk in the Light

Ask God to shine the light of His Holy Spirit on any area of your heart in need of housecleaning. Ask Jesus to clean house by immediately confessing trespasses. Submit to God's will, and stay in right relationship with Him moment by moment so nothing blocks your communication. Keep in proper submission to people who have spiritual authority over you. Make sure all your personal, family, and business relationships are in order, since the kingdom of God is a kingdom of righteous, loving relationships with God, our neighbors, and ourselves.

6. Get a Clue!

Understand that a God-given vision is getting a glimpse of what God wants to do through you. When God gives you a vision, He will give the faith and the means to see it happen as you follow Him.

7. Think Big

Expect that any vision from God is going to be bigger

than any dream you could ever imagine. Depend on God's resources rather than what you have on hand or in view. If you can see your way clear to accomplish the vision, it is probably not of God.

8. Mission Impossible?

Don't dismiss "impossible" options. Likewise, do not assume that the opening of promising new doors means God wants you to walk through them. Pray and ask God to confirm His direction.

9. Expect Confirmation

God sometimes confirms His message through a persistent, deeper sense of "knowing," or He may speak through scripture reading or various circumstances of life. On occasion, He confirms His guidance through other people, and often through a combination of means. When you sense God is speaking, do not be afraid to ask Him for confirmation and correct understanding. Once you receive confirmation and correct understanding, move ahead in courage to obey what you have heard. When you have confidence about God's will for a particular situation, it becomes easier to persist in prayer, faith, and action toward its accomplishment. An often-repeated pattern for me is:

    A. Confirmation through a passage of scripture that seems to come alive

    B. Support from my wife, Kris, or other loved ones

    C. The presence of a prayer burden for the project by our intercessory prayer group

    D. Agreement by our administrative team and our Valley Christian Schools board

10. Let God Speak for Himself

Do not be surprised when you cannot convince others to support a God-sized project. After all, a rational person might tell you God's plans seem impossible. Trust that He knows how to communicate with people who are needed for the project in ways personally meaningful to them.

11. Pay the Price

As God leads, be willing to sacrifice and give all toward the fulfillment of His purposes. When God wants to stretch your faith, the process is often uncomfortable, or even painful, requiring you to see and do things differently and seemingly unnaturally. It is not unusual for you, a rational person, to question your sanity; after all, Noah built an ark on dry ground when it had never rained in the history of the world. Or perhaps you resonate with Moses, who was tasked with leading millions of people across the Red Sea without a single boat; or with aged Abraham and barren Sarah trying to have as many children as there are stars in the sky and grains of sand on the seashore. Trust Him to take care of your needs and your reputation in pursuit of the vision. Take heed: The more vision God gives, the more you are responsible to accomplish what He has shown you. As Jesus said, "... to whom much is given, from him much will be required."[164]

12. Wait Upon the Lord

Since only God can do His work, "wait on the Lord" to do it. You cannot force progress even if you try. Position yourself for God to act, then watch and wait expectantly for what God will do. Allow time for God to do His work in His way. Allow Him to teach you through trials and challenges. Wait, but do not give up on the vision. God often gives progressive disclosure to His vision. Oftentimes, the larger the vision, the longer the lead time between seeing the vision and doing the vision. The lead time allows for adequate prayer, personal spiritual growth, and planning.

We were led to purchase the land for Valley Christian Schools ten years before God opened the door for city approvals and for construction to begin. The Skyway campus vision seemed dead and buried. But about the time I began to question whether I had misunderstood God's vision, God powerfully resurrected the project. I have discovered that God often allows all to appear lost right before He shows up and does His miraculous work. I call them "Cliff hangers"! It is a great reminder that He is God and He uses these circumstances to grow our faith.

13. Forget Plan B

Insist on going forward according to God's "A Team" plans. When obstacles or setbacks arise, pray and ask God to show you how He wants to deal with the situation. Believe that He does not want to settle for Plan B. Do not succumb to fear. God's vision is never lacking His provision. Be open to creative and unprecedented solutions. Remember, "Plans made in heaven are never ten feet too short!"[165]

14. Call In the Air Force

The Bible refers to Satan as "the mighty prince of the power of the air."[166] The enemy always opposes God's work. Remember Paul's admonition: "For we are not fighting against people made of flesh and blood, but against the evil rulers and authorities of the unseen world, against those mighty powers of darkness who rule this world, and against wicked spirits in the heavenly realms."[167]

God appoints prayer intercessors to call in the "air cover" of His angelic hosts for His faithful warriors on the front lines. Watch for and honor the intercessors God assigns to pray for you and the vision you share. It is very helpful to pray weekly with an intercessory team as God leads. Keep your prayer team informed of your vision, your prayer requests, and how God is answering prayer, so they can pray strategically. Allow God to guide corporately as well as individually. "Pray at all times and on every occasion in the power of the Holy Spirit. Stay alert and be persistent in your prayers for all Christians everywhere. And pray for me, too."[168]

The enemy is no match for God's angelic air force, and the Lord will defeat "the mighty prince of the power of the air" through prayer and the air cover of His angelic hosts. Every phase of God's work at Valley Christian Schools required a breakthrough in prayer to achieve success. When circumstances, human weaknesses, and dark forces seem to block God's purposes, partner with God-appointed prayer intercessors to call in the air force—God's angelic hosts!

"Praise Him, all His angels; praise Him, all His hosts!"[169]

"Restore us, O Lord God of hosts; cause Your face to shine, and we shall be saved!"[170]

"The Lord of hosts is with us; the God of Jacob is our refuge."[171]

God assigns His angels to watch over us as children, and they are at His command to help us achieve His purposes throughout our lives as we pray and seek to serve Him. "See that you don't look down on one of these little ones, because I tell you that in heaven their angels continually view the face of My Father in heaven."[172]

15. *Keep the Faith*

Do not allow obstacles to stop you or to damage your faith. Your faith will soar if instead you see obstacles as opportunities for God to demonstrate His miraculous power. Let Him reassure you about His desire and intention to accomplish His highest purposes in whatever way He chooses. Faith is a gift of the Holy Spirit, and God gives us the gift for each of His works. We cannot manufacture miracle-working faith. "The Spirit gives special faith. . . ."[173]

16. *Duke It Out*

Give yourself permission to wrestle with your doubts and to work through the "why" questions. Ask God to help you understand scriptural truths that apply to your situation. Ask God for the faith to make a wholehearted commitment to move forward in the face of unanswered questions like, "Where will we get the money?"

17. *Tap Great Talent*

Ask God to help you do the homework needed to discover and engage the finest talent to help move the vision forward. Ask "the Lord of the harvest to send out laborers into His harvest."[174] The initial price tag is usually higher, but quality usually improves the bottom line before long.

18. No Secrets

Always share the vision God gave you with those who will listen. On more than one occasion, I have shared God's vision with people of seemingly modest means who eventually gave tens of thousands—and even millions—of dollars in response to God's leading. Be faithful to share the vision, but understand that it is only God who can lead people to give their time, talent, and treasure from their hearts.

19. Aim For the Stars

Aim for excellence in everything you do. Ultimately, true excellence is the nature, character, and works of God. Anything we do truly reflecting excellence requires the work of God and is by definition "supernatural." Pursuing His excellence opens the door to experiencing His supernatural works in your everyday life—naturally.

20. Journal the Journey

Periodically document the ways God has supernaturally worked through your life. Honor Him for His faithfulness, and allow these accounts to bring you and others into a new dimension of faith in and love for God. Later in life when you face doubts and difficulties, written testimonies of what God has accomplished through you will be a great encouragement. Recorded details of God's miraculous works will speak to you, your children, and their children, and teach others about His faithfulness.

The twenty principles and practices listed above are illustrated by the great miraculous events God engineered to develop Valley

Christian Schools. Your personal stories of how God discloses His miraculous Quest for Excellence through your life, family, and career will be different, but the principles remain constant.

In the Quest for Excellence, the highest standard for excellence is understood as the nature, character, and works of God. The Excellence Brings Influence strategy prepares students to reshape their culture by bringing goodness, peace, and joy to their families, schools, communities, and beyond. Their communities and the world benefit through the students' personal Quests for Excellence and their emerging professional spheres, including business, education, engineering, entertainment, finance, law, politics, media, medicine, science, and all professions of influence.

In a nutshell, I propose that the extraordinary quality of education available to more than 2,500 students at Valley Christian Schools can become available to schoolchildren across America and around the world. There is no limit to what God can and will do for those who believe.

Neither VCS nor I have a corner on the market of educational excellence. Our schools and their quality of education for our children can be only as robust as the values and truths we teach. And the universal values of our Founding Fathers are available to benefit all school students everywhere!

For me, there is one pivotal question upon which the door of educational opportunity swings for every student in America and around the world. Are you ready? Here it is:

Can we rely on the self-evident truths our Founding Fathers preserved in the Declaration of Independence to serve as a proven rudder and moral compass steering our schools toward quality education?

It is a simple question with potentially profound implications. My goal is for every reader to have a clear strategy on how to build a culture of goodness, peace, and joy in their local schools, in an environment of academic excellence.

Our journey at VCS has been peppered with huge obstacles and heartaches, but also joys and triumphs. Our Creator remains faithful to guide us as we pursue the Quest for Excellence for our children, our families, our communities, our nation, and schools around the world. They deserve it! Every single child is irreplaceable in God's eyes. It is our task and our privilege to answer His call and, as parents and educators, to encourage every student to discover his or her personal Quest for Excellence.[175]

It bears repeating: At the heart of the Quest for Excellence is the crucial definition of excellence. There could be no higher standard or more accurate definition of excellence than the person of God Himself, whose name is "Excellent."[176] For our purposes, then, excellence is defined as the nature, character, and works of God—a standard beyond the reach of any mortal. This is why we have a *Quest* for Excellence. It's about following Jesus and becoming like Jesus, which is a lifelong journey. Indeed, as John the Apostle wrote, "we know that when Christ appears, we shall be like him. . . ."[177]

There *is* hope for America's schools. There *is* a bright future for America's children—as the Quest for Excellence continues!

ACKNOWLEDGMENTS

SINCERE APPRECIATION is expressed to those who helped make *The Quest Continues* a reality by contributing to the story or assisting with editing. Among them:

My precious and loving wife, Kris, read and patiently listened to my meanderings while discussing many of the ideas in the book.

Mike Annab, a great friend and son-in-law, assisted with editing.

Emily Annab, our eldest grandchild, first suggested the title *The Quest Continues*.

Pam Watson, my executive assistant at Valley Christian Schools (VCS), first read the unedited manuscript and encouraged me to move forward toward publication. She also greatly assisted with final editing.

Jane Rumph served as the final editor of both *Quest for Excellence* and *The Quest Continues*.

Kyle Duncan assisted in the organization of the two parts of this book and significant editing.

Debby Alten did a complete edit of the manuscript.

Peter Gloege of LOOK Design Studio designed the cover and the entire format of the book.

Patrick Judd of PLJ Communications served as my publishing consultant.

The Valley Christian Board of Directors members past and present since 2006, including Vera Shantz (Chair), Michael Sprauve (Vice Chair), Dan Burford (Secretary), Michael Ainslie, Susan Bagley, Stephen McMinn, Jerry Merza, Eric Phelps, Robert Rubino, Don Watson, and Rick Watson have provided extraordinary Valley Christian Schools board governance, without which this book could not exist.

Valley Christian Schools' Senior Leadership Team—including (in alphabetical order) Michael Annab, Director of IT; Lisa Arnett, Junior High Principal; Kimberly Ellefsen, Director of Marketing; Claude Fletcher, Chancellor Emeritus; Troy Gunter, VP/Director K–12 Conservatory of the Arts; Gabe Guven, Elementary Principal; Shirley Hitchcock, Director of Accreditation/Curriculum; Mike LaBarbera, Extend the Gift Advancement Director; Mark Lodewyk, High School Principal; Karina McCann, Administrative Assistant; Steve McMinn, VP/COO; Eric Scharrenberg, VP K–12 Athletics and Physical Education; Ken Shilling, VP/CFO; Werner Vavken, VP/Director K–12 Applied Math, Science, and Engineering Institute (AMSE) and VCS Faculty/Staff Chaplain; and Pam Watson, Executive Assistant to the President—all passionately pursue the Quest for Excellence™. In addition, Robert Bridges, retired Junior High Principal; Don Shipley, retiring VP/CFO; and Joel Torode, retired High School Principal, each made significant leadership contributions to the journey recorded in *The Quest Continues*.

Valley Christian Board Chaplain, Ed Silvoso, continues as a guiding light for transformation at Valley Christian Schools and beyond.

Prayer intercessors Sheri Vavken (Lead Intercessor) and her husband, Werner, Kris Daugherty, Zane Daugherty, Dean and Bev Deaton, Joan Keller, Danny and Hannah Kim, Sonny Lara, Victor Pioli, and Joel and Sue Torode provide the spiritual air cover to enable what God is accomplishing as the Quest for Excellence™ continues.

The Quest Institute for Quality Education Board of Directors, including Susan Bagley, Robert Rubino, Vera Shantz, Mike Sprauve, Werner Vavken, and Rick Watson, has pursued its mission to develop and sustain premier comprehensive schools in support of the Quest for Excellence through Academic Achievement, Artistic Beauty, and Athletic Distinction, while upholding the values of our Founding Fathers.

AMSE (Applied Math, Science, and Engineering) Advisory Board members, past and present, include NASA astronaut Yvonne Cagle, Brian Cronquist, Jean Fairweather, Larry Fennern, Stephen Ferrero, Ani Karmarkar, Danny Kim, Yoon Berm Kim, Doug McNeil, Bob Monteverde, Eric Phelps, Jon Prange, Tom Rivellini, Bruce D. Roth, Dan Saldana, Werner Vavken, and Jim Young.

Cindy Nardi, Valley Christian High School (VCHS) teacher, serves as the point person to lead hundreds of VCS students as Junior University and Lighthouse Initiative mentors for students in local public schools.

Karina McCann, my administrative assistant, helped facilitate the entire Junior University and Lighthouse Initiative in recent years.

Cathy Manthey, Valley Splash Director of Aquatics, gave birth to the "Splish! Splash! Learn to Swim" program for socioeconomically disadvantaged public school students.

John Mark Cooley of CooleySublett PLC, general counsel for Valley Christian Schools and the Quest Institute, provided invaluable legal guidance as we pursued the vision for Junior University and the Lighthouse Initiative.

Public school leaders Dr. Ricardo Balderas, Dr. Maria Dehghanfard, Joshua Greene, Carla Haakma, Bettina Lopez, Liz Nandakumar, and Dr. John Porter led in the development of the Junior University and Lighthouse Initiative in partnership with Valley Christian Schools.

Principal Jerry Merza and his wife, Lyn, walked with us on a wonderful transformation journey at Hellyer Elementary School and beyond.

Tara Davis, founder and principal of Faith Christian Academy in Coalinga, California, helped me discover that God can build great schools in small places.

Adele Willson and Lynn Eller of Slaterpaull Architects created a beautiful design of the Conservatory of the Arts building.

Key Bank of America professionals including Doug Brown, Daniel Dryzin, Anna Jenkins, Mike Moss, Marianna Pisano, and Mark Slater believed in the VCS mission and funded $38 million in tax-exempt bonds in 2003 to construct the elementary campus while retiring VCS's obligation to its previous lender; they also issued $20 million in tax-exempt bonds in 2008 to build the Valley Christian Human Performance Center and the Conservatory of the Arts in the face of the Great Recession.

Key Wells Fargo professionals including Cynthia Bouldt, Doug Brown, Chris Gernhard, Warren Guinane, Mark Haggen, Mystique Pearson, Keri Rees, Mark Slater, Rob Swanson, and Kaylin Tabb provided $58 million in tax-exempt bond funding to retire Bank of America bonds in 2012. Note: Doug Brown and Mark Slater moved their careers from Bank of America to Wells Fargo Bank and greatly assisted VCS while serving at both banks.

Richard Furtado of South Bay Construction, a VCS alumni parent who constructed all of the Skyway campus between 1998 and 2002, built Phase 1 of the Conservatory of the Arts, including 55,000 square feet, in 2011 for almost $200 per square foot less than the next pricing offered by another reputable construction firm. The savings Richard provided came to just over $10 million on the conservatory building.

Brian Brager of New Technology Specialists, a VCS alumnus, completed Phase 2 of the Conservatory of the Arts, including the first and fourth floors, at a savings of about $1.7 million. The lower floor was finished for the opening of the 2012-13 school year and the fourth floor for the 2013–14 school year.

Pepperdine University's Chancellor (now Emeritus) Charles B. Runnels was very instrumental during my early years at Valley Christian Schools in establishing the VCS mentality on "excellence" and the broader vision of using adversity to challenge us toward achieving even greater accomplishments.

Friends of VCS have significantly contributed their time, talent, and treasure to help fund the school's operations and development.

ENDNOTES

All websites accessed as of March 6, 2015

Chapter 1

1. "Who Really Sank the Bismarck?," http://abcnews.go.com/WNT/story?id=129972&page=1

2. *Ibid.*

3. "The Fairey Swordfish, Albacore, & Barracuda," http://www.airvectors.net/avsword.html

4. *Ibid.*

5. "I Sank the Bismarck . . .," http://www.dailymail.co.uk/news/article-1191813/Pilot-sank-Bismarck-tells-tale-70-years.html

6. "German battleship *Bismarck*," Wikipedia, http://en.wikipedia.org/wiki/German_battleship_Bismarck

7. "British Prime Minister Winston Churchill issued the order 'Sink the Bismarck!,'" HLR Gazette Archives, http://www.hlrgazette.com/2011-articles/145-may-7-2011/1537-british-prime-minister-winston-churchill-issued-the-order-sink-the-bismarck.html

8. *"Bismarck's* Final Battle," Part 2, William H. Garzke, Jr., and Robert O. Dulin, Jr., http://www.navweaps.com/index_inro/INRO_Bismarck_p2.htm

9. "Bismarck receiving first torpedo," http://www.dailymail.co.uk/news/article-2247003/Bismarck-receiving-torpedo-Rare-photos-chronicle-race-sink-pride-Hitlers-fleet.html#ixzz2ozzZ38Dh

10. See Romans 8:31.

11. The phrase "goodness, peace, and joy" comes from Romans 14:17, New Living Translation (NLT).

12. "For there is no partiality with God" (Romans 2:11).

13. Colossians 3:23, KJV

14. From John 14:14

15. From James 1:5

Chapter 2

16. *Democracy in America,* Volume I 1835, http://www.gutenberg.org/files/815/815-h/815-h.htm, Introductory Chapter, paragraph 23

17. Abington Township School District v. Schempp, 1963

18. Congressional Prayer Caucus Foundation, December 11, 2013, "The Effects of Removing Prayer and the Bible From the Schools in 1962," http://cpcfoundation.wordpress.com/2013/12/11/the-effects-of-removing-prayer-and-the-bible-from-the-schools-in-1962/

19. *Democracy in America,* Volumes I 1835 and II 1840, Kindle, Loc 6326

20. *Democracy in America,* Volumes I 1835 and II 1840, Kindle, Loc 852

21. "Jefferson's Formal Education," *Thomas Jefferson Encyclopedia,* http://www.monticello.org/site/research-and-collections/jeffersons-formal-education. This article is based on Gaye Wilson, Monticello Research Report, December 1999.

22. "William Small," *Thomas Jefferson Encyclopedia,* http://www.monticello.org/site/jefferson/william-small

23. U.S. Department of Education, http://www2.ed.gov/about/offices/list/oii/nonpublic/statistics.html#private

Chapter 3

24. National Center for Educational Statistics, Fast Facts, http://nces.ed.gov/fastfacts/display.asp?id=1

25. "U.S. Education Spending Tops Other Countries," Students First, posted by Cameron Conrad on July 3, 2013, http://www.studentsfirst.org/blogs/entry/u.s.-education-spending-tops-other-countries

26. Tinker v. Des Moines Independent Community School District, 393 U.S. 503 (1969)

27. *Ibid.*

28. Socrates, http://www.bartleby.com/348/authors/506.html

29. Plato, http://www.goodreads.com/quotes/85597-education-is-teaching-our-children-to-desire-the-right-things

30. George Washington, in a letter to the Episcopal Church, http://www.sonofthesouth.net/revolutionary-war/general/george-washington-letter-episcopals.htm

31. *Ibid.*

32. "Top Schools of the Silicon Valley Region," Innovate Public Schools, December 2013, Originally posted at www.InnovateSchools.org. Available via moopdf.net/file/top-schools-of-the-silicon-valley-region-innovate-public-36709.html

33. From Proverbs 21:1

34. From Proverbs 31:9, NASB

Chapter 4

35. At the time Ed Silvoso introduced us to LUYW, the Sanchezes were part of his ministry.

36. The Quest Institute for Quality Education, www.TheQuestInstitute.com. The VCS board of directors and I had founded the Quest Institute (QI) in 2006 to serve as a conduit for VCS's innovations and intellectual properties to flow outward to member schools and organizations. The QI promotes best educational practices and the values of our Founding Fathers in schools and organizations. VCS and the QI later trained Girl Scout mentors to lead a team of Hawaiian Girl Scouts to design and build a successful science experiment launched onto the International Space Station—but the amazing VCS on-campus space program is a story for another chapter.

37. http://www.youtube.com/watch?v=fvzH2FBD-o8. See also a student-made video about the Junior University and Lighthouse Initiative at http://www.youtube.com/watch?v=jVWWgK57fsc.

38. From Mark 9:24; see story in Mark 9:14–29.

39. Matthew 18:20

Chapter 6

40. Psalm 127:1, NIV

41. John Mark Cooley's email is reproduced here in its entirety:

From: John M. Cooley
Sent: Monday, May 13, 2013 2:46 PM
To: Cliff Daugherty

Dr. Daugherty,

I am writing to follow up on our prior conversation regarding the Valley Christian Schools ("Valley") Splish/Splash swim program.

Assuming the particular school, or school district, has a practice of partnering with other community programs to provide opportunities to students and distributes communications informing parents of those opportunities, then disseminating a brochure or flyer to parents on Valley's Splish/Splash program would not be prohibited. Under a series of cases, the United States Supreme Court has recognized that where access/facilities/communications are made available to other secular groups, then a school district must also make the same opportunities available to religious groups on equal terms. For example, in *Good News Club v. Milford Central School District*, 533 U.S. 98 (2001), the U.S. Supreme Court addressed a school district's denial to permit an adult-initiated, adult-led after-school religious club. The Court found the district's exclusion of the club, simply on the basis of its religious content, constituted impermissible

viewpoint discrimination in violation of the First Amendment to the United States Constitution ("First Amendment"). Other cases confirm that the First Amendment requires neutrality toward, not hostility against, subject matter which merely happens to be addressed from a religious perspective.

Following the *Milford* case, other courts have addressed various aspects of this issue. In fact, the Ninth Circuit Court of Appeals addressed this precise issue (distribution of a flyer for a summer camp) in *Hills v. Scottsdale Unified Sch. Dist.*, 329 F.3d. 1044 (9th Cir. 2003) (*per curiam*). I have attached a copy of this case to this email. The Ninth Circuit Court of Appeals covers California and, therefore, this decision would be controlling precedent.

In *Hills*, as in this situation, a summer camp program sought to distribute a flyer informing parents of the availability of the summer camp program, which would include religious content. The School District refused to distribute the flyer due to the Christian nature of the summer camp program. The program was run by an Arizona non-profit and the brochure advertised a camp that offered various classes in outdoor activities, along with Bible classes. The Ninth Circuit Court of Appeals found the School District's refusal to allow the flyer to be distributed through the school constituted unconstitutional viewpoint discrimination in violation of the First Amendment. As the Court provided, **"the District's exclusion of Hills's summer camp brochure because it offered Bible Classes from a Christian perspective . . . constitutes impermissible viewpoint discrimination"** 329 F.3d at 1052 (emphasis added). The Court went on to recognize that if the District allows other organizations to distribute similar information, "then [it] cannot refuse to distribute literature advertising an off-campus summer program because it is taught from a Christian perspective" *Id.* at 1053.

The Court in *Hills* did recognize that the flyer would have contained a disclaimer that the School District "neither endorses nor sponsors the organization or activity represented in this document. The distribution of this material is provided as a community service." The Ninth Circuit did not elaborate on whether this specific language is required or not, but some disclaimer, consistent with the above, should be provided. Since there are no other cases, it is unclear what, if any, effect altering the language of the disclaimer would have. The primary purpose is to demonstrate that the activity is not one which has the imprimatur or coercion of the school or school district. If there are concerns regarding the precise wording of the disclaimer, the following is another potential alternative for consideration:

"The program referenced in this brochure is sponsored by the Quest Institute for Quality Education and Valley Christian Schools as a community service. The Franklin–McKinley School District is not sponsoring or supervising the activity and is providing this information as a community service. Participation is at the discretion of parents."

I hope this assists Valley in answering any questions or concerns the school or school district may have in this situation. Please let me know if you need anything further regarding this matter.

Best Regards,
John M.

John Mark Cooley, Esq.
CooleySublett PLC
Colonnade Corporate Center
2965 Colonnade Drive, Suite 200
Roanoke VA 24018

42. http://www.lightupyourworld.org/

Chapter 7
43. Socrates, http://www.quoteopia.com/famous.php?quotesby=socrates

Chapter 8
44. Proverbs 16:3. The NKJV uses the word "thoughts" and the NASB uses the word "plans." Both translation of the Hebrew word are important to understanding the more complete meaning.
45. Psalm 37:23
46. From Colossians 2:2–3
47. See Matthew 17:5.
48. John 14:12–14
49. John 15:4–5
50. See Matthew 22:37.

Chapter 9
51. John 15:7
52. Joshua 1:8
53. From Psalm 1:2–3
54. Proverbs 4:5–8
55. Proverbs 9:10
56. From Colossians 1:27
57. Colossians 1:16–17
58. 1 Corinthians 2:16
59. From John 3:13
60. Colossians 2:9
61. See John 1:3, 3:1–21.
62. Isaiah 55:9
63. 2 Timothy 1:12
64. From Matthew 7:23
65. Matthew 25:21

66. Hebrews 13:20–21
67. Luke 18:27
68. From Luke 22:42
69. From Luke 11:2
70. See John 5:19.
71. Matthew 22:37
72. John 14:15, 21
73. From Philippians 4:19
74. Matthew 6:10
75. See John 14:14.
76. From Colossians 1:10
77. From 2 Thessalonians 1:11
78. Matthew 11:29
79. From Colossians 3:23
80. Psalm 37:4
81. Proverbs 16:2–4, NASB
82. Romans 14:17, NLT

Chapter 10
83. Proverbs 29:18, KJV
84. From Luke 12:48

Chapter 11
85. Matthew 6:21
86. From Acts 20:35
87. Matthew 6:21
88. James 1:5
89. From Acts 20:35
90. Luke 4:18–19, NIV
91. See Acts 10:34.
92. Philippians 2:13

Chapter 12
93. Matthew 5:14
94. From Romans 14:17, NLT
95. From Romans 10:13

Chapter 13
96. Isaiah 43:19, NASB
97. See Leviticus 25:8.
98. The word "children" is taken from the NKJV; the remainder of the passage is NASB.
99. 3-17-09
100. 3-17-09
101. 3-17-09
102. Philippians 4:19

Chapter 14
103. From Proverbs 3:6
104. http://www.readwriteweb.com/start/2010/02/silicon-valley-2009-job-loss.php

105. See 1 Corinthians 10:13.

106. See Mark 9:14–27, NKJV.

107. Dated week of 7-13-09

Chapter 15

108. From Leviticus 19:3, NLT

109. See John 14:12–14.

110. From Isaiah 43:1

111. From Isaiah 43:6

112. From Isaiah 43:19

113. From Isaiah 49:20

114. From Isaiah 49:25

Chapter 16

115. James 1:2

116. As described by the Apostle Paul in Romans 14:17 (NLT)

117. From James 5:16

118. VCS made a $200,000 initial payment for the land from the $20 million bond proceeds, with the balance to be paid to the church over five years.

Chapter 17

119. Confirmed by an email of 11-09-2009 to the prayer intercessors and VCS board

120. Isaiah 66:2, NASB

121. Ephesians 6:12

122. From Leviticus 25:10

Chapter 18

123. From James 1:17, NIV

124. From Zechariah 4:6

125. From Matthew 28:19, NLT

Chapter 19

126. Zechariah 4:10, NLT

Chapter 21

127. From John 10:10

128. John 3:16

129. John 1:1–3

130. From John 14:9

131. John 10:30

132. Summarized and slightly edited for this book

133. http://www.youtube.com/watch?v=3ezKgLxbz2M

134. For more information, visit http://www.vcs.net/page.cfm?p=742; also click on the image of the brochure "College Begins Here" describing the cost savings and benefits.

135. Echoing John 1:46

Chapter 22

136. The term "'Big Hairy Audacious Goal' was proposed by James Collins and Jerry Porras in their 1994 book entitled *Built to Last: Successful Habits of Visionary Companies*. A BHAG encourages companies to define visionary goals that are more strategic and emotionally compelling." See http://en.wikipedia.org/wiki/Big_Hairy_Audacious_Goal

137. Michelle Roth helped compose the following announcement to move the project forward:

Nanotechnology Comes to Valley Christian Schools!
By Michelle Roth and Clifford Daugherty, Ed.D

While summer sizzles, Valley Christian Schools launches another exciting, groundbreaking innovation for students. Valley Christian Schools joins the ranks of Columbia, Cornell, Dow Chemical, IBM, MIT, UC Berkeley and William and Mary, with the addition of a nanotechnology lab featuring two Atomic Force Microscopes (AFMs). The lab will greet students as they return to classes for the 2010–11 school year.

Dr. Daugherty, VCS President, credits Dr. Bruce Roth for the vision and courage to launch the nation's first high school AFM lab. Dr. Bruce Roth, Vice President of Discovery Chemistry at Genentech Small Molecule Discovery, serves as an Advisory Board member for VCS's Applied Math, Science and Engineering Institute (AMSE).

What is nanotechnology? "Nanos" in the Greek means "dwarf," but in scientific applications it is a prefix for the study of objects that are very, very, very, very, very small! Nano-scale objects are one/one-billionth of a meter (1/1,000,000,000) in size and can be manmade (ridges in DVDs) or natural products like viruses, molecules, chromosomes or DNA. Such objects require the use of highly specialized microscopes to make them visible. Visualization of such small objects requires the use of an electron microscope or the more advanced AFM.

Bob Monteverde, Marketing Manager at Nanounity, a company that distributes and services advanced microscopes, said, "Nanounity is pleased to support Valley Christian as the first high school in the nation to offer students a research grade AFM." The nation's first high school nanotechnology lab includes the 2009 award winning Solver Next and a mobile training microscope called the "Nano-educator."

Staff training began in earnest, under the leadership of Michelle Roth, VCHS Biotechnology instructor. Mrs. Roth is building on her experience as a university electron microscope technician with Nanounity training this summer. With Nanounity support, she will assist students and faculty with AFM training on the Skyway campus during the 2010–11 school year.

The microscopes will directly support the research projects of AMSE students, but the technology is available for instruction and demonstration for all Valley Christian students in grades K–12. Mrs. Roth emphasizes, "Valley Christian's nanotechnology curriculum initiative is to inspire and support students across grade levels with cross curriculum applicability. This equipment is an investment in our students and is meant to inspire them to explore God's creation and to excel in their scientific learning through the fascinating world of nanotechnology."

138. See http://www.vcs.net/page.cfm?p=846 for more information about the AMSE Advisory Board.

139. By the 2014–15 school year, just over 400 high school students enrolled as majors or minors in the AMSE Institute, alongside more than 450 students enrolled as majors or minors in the Conservatory of the Arts.

140. http://spacenews.com/10-who-made-difference-space-bob-twiggs-professor-emeritus-stanford-university/ and http://insiderlouisville.com/business/space/

Chapter 23

141. Joshua Greene is E.L.D. Teacher, 504 Coordinator, CAS Hours Coordinator, and Junior University/Community Service Opportunities Coordinator at Andrew P. Hill High School.

142. www.The-Firehouse.org

143. Andrew P. Hill High School 2012–13 School Accountability Report Card, page 11. See http://www.esuhsd.org/documents/A%20-%20Update%202012/Students%20-%20Parents/Instruction/Testing%20-%20Accountability/SARCs/SARC2014/AH2013_School_Accountability_Report_Card_Andrew_P._Hill_High_School_20140103.pdf

144. http://www.lightupyourworld.org

145. Customer satisfaction is a score from 0 to 100 percent, and the overall score following the summer LUYW program was 84 percent. One of the four questions measuring customer satisfaction asks, "I feel I benefited from this program," and only 3 percent of the respondents indicated they did not benefit from LUYW.

Service productivity is determined by asking

the youth whether they changed for the better because of the program services. Seven questions measured asset development, and the overall score for asset development service productivity was 61 percent. (The national benchmark for performance on service productivity is 60 percent.) On one of the questions, 82 percent of youth answered: "Because of this program, my understanding of who I am and what I can do is: Better."

Youth were also asked eight questions based on the LUYW curriculum about specific targeted changes and behaviors. The overall score for the LUYW-specific target changes service productivity was 68 percent. One of the questions asked, "Because of this program, I understand my true value," and 75 percent answered "More."

LUYW youth participants who are receiving mentoring and coaching services are being surveyed twice during the 2014–15 school year.

146. See http://www.youtube.com/watch?v=lAHeJDF5780 for a video of the complete concert.

147. See http://www.youtube.com/watch?v=hZWVjG1Wd3o for a four-minute clip of the jazz ensemble.

148. See the "Declaration" video at http://www.youtube.com/watch?v=sSn-KtlTAIg. Obtain "Declaration" song videos produced by Valley Christian Schools through the Quest Institute for Quality Education. Member schools or organizations may obtain the videos at cost to the Quest Institute.

149. See Galatians 5:22–23, 1 Corinthians 13:13, Romans 14:17 (NLT).

150. See Proverbs 4:5–8, Matthew 11:29.

151. Hebrews 11:6

Conclusion

152. MailOnline, also known as dailymail.co.uk, is the world's most visited newspaper website, according to ComScore, whose methodology gave the site 50.1 million unique visitors for October 2012, ahead of the previous leader, The New York Times website, which received 48.7 million visitors in the same month. See http://en.wikipedia.org/wiki/Mail_Online

153. http://www.dailymail.co.uk/news/article-1191813/Pilot-sank-Bismarck-tells-tale-70-years.html. See also http://www.dailymail.co.uk/news/article-2247003/Bismarck-receiving-torpedo-Rare-photos-chronicle-race-sink-pride-Hitlers-fleet.html#ixzz2ozzZ38Dh

154. From Romans 8:31

155. "The Fairey Swordfish, Albacore, & Barracuda," http://www.airvectors.net/avsword.html

156. Ephesians 2:2

157. Ephesians 1:19–21

158. Ephesians 3:14–21

159. *Foxe's Book of Martyrs,* Chapter 2

160. 1 Corinthians 16:9

161. http://www.huffingtonpost.com/2012/11/27/best-education-in-the-wor_n_2199795.html

162. From 2 Corinthians 4:4, NASB

The Twenty Indispensable Principles

163. Ezekiel 36:26–27, NLT

164. From Luke 12:48

165. The "ten feet too short" quotation is from the miracle described in Chapter 11 of *Quest for Excellence* about how the oversized Olympic pool and the baseball field were both built on space that initially was "ten feet too short."

166. From Ephesians 2:2, NLT

167. Ephesians 6:12, NLT

168. Ephesians 6:18–19a, NLT

169. Psalm 148:2

170. Psalm 80:19

171. Psalm 46:11

172. Matthew 18:10, HCSB

173. From 1 Corinthians 12:9, NLT

174. From Luke 10:2

175. See Proverbs 22:6.

176. See Psalm 8:1, 9; Hebrews 1:4.

177. From 1 John 3:2, NIV

DR. CLIFFORD DAUGHERTY joined Valley Christian Schools in San Jose, California, as president and superintendent in July 1986. Under his leadership, enrollment has tripled, and VCS now serves approximately 2,700 K–12 students, including more than 1,500 in the high school. During his tenure, permanent facilities have been constructed for all three schools, with a current value of more than $150 million. Dr. Daugherty also serves as founding president of the Quest Institute for Quality Education and of Neighborhood Christian Preschools in Silicon Valley, was founding principal at Los Altos Christian School, and founded the Santa Clara County Christian School Association. He sits on the Board of Trustees of William Jessup University. He has authored *Quest for Excellence*, the first volume in a two-book series with *The Quest Continues*, and *Fly With Your Dreams*.

Dr. Daugherty received his B.S. in English Literature, Bible and Theology from Bethany College, his M.A. in Public School Administration from San Jose State University, and his Ed.D. in Private School Administration and Special Education from the University of San Francisco. He holds lifetime California and ACSI Teaching and Administrative credentials.

He and his wife, Kris, have two children and five grandchildren.

CONTACT INFORMATION
If you are interested in learning more about the Quest for Excellence in your professional sphere of influence, contact the Quest Institute for Quality Education at **408-513-2503** *or visit* **www.TheQuestInstitute.com.**

Clifford E. Daugherty, Ed.D. • President/Superintendent
Valley Christian Schools • 100 Skyway Drive • San Jose CA 95111
president@valleychristian.net

THE QUEST CONTINUES
Paperback: ISBN: 978-0-9964207-2-3
eBook: ISBN: 978-0-9964207-3-0
Audio: ISBN: 978-0-9964207-4-7

QUEST FOR EXCELLENCE
Paperback: ISBN: 978-0-9964207-0-9
eBook: ISBN: 978-0-9964207-1-6
Audio: ISBN: 978-0-9964207-5-4

...AND FOR CHILDREN:

Fly With Your Dreams: The Quest for Goodness, Peace, and Joy is an illustrated book about dreams coming true. Follow the white dove of Goodness, Peace, and Joy as she takes flight from Far East China in the 8th century BC and lands nearly 28 centuries later at the Pasadena Tournament of Roses® parade in California, USA on January 1, 2013. The true stories in this book are intended to inspire children and adults of all ages, from around the world, to dream and imagine their own stories taking flight. Dreams harness powerful energies to encircle the earth with Goodness, Peace, and Joy as dreams become reality. No matter where you live, what you do, or whether you are young or old, you can have dreams that come true.

ISBN: 978-0-9964207-6-1